Turn-of-the-Century
Doors, Windows and Decorative Millwork
The Mulliner Catalog of 1893

The Mulliner Box & Planing Co.

Dover Publications, Inc.
New York

Published in Canada by General Publishing Company, Ltd., 30 Lesmill Road, Don Mills, Toronto, Ontario.

Published in the United Kingdom by Constable and Company, Ltd., 3 The Lanchesters, 162–164 Fulham Palace Road, London W6 9ER.

Bibliographical Note

This Dover edition, first published in 1995, is an unabridged and unaltered republication of the work originally published by Rand, McNally & Company, Chicago, 1893, under the title *Combined Book of Sash, Doors, Blinds, Mouldings, Stair Work, Mantels, and All Kinds of Interior and Exterior Finish* (etc.; see reproduction of original title page, opposite). The original edition gave the company name only on the cover, with the company address "Quincy, Illinois."

Library of Congress Cataloging-in-Publication Data

Combined book of sash, doors, blinds, mouldings, stair work, mantels, and all kinds of interior and exterior finish.

Turn-of-the-century doors, windows, and decorative millwork : the Mulliner catalog of 1893 / the Mulliner Box & Planing Co.

p.   cm.

Originally published: Combined book of sash, doors, stair work, mantels, and all kinds of interior and exterior finish. Chicago : Rand McNally, 1893.

ISBN 0-486-28514-6 (pbk.)

1. Woodwork—United States—Catalogs. 2. Woodwork—Canada—Catalogs. 3. Architecture, Victorian—United States. 4. Architecture, Victorian—Canada. 5. Architecture—Details. I. Mulliner Box & Planing Co.

TH1155.C66   1995

724'.5—dc20

94-23833
CIP

Manufactured in the United States of America

Dover Publications, Inc., 31 East 2nd Street, Mineola, N.Y. 11501

COMBINED BOOK

OF

SASH, DOORS, BLINDS

MOULDINGS, STAIR WORK, MANTELS,

AND ALL KINDS OF INTERIOR AND EXTERIOR FINISH.

GLASS LISTS,

LATEST STYLES, ELEVATIONS, DESIGNS, ETC.,

OF

EMBOSSED, GROUND, AND CUT GLASS

BRACKETS, SCROLL AND TURNED WORK, WOOD DRAPERY, STORE FRONTS, CORNER
BLOCKS AND BEADS, PLINTH BLOCKS, SAWED AND TURNED BALUSTRADES,
DOOR AND WINDOW FRAMES, PULPITS, PEW ENDS, ETC.

ALSO REVISED EDITION

NEW UNIVERSAL MOULDING BOOK

GIVING FULL SIZE OF MOULDINGS, AND THEIR EXACT MEASUREMENT IN INCHES
ON EACH MOULDING.

———————

Adopted by the Wholesale Sash, Door and Blind Manufacturers' Association of the Northwest,
December 5, 1892.

———————

CHICAGO:
PUBLISHED BY RAND, McNALLY & COMPANY,
Printers, Engravers, and Electrotypers.
1893.

[Original title page]

INDEX.

INDEX.

INDEX.

Order by Number Only.

Do not Cut the Book.

DIRECTIONS FOR ORDERING.

Please observe the following Directions in giving orders, as it will often avoid errors and unnecessary delays.

Orders for Sash should state the size of the glass, number of lights in window, thickness, whether plain or check rail, glazed or unglazed. For segment or circle corner windows, always give the radius of the segment and circle corner, otherwise we shall make our regular radius, which is the width of the window. For circle head, segment head, and circle corner windows, always state whether they are wanted to finish circle inside and outside, like Plans 1 and 3, on page 11, or to finish circle on outside only, as Plans 2 and 4 on same page; also, where frames are made, we should have width and height of frame in the clear, and if not regular Western sizes give size of openings.

Orders for Doors should state size, thickness, number of panels and quality; if moulded, say if one or both sides, flushed or raised moulding ; if more than five panels make sketch.

Orders for Outside Blinds should state size of glass, number of lights in window, thickness of blinds, stationary or rolling slats; if for segment head windows, give radius of segment; also state if for wood or brick building.

Orders for Inside Blinds should state exact size of opening, the number of folds (width of box, if any), and if panels or slats, and where blinds are to be cut.

Orders for Frames should state whether for a frame or brick building; if for a brick building, give thickness of wall; if for a frame building, give width of studding, and whether outside or inside, or both. For Window Frames, state if for plain or check rail sash, with or without pulleys. For inside door jambs, give the width of the jamb.

Orders for Mouldings should give plainly the number of the Moulding. We use the new Universal Book. (*See Page 277.*)

PLEASE NOTE THE FOLLOWING.

It is economy to conform to regular sizes and styles as much as possible.

Be explicit in giving orders and state fully your wants. Do not assume that we know them.

When ordering work outside of regular styles, as given in this book, give sketch or section. A rude drawing will often answer the purpose.

Plans and drawings in detail should accompany all complicated orders, and specification giving bill of items, sizes, and the quality of material required, thereby saving delay and cost of alterations.

In ordering Sash, Doors, and Blinds *always give the width first.* Use terms, when practicable, as given in this book.

GRADES OF

SASH, DOORS, AND BLINDS,

Adopted by the Wholesale Sash, Door, and Blind Manufacturers'

Association of the Northwest.

DOORS.

No. 1 Doors.—Workmanship on No. 1 Doors must be good. Stiles, rails, and panels must be clear, except that white sap and water stain caused by cross-piling lumber is admitted, and small pin knots not exceeding one-fourth ($\frac{1}{4}$) inch in diameter may be allowed. The Standard No. 1 Door may be pinned and the wedges glued, or glued tenons without pins.

No. 2 Doors.—No. 2 Doors may contain knots not larger than one (1) inch in diameter, and may contain blue sap on two (2) sides, and may contain gum spots showing on one (1) side. Other small defects may be allowed, but the total number of defects (not including blue sap) shall not exceed ten (10) in number on each side, and blue sap must not exceed fifty (50) per cent. of any piece of the door. Workmanship must be good, though slight defects therein may be allowed where the quality averages fair. Shaky lumber shall not be admitted. No part of a No. 2 Door, except the top rail, short muntins and short panels, shall be free from some defect.

No. 3 Doors.—No. 3 Doors may contain double the amount of defects that are allowed in No. 2, and the knots and other defects may be coarser. Worm-eaten lumber may be admitted if showing on one side only. Workmanship may be defective, but not enough so to destroy the strength of the door.

WINDOWS.

Check Rail Windows may contain not to exceed two (2) knots in each piece of the sash, said knots not to exceed three-eighths ($\frac{3}{8}$) inch in diameter. White sap and a small amount of blue sap may be admitted. Workmanship must be good.

Plain Rail Windows and Sash may contain blue sap and (small) knots. Shaky lumber not admissible.

BLINDS.

Outside Blinds must be made of clear lumber, except that small pin knots in the stiles and rails and white sap may be admitted. Shaky lumber is not admitted. Workmanship must be good.

CIRCLE AND SEGMENT TOP WINDOWS.

Fig. 1.

For Window Frames, Circle
inside and outside.

Fig. 2.

For Window Frames, Circle
outside, Square inside.

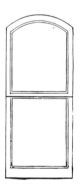

Fig. 3.

For Window Frames, Segment
inside and outside.

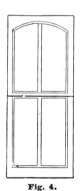

Fig. 4.

For Window Frames, Segment
outside, Square inside.

Windows made in the above forms can be filled with any number of lights required.

N. B.—A Window indicates two pieces. A Sash indicates one piece. A pair of Blinds indicates two pieces. A Blind indicates one piece. A set of Sash or Blinds indicates more than two pieces, and order should be accompanied with elevation.

PLAIN RAIL SASH.

Eight-Lighted Windows.

Size of Glass.	Thickness.	Price per Window, Open.	Price per Window, Glazed.	Size of Window.				
Inches.	Inches.	$ cts.	$ cts.	Ft.	In.		Ft.	In.
8 × 10	1 1-8	.63	1.50	1	8½	×	3	9¼
8 × 12	"	.66	1.70	1	8½	×	4	6
8 × 14	"	.73	1.95	1	8½	×	5	2
8 × 16	"	.77	2.15	1	8½	×	5	10
9 × 12	"	.73	1.90	1	10½	×	4	6
9 × 14	"	.77	2.15	1	10½	×	5	2
9 × 16	"	.83	2.40	1	10½	×	5	10
10 × 12	"	.75	2.05	2	0½	×	4	6
10 × 14	"	.79	2.30	2	0½	×	5	2
10 × 16	"	.84	2.85	2	0½	×	5	10
10 × 18	"	.93	3.15	2	0½	×	6	6
12 × 14	"	.89	2.95	2	4½	×	5	2
12 × 16	"	.97	3.30	2	4½	×	5	10
12 × 18	"	1.04	3.65	2	4½	×	6	6

Twelve-Lighted Windows.

Size of Glass.	Thickness.	Price per Window, Open.	Price per Window, Glazed.	Size of Window.				
Inches.	Inches.	$ cts.	$ cts.	Ft.	In.		Ft.	In.
7 × 9	1 1-8	.53	1.55	2	1	×	3	4½
8 × 10	"	.68	1.95	2	4	×	3	9¼
8 × 12	"	.72	2.25	2	4	×	4	6
8 × 14	"	.79	2.60	2	4	×	5	2
8 × 16	"	.86	2.95	2	4	×	5	10
9 × 12	"	.81	2.55	2	7	×	4	6
9 × 13	"	.84	2.70	2	7	×	4	10
9 × 14	"	.84	2.90	2	7	×	5	2
9 × 15	"	.88	3.05	2	7	×	5	6
9 × 16	"	.90	3.20	2	7	×	5	10
9 × 18	"	.95	3.95	2	7	×	6	6
10 × 12	"	.83	2.75	2	10	×	4	6
10 × 14	"	.86	3.10	2	10	×	5	2
10 × 15	"	.90	3.30	2	10	×	5	6
10 × 16	"	.94	3.90	2	10	×	5	10
10 × 18	"	1.00	4.35	2	10	×	6	6
10 × 20	"	1.10	4.80	2	10	×	7	2
12 × 14	"	1.07	4.20	3	4	×	5	2
12 × 16	"	1.13	4.65	3	4	×	5	10
12 × 18	"	1.21	5.15	3	4	×	6	6

1⅜ Plain Rail Windows, same price as 1⅜ Check Rail Windows.

Sizes not given above, extra price.

PANTRY CHECK RAIL SASH.

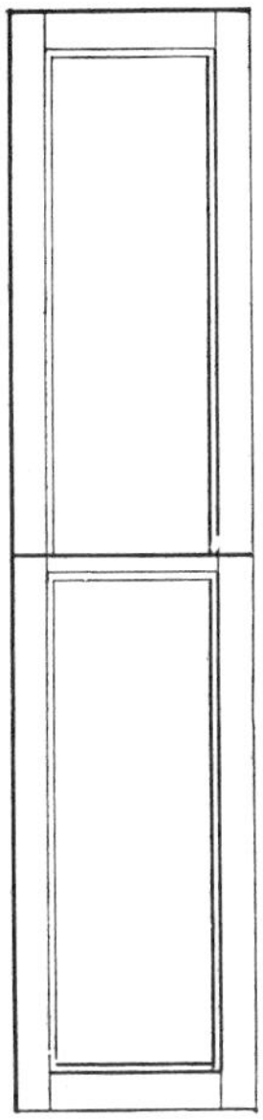

Two-Lighted Windows, One Light Wide.

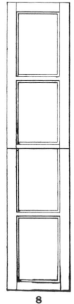

7

Size of Glass.	Thickness.	Price per Window, Open.	Price per Window, Glazed.	Size of Window.			
Inches.	Inches.	$ cts.	$ cts.	Ft.	In.	Ft.	In.
12 × 24	1 3-8	.74	1·75	1	4⅛ ×	4	6
12 × 26	"	.79	1·90	1	4⅛ ×	4	10
12 × 28	"	.84	2·10	1	4⅛ ×	5	2
12 × 30	"	.90	2·55	1	4⅛ ×	5	6
12 × 32	"	.97	2·70	1	4⅛ ×	5	10
12 × 34	"	1·03	2·85	1	4⅛ ×	6	2
12 × 36	"	1·11	3·05	1	4⅛ ×	6	6
14 × 24	"	.74	1·90	1	6⅛ ×	4	6
14 × 26	"	.79	2·05	1	6⅛ ×	4	10
14 × 28	"	84	2·60	1	6⅛ ×	5	2
14 × 30	"	.90	2·85	1	6⅛ ×	5	6
14 × 32	"	.97	3·00	1	6⅛ ×	5	10
14 × 34	"	1·03	3·25	1	6⅛ ×	6	2
14 × 36	"	1·11	3·45	1	6⅛ ×	6	6

Four-Lighted Windows, One Light Wide.

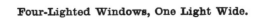

Size of Glass.	Thickness.	Price per Window, Open.	Price per Window, Glazed.	Size of Window.			
Inches.	Inches.	$ cts.	$ cts.	Ft.	In.	Ft.	In.
9 × 12	1 3-8	.74	1·40	1	1⅛ ×	4	6
9 × 14	"	.84	1·65	1	1⅛ ×	5	2
9 × 16	"	.97	1·85	1	1⅛ ×	5	10
12 × 14	"	.84	2·00	1	4⅛ ×	5	2
12 × 16	"	.97	2·35	1	4⅛ ×	5	10
12 × 18	"	1·11	2·65	1	4⅛ ×	6	6

All Check Rail Windows are plowed and bored.

8

CHECK RAIL SASH.

Two-Lighted Windows.

Size of Glass.	Thickness.	Price per Window, Open.	Price Glazed, Single Strength.	Price Glazed, Double Strength.	Size of Window.			
Inches.	Inches.	$ cts.	$ cts.	$ cts.	Ft.	In.	Ft.	In.
16 × 24	1 3-8	.74	1.90	2.40	1	8⅛ ×	4	6
16 × 26	"	.79	2.45	3.10	1	8⅛ ×	4	10
16 × 28	"	.84	2.60	3.25	1	8⅛ ×	5	2
16 × 30	"	.90	2.75	3.50	1	8⅛ ×	5	6
16 × 32	"	.97	3.00	3.75	1	8⅛ ×	5	10
16 × 34	"	1.03	3.20	4.00	1	8⅛ ×	6	2
16 × 36	"	1.11	3.35	4.25	1	8⅛ ×	6	6
18 × 24	"	.74	2.40	3.05	1	10⅛ ×	4	6
18 × 26	"	.79	2.55	3.20	1	10⅛ ×	4	10
18 × 28	"	.84	2.85	3.60	1	10⅛ ×	5	2
18 × 30	"	.90	2.90	3.65	1	10⅛ ×	5	6
18 × 32	"	.97	3.15	3.95	1	10⅛ ×	5	10
18 × 34	"	1.03	3.45	4.45	1	10⅛ ×	6	2
18 × 36	"	1.11	3.75	4.80	1	10⅛ ×	6	6
18 × 38	"	1.25	4.10	5.15	1	10⅛ ×	6	10
18 × 40	"	1.26	4.40	5.50	1	10⅛ ×	7	2
20 × 24	"	.74	2.60	3.30	2	0⅛ ×	4	6
20 × 26	"	.79	2.80	3.55	2	0⅛ ×	4	10
20 × 28	"	.84	3.00	3.85	2	0⅛ ×	5	2
20 × 30	"	.90	3.25	4.15	2	0⅛ ×	5	6
20 × 32	"	.97	3.60	4.70	2	0⅛ ×	5	10
20 × 34	"	1.03	3.65	4.75	2	0⅛ ×	6	2
20 × 36	"	1.11	4.25	5.35	2	0⅛ ×	6	6
20 × 38	"	1.25	4.35	5.50	2	0⅛ ×	6	10
20 × 40	"	1.26	4.75	6.00	2	0⅛ ×	7	2
22 × 24	"	.82	2.85	3.60	2	2⅛ ×	4	6
22 × 26	"	.87	3.05	3.85	2	2⅛ ×	4	10
22 × 28	"	.92	3.25	4.15	2	2⅛ ×	5	2
22 × 30	"	.99	3.60	4.70	2	2⅛ ×	5	6
22 × 32	"	1.05	3.95	5.15	2	2⅛ ×	5	10
22 × 34	"	1.11	4.25	5.40	2	2⅛ ×	6	2
22 × 36	"	1.20	4.65	5.95	2	2⅛ ×	6	6
22 × 38	"	1.33	4.80	6.05	2	2⅛ ×	6	10
22 × 40	"	1.37	5.45	7.10	2	2⅛ ×	7	2
22 × 42	"	1.47	5.55	7.20	2	2⅛ ×	7	6
22 × 44	"	1.58	6.25	8.10	2	2⅛ ×	7	10
22 × 46	"	1.68	6.35	8.20	2	2⅛ ×	8	2
22 × 48	"	1.79	6.50	8.30	2	2⅛ ×	8	6
24 × 24	"	.82	3.15	4.05	2	4⅛ ×	4	6
24 × 26	"	.87	3.20	4.10	2	4⅛ ×	4	10
24 × 28	"	.92	3.55	4.65	2	4⅛ ×	5	2
24 × 30	"	.99	3.90	5.05	2	4⅛ ×	5	6

Continued on next Page.

CHECK RAIL SASH.

Two-Lighted Windows.

Size of Glass.	Thickness.	Price Window Open,	Price Glazed, Single Strength.	Price Glazed, Double Strength.	Size of Window.				
Inches.	Inches.	$ cts.	$ cts.	$ cts.	Ft.	In.		Ft.	In.
24 × 32	1 3-8	1.05	4.15	5.30	2	4⅛	×	5	10
24 × 34	"	1.11	4.60	5.85	2	4⅛	×	6	2
24 × 36	"	1.20	4.65	5.95	2	4⅛	×	6	6
24 × 38	"	1.33	5.45	7.05	2	4⅛	×	6	10
24 × 40	"	1.37	5.50	7.10	2	4⅛	×	7	2
24 × 42	"	1.47	6.15	8.00	2	4⅛	×	7	6
24 × 44	"	1.58	6.30	8.10	2	4⅛	×	7	10
24 × 46	"	1.68	6.40	8.20	2	4⅛	×	8	2
24 × 48	"	1.79	7.90	10.05	2	4⅛	×	8	6
26 × 30	"	1.14	4.60	5.90	2	6⅛	×	5	6
26 × 32	"	1.21	4.70	5.95	2	6⅛	×	5	10
26 × 34	"	1.27	5.15	6.60	2	6⅛	×	6	2
26 × 36	"	1.35	5.45	7.05	2	6⅛	×	6	6
26 × 38	"	1.49	6.20	8.00	2	6⅛	×	6	10
26 × 40	"	1.52	6.25	8.05	2	6⅛	×	7	2
26 × 42	"	1.63	6.35	8.15	2	6⅛	×	7	6
26 × 44	"	1.73	7.20	9.35	2	6⅛	×	7	10
26 × 46	"	1.84	7.95	10.10	2	6⅛	×	8	2
26 × 48	"	1.94	8.05	10.20	2	6⅛	×	8	6
28 × 30	"	1.14	4.60	5.90	2	8⅛	×	5	6
28 × 32	"	1.21	5.10	6.55	2	8⅛	×	5	10
28 × 34	"	1.27	5.35	7.00	2	8⅛	×	6	2
28 × 36	"	1.35	6.05	7.90	2	8⅛	×	6	6
28 × 38	"	1.49	6.20	8.00	2	8⅛	×	6	10
28 × 40	"	1.52	6.25	8.05	2	8⅛	×	7	2
28 × 42	"	1.63	7.10	9.25	2	8⅛	×	7	6
28 × 44	"	1.73	7.85	10.00	2	8⅛	×	7	10
28 × 46	"	1.84	7.95	10.10	2	8⅛	×	8	2
28 × 48	"	1.94	9.30	11.85	2	8⅛	×	8	6
30 × 32	"	1.37	5.45	7.10	2	10⅛	×	5	10
30 × 34	"	1.43	6.10	7.95	2	10⅛	×	6	2
30 × 36	"	1.51	6.20	8.05	2	10⅛	×	6	6
30 × 38	"	1.65	6.35	8.20	2	10⅛	×	6	10
30 × 40	"	1.68	7.15	9.30	2	10⅛	×	7	2
30 × 42	"	1.79	7.90	10.05	2	10⅛	×	7	6
30 × 44	"	1.89	8.00	10.15	2	10⅛	×	7	10
30 × 46	"	2.00	9.35	11.90	2	10⅛	×	8	2
30 × 48	"	2.10	9.45	12.00	2	10⅛	×	8	6
30 × 50	"	2.26	9.60	12.20	2	10⅛	×	8	10

For Windows 1¾ inches, add **80 cents** each to above list.
Segment Head, 1⅜ thick, add 60 cents; 1¾ thick, add 80 cents to list.
Half Circle Head, 1⅜ thick, add $1.20; 1¾ thick, add $1.50 to list.
Sizes not given, **extra** price.
All Check Rail Windows plowed and bored.
Windows prepared for Oil Finish, add 30 cents to list.
For Windows glazed with A. A. Glass, add 10 per cent. to 1⅜ list.
MARGINAL LIGHT SASH—For unglazed Marginal Light Sash, add 10 cents per light to list of open Sash.

CHECK RAIL SASH.

Four-Lighted Windows.

Size of Glass.	Thickness.	Price per Window, Open.	Price Glazed, Single Strength.	Price Glazed, Double Strength.	Size of Window.			
Inches.	Inches.	$ cts.	$ cts.	$ cts.	Ft.	In.	Ft.	In.
10 × 20	1 3-8	.63	1.85		2	1	× 3	10
10 × 22	"	.68	2.00		2	1	× 4	2
10 × 24	"	.74	2.25		2	1	× 4	6
10 × 26	"	.79	2.40		2	1	× 4	10
10 × 28	"	.84	2.55		2	1	× 5	2
10 × 30	"	.90	2.75		2	1	× 5	6
10 × 32	"	.97	3.50		2	1	× 5	10
10 × 34	"	1.03	3.80		2	1	× 6	2
10 × 36	"	1.11	4.00		2	1	× 6	6
12 × 20	"	.71	2.20		2	5	× 3	10
12 × 22	"	.77	2.40		2	5	× 4	2
12 × 24	"	.82	2.60		2	5	× 4	6
12 × 26	"	.87	2.80		2	5	× 4	10
12 × 28	"	.92	2.95		2	5	× 5	2
12 × 30	"	.99	3.80		2	5	× 5	6
12 × 32	"	1.05	4.00		2	5	× 5	10
12 × 34	"	1.11	4.25		2	5	× 6	2
12 × 36	"	1.20	4.50		2	5	× 6	6
12 × 38	"	1.28	4.80		2	5	× 6	10
12 × 40	"	1.37	5.25		2	5	× 7	2
12 × 42	"	1.47	5.60		2	5	× 7	6
12 × 44	"	1.58	6.20		2	5	× 7	10
12 × 46	"	1.68	6.50		2	5	× 8	2
12 × 48	"	1.79	6.60		2	5	× 8	6
14 × 24	"	.98	3.00		2	9	× 4	6
14 × 26	"	1.03	3.25		2	9	× 4	10
14 × 28	"	1.08	4.05		2	9	× 5	2
14 × 30	"	1.14	4.45		2	9	× 5	6
14 × 32	"	1.21	4.70	6.05	2	9	× 5	10
14 × 34	"	1.27	5.00	6.45	2	9	× 6	2
14 × 36	"	1.35	5.35	6.90	2	9	× 6	6
14 × 38	"	1.43	5.55	7.25	2	9	× 6	10
14 × 40	"	1.52	5.95	7 80	2	9	× 7	2
14 × 42	"	1.63	6.85	8.75	2	9	× 7	6
14 × 44	"	1.73	6.95	8.85	2	9	× 7	10

Continued on next Page.

CHECK RAIL SASH.

Four-Lighted Windows.

Size of Glass.			Thickness.	Price per Window, Open.	Price Glazed, Single Strength.	Price Glazed, Double Strength.	Size of Window.				
Inches.			Inches.	$ cts.	$ cts.	$ cts.	Ft.	In.		Ft.	In.
14	×	46	1 3-8	1 84	7.50	9.60	2	9	×	8	2
14	×	48	"	1 94	7.90	10.25	2	9	×	8	6
15	×	24	"	1.13	3.45	4.35	2	11	×	4	6
15	×	26	"	1.19	4.25	5.40	2	11	×	4	10
15	×	28	"	1.24	4.65	5.95	2	11	×	5	2
15	×	30	"	1.30	4.90	6.30	2	11	×	5	6
15	×	32	"	1.37	5.20	6.70	2	11	×	5	10
15	×	34	"	1.43	5.55	7.15	2	11	×	6	2
15	×	36	"	1.51	6.10	8.00	2	11	×	6	6
15	×	38	"	1.60	6.20	8.10	2	11	×	6	10
15	×	40	"	1 68	7.05	9.00	2	11	×	7	2
15	×	42	"	1.79	7 65	9.80	2	11	×	7	6
15	×	44	"	1.89	7.75	9.90	2	11	×	7	10
15	×	46	"	2.00	8.80	11.45	2	11	×	8	2
15	×	48	"	2.10	8.90	11.55	2	11	×	8	6

For Segment Head Windows, 1⅜ thick, add 60 cents; 1¾ thick, add 80 cents to list.

Half Circle Head, 1⅜ thick, add $1.20; 1¾ thick, add $1.50 to list.

Open Sash made for glass 11 inches wide, same price as 12-inch.

Open Sash made for glass 13 or 13½ inches wide, same price as 14-inch.

For price of 1⅛-inch Check Rail Windows deduct 10 per cent. from the list price of 1⅜ Open Check Rail Sash, same size.

For price of 1⅛-inch 4-Light Plain Rail Sash deduct 12½ per cent. from the list price of 1⅜ Open Check Rail Sash, same size.

All Check Rail Windows plowed and bored.

☞N. B.—In figuring percentage as above, when fractions are 5 mills or more, call it 1 cent; if less than 5 mills, omit.

Sizes not given above, extra price.

1⅜ Plain Rail Windows, same price as 1⅜ Check Rail.

Windows prepared for Oil Finish, add 30 cents to the list.

For 1¾-inch Windows, where not listed, add 80 cents to list of 1⅜-inch, same size.

PLEASE NOTICE.

We ship all orders for Windows GLAZED, unless ordered Open.

CHECK RAIL SASH.

Four-Lighted Windows.

Size of Glass.	Thickness.	Price per Window, Open.	Price Glazed, Single Strength.	Price Glazed, Double Strength.	Size of Window.			
Inches.	Inches.	$ cts.	$ cts.	$ cts.	Ft.	In.	Ft	In.
12 × 30	1 3-4	1.79	4.60	5 65	2	5	× 5.	6
12 × 32	"	1.85	4.80	5.95	2	5	× 5	10
12 × 34	"	1.91	5.05	6.20	2	5	× 6	2
12 × 36	"	2.00	5.30	6.55	2	5	× 6	6
12 × 38	"	2.08	5.60	6.95	2	5	× 6	10
12 × 40	"	2.17	6.05	7.60	2	5	× 7	2
12 × 42	"	2.27	6.40	8.15	2	5	× 7	6
12 × 44	"	2.38	7.00	8.70	2	5	× 7	10
12 × 46	"	2.48	7.30	9.30	2	5	× 8	2
12 × 48	"	2.59	7.40	9 40	2	5	× 8	6
14 × 30	"	1.94	5.25	6.50	2	9	× 5	6
14 × 32	"	2.01	5.50	6.85	2	9	× 5	10
14 × 34	"	2.07	5.80	7.25	2	9	× 6	2
14 × 36	"	2.15	6.15	7.70	2	9	× 6	6
14 × 38	"	2.23	6.25	8.05	2	9	× 6	10
14 × 40	"	2.32	6.75	8.60	2	9	× 7	2
14 × 42	"	2.43	7.65	9.55	2	9	× 7	6
14 × 44	"	2.53	7.75	9.65	2	9	× 7	10
14 × 46	"	2.64	8.30	10.40	2	9	× 8	2
14 × 48	"	2.74	8.70	11.05	2	9	× 8	6
15 × 32	"	2.17	6.00	7.50	2	11	× 5	10
15 × 34	"	2.23	6.35	7.95	2	11	× 6	2
15 × 36	"	2.31	6.90	8.80	2	11	× 6	6
15 × 38	"	2.40	7.00	8.90	2	11	× 6	10
15 × 40	"	2.48	7.85	9.80	2	11	× 7	2
15 × 42	"	2 59	8.45	10.60	2	11	× 7	6
15 × 44	"	2.69	8.55	10.70	2	11	× 7	10
15 × 46	"	2.80	9.60	12.25	2	11	× 8	2
15 × 48	"	2.90	9.70	12.35	2	11	× 8	6

For 1¾ inch Windows, where not listed, add 80 cents to list of 1⅜ inch, same size.

CHECK RAIL SASH.

Eight-Lighted Windows.

Size of Glass.	Thickness.	Price per Window, Open.	Price Glazed, Single Strength.	Size of Window.			
Inches.	Inches.	$ cts.	$ cts.	Ft. In.		Ft. In.	
9 × 12	1 3-8	.79	1.95	1 11	×	4 6	
9 × 14	"	.92	2.30	1 11	×	5 2	
9 × 16	"	1.02	2.55	1 11	×	5 10	
9 × 18	"	1.15	3.15	1 11	×	6 6	
10 × 12	"	.79	2.10	2 1	×	4 6	
10 × 14	"	.92	2.40	2 1	×	5 2	
10 × 16	"	1.02	3.00	2 1	×	5 10	
10 × 18	"	1.15	3.40	2 1	×	6 6	
10 × 20	"	1.31	3.80	2 1	×	7 2	
12 × 14	"	.97	3.05	2 5	×	5 2	
12 × 16	"	1.10	3.45	2 5	×	5 10	
12 × 18	"	1.25	3.90	2 5	×	6 6	
12 × 20	"	1.42	4.40	2 5	×	7 2	
14 × 16	"	1.27	4.05	2 9	×	5 10	
14 × 18	"	1.40	4.50	2 9	×	6 6	
14 × 20	"	1.57	5.00	2 9	×	7 2	
14 × 22	"	1.78	5.50	2 9	×	7 10	
14 × 24	"	1.99	6.05	2 9	×	8 6	
10 × 16	1 3-4	1.85	3.85	2 1	×	5 10	
10 × 18	"	1.99	4.20	2 1	×	6 6	
10 × 20	"	2.15	4.65	2 1	×	7 2	
12 × 14	"	1.81	3.90	2 5	×	5 2	
12 × 16	"	1.94	4.30	2 5	×	5 10	
12 × 18	"	2.08	4.70	2 5	×	6 6	
12 × 20	"	2.25	5.25	2 5	×	7 2	
12 × 22	"	2.36	5.65	2 5	×	7 10	
12 × 24	"	2.57	6.15	2 5	×	8 6	
14 × 16	"	2.18	5.00	2 9	×	5 10	
14 × 18	"	2.24	5.30	2 9	×	6 6	
14 × 20	"	2.41	5.85	2 9	×	7 2	
14 × 22	"	2.62	6.35	2 9	×	7 10	
14 × 24	"	2.83	6.90	2 9	×	8 6	

Segment Head, 1⅜ inches thick, add 60 cents; 1¾ inches thick, add 80 cents to list.
Half Circle Head, 1⅜ inches thick, add $1.20; 1¾ inches thick, add $1.50 to list.
Sizes not given above, extra price.
1⅜ inch Plain Rail Windows, same price as 1⅜ Check Rail.
All Check Rail Windows plowed and bored.

CHECK RAIL SASH.

Twelve-Lighted Windows.

Size of Glass.	Thickness.	Price per Window, Open.	Price Glazed, Single Strength.	Size of Window.			
Inches.	Inches.	$ cts.	$ cts.	Ft.	In.	Ft.	In.
8 × 10	1 3-8	.87	2.15	2	4½ ×	3	10
8 × 12	"	.97	2.50	2	4½ ×	4	6
8 × 14	"	1.08	2.90	2	4½ ×	5	2
8 × 16	"	1.21	3.30	2	4½ ×	5	10
9 × 12	"	1.13	2.85	2	7½ ×	4	6
9 × 13	"	1.18	3.05	2	7½ ×	4	10
9 × 14	"	1.24	3.30	2	7½ ×	5	2
9 × 15	"	1.30	3.50	2	7½ ×	5	6
9 × 16	"	1.36	3.70	2	7½ ×	5	10
9 × 18	"	1.51	4.50	2	7½ ×	6	6
10 × 12	"	1.29	3.20	2	10½ ×	4	6
10 × 14	"	1.39	3.65	2	10½ ×	5	2
10 × 15	"	1.46	3.90	2	10½ ×	5	6
10 × 16	"	1.52	4.50	2	10½ ×	5	10
10 × 18	"	1.67	5.00	2	10½ ×	6	6
10 × 20	"	1.84	5.55	2	10½ ×	7	2
10 × 22	"	2.05	6.05	2	10½ ×	7	10
10 × 24	"	2.26	6.70	2	10½ ×	8	6
12 × 14	"	1.71	4.85	3	4½ ×	5	2
12 × 16	"	1.84	5.35	3	4½ ×	5	10
12 × 18	"	1.98	5.90	3	4½ ×	6	6
12 × 20	"	2.15	6.60	3	4½ ×	7	2
12 × 22	"	2.36	7.30	3	4½ ×	7	10
12 × 24	"	2.57	7.95	3	4½ ×	8	6

For price of 1¾-inch Windows, add 80 cents each to above list.

All Check Rail Windows plowed and bored.

For price of 1⅛-inch Check Rail Sash, deduct 10 per cent. from the list price of 1⅜-inch Open Check Rail Sash, same size.

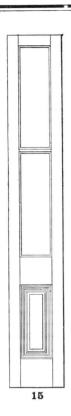

15

SIDE LIGHTS FOR DOORS.

With Moulded Panel Below.

Width.	Height.		Thickness.	Price per Pair, Unglazed.	Price per Pair, Glazed.
Inches.	Ft.	In.	Inches.	$ cts.	$ cts.
12	6	10	1 3-8	3.20	4.70
12	7	0	"	3.20	4.90
12	7	6	"	3.40	5.25
14	6	10	"	3.40	5.25
14	7	0	"	3.60	5.50
14	7	6	"	3.90	5.90
14	8	0	"	4.25	6.50

Prices are for either two or three lights in each sash.
10-inch same price as 12-inch.   Subject to Door Discount.

FIFTEEN AND EIGHTEEN LIGHTED WINDOWS.

For 15-Light Windows, unglazed, add to open list of 12-Light, one-third.
For 18-Light Windows, unglazed, add to open list of 12-Light, two-thirds.
For 15-Light Windows, glazed, add to glazed list of 12-Light, one-quarter.
For 18-Light Windows, glazed, add to glazed list of 12-Light, one-half.

21

FOUR-LIGHT BARN SASH.

Size of Glass.	Thickness.	Price per Sash, Open.	Price per Sash, Glazed.
Inches.	Inches.	cts.	$ cts.
8 × 10	1 1-8	.32	.90
9 × 12	"	.38	1.10
9 × 14	"	.45	1.30
9 × 16	"	.45	1.45
10 × 12	"	.43	1.25
10 × 14	"	.50	1.45

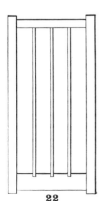

22

HOT BED SASH.

Made for 6 or 7 inch Glass.   Odd Sizes, extra price.

Size of Sash.				Thickness.	Price Each Sash, Open.	Price Each Sash, Glazed.
Ft.	In.	Ft.	In.	Inches.	$ cts.	$ cts.
3	0 ×	6	0	1⅜	2.00	4.85
3	0 ×	6	0	1¾	2.80	5.65

CELLAR SASH.

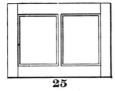

25

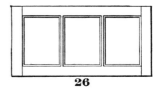

26

Two Lights.

Size of Glass.	Thickness.	Price, Open.	Price, Single Glazed.	Price, Double Glazed.	Size of Sash.			
Inches.	Inches.	cts.	$ cts.	$ cts.	Ft.	In.	Ft.	In.
10 × 12	1 3-8	.35	.80	1.25	2	1 ×	1	4
10 × 14	"	.35	.90	1.35	2	1 ×	1	6
10 × 16	"	.45	1.10	1.75	2	1 ×	1	8
10 × 18	"	.45	1.20	1.95	2	1 ×	1	10
12 × 12	"	.40	.95	1.50	2	5 ×	1	4
12 × 14	"	.45	1.15	1.85	2	5 ×	1	6
12 × 16	"	.45	1.25	2.05	2	5 ×	1	8
12 × 18	"	.50	1.35	2.20	2	5 ×	1	10
12 × 20	"	.55	1.50	2.45	2	5 ×	2	0
14 × 16	"	.50	1.40	2.30	2	9 ×	1	8
14 × 18	"	.55	1.55	2.55	2	9 ×	1	10
14 × 20	"	.60	1.70	2.80	2	9 ×	2	0
14 × 22	"	.65	1.80	2.95	2	9 ×	2	2
14 × 24	"	.70	1.95	3.20	2	9 ×	2	4

Three Lights.

Size of Glass.	Thickness.	Price, Open.	Price, Single Glazed.	Price, Double Glazed.	Size of Sash.			
Inches.	Inches.	cts.	$ cts.	$ cts.	Ft.	In.	Ft.	In.
7 × 9	1 1-8	.25	.75	1.25	2	1 ×	1	1
8 × 10	"	.30	.85	1.40	2	4 ×	1	2
9 × 12	"	.35	1.00	1.65	2	7 ×	1	4
9 × 13	"	.35	1.05	1.75	2	7 ×	1	5
9 × 14	"	.40	1.15	1.90	2	7 ×	1	6
9 × 15	"	.40	1.15	1.90	2	7 ×	1	7
9 × 16	"	.45	1.25	2.05	2	7 ×	1	8
10 × 12	"	.40	1.15	1.90	2	10 ×	1	4
10 × 14	"	.40	1.25	2.10	2	10 ×	1	6
10 × 15	"	.40	1.25	2.10	2	10 ×	1	7
10 × 16	"	.45	1.45	2.45	2	10 ×	1	8
12 × 12	"	.40	1.20	2.00	3	4 ×	1	4
12 × 14	"	.45	1.50	2.55	3	4 ×	1	6
12 × 16	"	.45	1.65	2.85	3	4 ×	1	8
12 × 18	"	.50	1.80	3.10	3	4 ×	1	10

TRANSOM SASH.

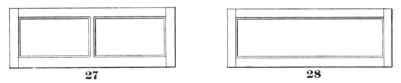

27   28

One and Two Lights.

Size of Sash.			Thickness.	Price per Sash, Open.	Price Two Light Glazed.	Price One Light Glazed.	Price One Light Glazed, Double Strength.
Ft.	In.	In.	Inches.	cts.	$ cts.	$ cts.	$ cts.
2	6 ×	12	1 3-8	.35	.85	1.05	
2	6 ×	14	"	.40	.95	1.15	
2	6 ×	16	"	.40	1.10	1.30	
2	8 ×	12	"	.45	.95	1.15	
2	8 ×	14	"	.45	1.05	1.25	
2	8 ×	16	"	.45	1.20	1.40	
2	8 ×	18	"	.45	1.30	1.50	
2	10 ×	14	"	.50	1.10	1.30	
2	10 ×	16	"	.50	1.30	1.50	
2	10 ×	18	"	.50	1.45	1.65	
2	10 ×	20	"	.50	1.60	1.80	
3	0 ×	14	"	.50	1.20	1.40	
3	0 ×	16	"	.55	1.40	1.60	
3	0 ×	18	"	.55	1.50	1.80	
3	0 ×	20	"	.60	1.70	2.00	
3	6 ×	20	"	.70	2.00	2.30	2.85
3	6 ×	22	"	.75	2.20	2.60	3.25
3	6 ×	24	"	.80	2.65	2.75	3.55
4	0 ×	16	"	.70	1.75	2.15	2.65
4	0 ×	18	"	.75	1.90	2.40	3.05
4	0 ×	20	"	.80	2.25	2.75	3.55
4	0 ×	22	"	.85	2.70	3.10	4.10
4	0 ×	24	"	.90	3.00	3.40	4.50

For Transoms 1¾ thick, 3–0x20 and under, add 40 cents; larger sizes add 80 cents to above list.
For Circle End Transoms 1⅜ thick, add 65 cents to list.
For Circle End Transoms 1¾ thick, add 90 cents to list.
For Block Corner Transoms, add 60 cents to list.
Intermediate sizes will be charged at price of size next larger.
Segment Top, 1⅜ inches thick, 4 feet and under in width, add 60 cents to list.
Segment Top, 1⅜ inches thick, over 4 feet in width, add 80 cents to list.
Segment Top, 1¾ inches thick, 4 feet and under in width, add 85 cents to list.
Segment Top, 1¾ inches thick, over 4 feet in width, add $1.10 to list.
For Circle Top add twice as much as for Segment.

TRANSOM SASH.

One and Two Lights.

Size of Sash.			Thickness.	Price per Sash, Open.	Price Two Light Glazed.	Price One Light Glazed.	Price One Light Glazed, Double Strength.
Ft.	In.	In.	Inches.	$ cts.	$ cts.	$ cts.	$ cts.
4	6 ×	18	1⅜	.85	2.20	2.90	3.80
4	6 ×	20	"	.90	2.95	3.20	4.20
4	6 ×	22	"	.95	3.10	3.50	4.65
4	6 ×	24	"	1.00	3.35	3.95	5.10
5	0 ×	18	"	1.00	2.85	3.70	4.60
5	0 ×	20	"	1.05	3.20		5.05
5	0 ×	22	"	1.10	3.50		5.65
5	0 ×	24	"	1.15	3.70		6.40
5	0 ×	26	"	1.20	3.95		6.65
5	6 ×	18	"	1.15	3.25		5.15
5	6 ×	20	"	1.20	3.55		5.75
5	6 ×	22	"	1.25	3.80		6 60
5	6 ×	24	"	1.30	4.45		6.70
5	6 ×	26	"	1.35	4.90		7.80
5	6 ×	28	"	1.40	5.35		8.15
5	6 ×	30	"	1.45	5.85		9.90
6	0 ×	20	"	1.35	3.90		6.05
6	0 ×	22	"	1.40	4 35		7.10
6	0 ×	24	"	1.45	4.55		8.15
6	0 ×	26	"	1.50	5 40		8 25
6	0 ×	28	"	1.55	5 90		11.05
6	0 ×	30	"	1.60	6.50		11.10
6	0 ×	32	"	1.65	6 80		12.15
6	0 ×	34	"	1.70	7.55		12.25

For Transoms 1¾ thick, 3–0x20 and under, add 40 cents; larger sizes add 80 cents to above list.
For Circle End Transoms 1⅜ thick, add 65 cents to list.
For Circle End Transoms 1¾ thick, add 90 cents to list.
For Block Corner Transoms, add 60 cents to list.
Intermediate sizes will be charged at price of size next larger.
Segment Top, 1⅜ inches thick, 4 feet and under in width, add 60 cents to list.
Segment Top, 1⅜ inches thick, over 4 feet in width, add 80 cents to list.
Segment Top, 1¾ inches thick, 4 feet and under in width, add 85 cents to list.
Segment Top, 1¾ inches thick, over 4 feet in width, add $1.10 to list.
For Circle Top add twice as much as for Segment.

TRANSOM SASH.

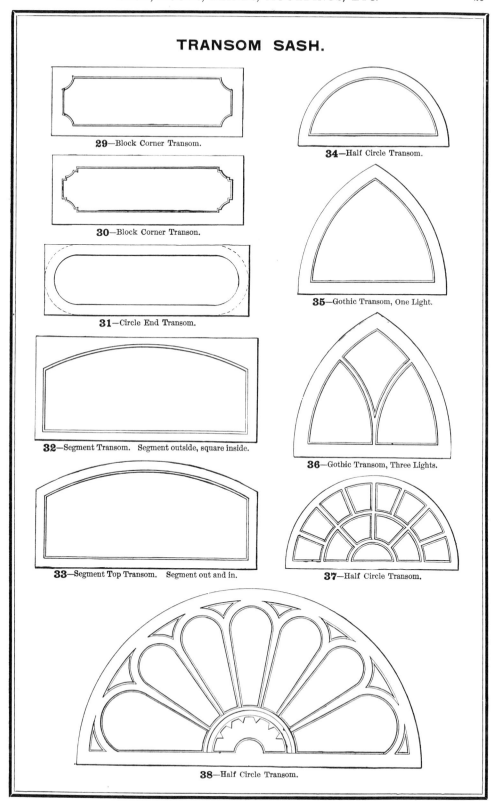

29—Block Corner Transom.

30—Block Corner Transom.

31—Circle End Transom.

32—Segment Transom. Segment outside, square inside.

33—Segment Top Transom. Segment out and in.

34—Half Circle Transom.

35—Gothic Transom, One Light.

36—Gothic Transom, Three Lights.

37—Half Circle Transom.

38—Half Circle Transom.

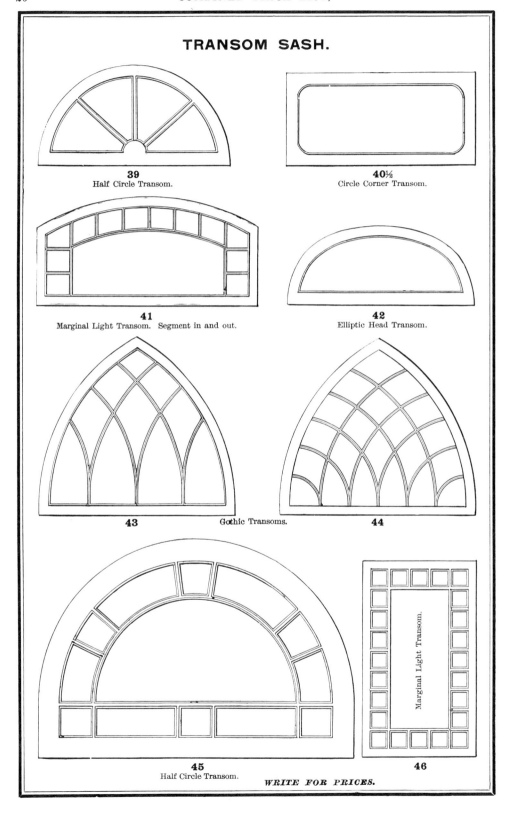

TRANSOM SASH.

39
Half Circle Transom.

40½
Circle Corner Transom.

41
Marginal Light Transom. Segment in and out.

42
Elliptic Head Transom.

43   Gothic Transoms.   **44**

45
Half Circle Transom.

Marginal Light Transom.

46

WRITE FOR PRICES.

GOTHIC WINDOWS.

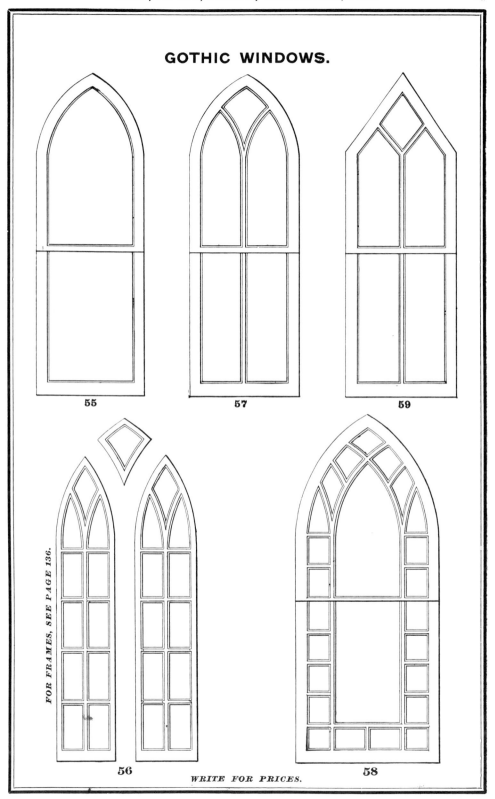

55

57

59

FOR FRAMES, SEE PAGE 136.

56

58

GLAZED STORM SASH.

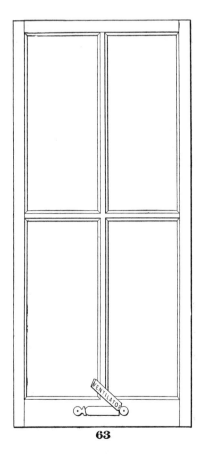

63

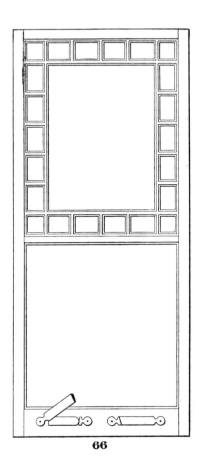

66

PLEASE NOTICE.

We make our Storm Sash with $2\frac{1}{4}$-inch Stiles. If 3-inch Stiles are wanted, order must so state, otherwise we will send our regular width. We can make one or more Ventilators in bottom rail of each Sash, as per cut above. Price 10 cents each, net.

IF VENTILATORS ARE WANTED, ORDER MUST SO STATE.

Place your order for Storm Sash early.

STORM SASH.

Two-Lighted Windows.

Size of Glass.			Thickness.	Price per Sash, Open.	Price Glazed, Single Strength.	Size of Sash, with 2¼-inch Stiles.				
Inches.			Inches.	$ cts.	$ cts.	Ft.	In.		Ft.	In.
16	×	24	1 1-8	.99	2.15	1	8⅛	×	4	7
16	×	26	"	1.04	2.70	1	8⅛	×	4	11
16	×	28	"	1.09	2.85	1	8⅛	×	5	3
16	×	30	"	1.20	3.05	1	8⅛	×	5	7
16	×	32	"	1.27	3.30	1	8⅛	×	5	11
16	×	34	"	1.33	3.50	1	8⅛	×	6	3
16	×	36	"	1.46	3.70	1	8⅛	×	6	7
18	×	24	"	.99	2.65	1	10⅛	×	4	7
18	×	26	"	1.04	2.80	1	10⅛	×	4	11
18	×	28	"	1.09	3.10	1	10⅛	×	5	3
18	×	30	"	1.20	3.20	1	10⅛	×	5	7
18	×	32	"	1.27	3.45	1	10⅛	×	5	11
18	×	34	"	1.33	3.75	1	10⅛	×	6	3
18	×	36	"	1.46	4.10	1	10⅛	×	6	7
18	×	38	"	1.60	4.45	1	10⅛	×	6	11
18	×	40	"	1.66	4.80	1	10⅛	×	7	3
20	×	24	"	.99	2.85	2	0⅛	×	4	7
20	×	26	"	1.04	3.05	2	0⅛	×	4	11
20	×	28	"	1.09	3.25	2	0⅛	×	5	3
20	×	30	"	1.20	3.55	2	0⅛	×	5	7
20	×	32	"	1.27	3.90	2	0⅛	×	5	11
20	×	34	"	1.33	3.95	2	0⅛	×	6	3
20	×	36	"	1.46	4.60	2	0⅛	×	6	7
20	×	38	"	1.60	4.70	2	0⅛	×	6	11
20	×	40	"	1.66	5.15	2	0⅛	×	7	3
22	×	24	"	1.07	3.10	2	2⅛	×	4	7
22	×	26	"	1.12	3 30	2	2⅛	×	4	11
22	×	28	"	1.17	3.50	2	2⅛	×	5	3
22	×	30	"	1.29	3.90	2	2⅛	×	5	7
22	×	32	"	1.35	4.25	2	2⅛	×	5	11
22	×	34	"	1.46	4.55	2	2⅛	×	6	3
22	×	36	"	1.55	5 00	2	2⅛	×	6	7
22	×	38	"	1.68	5.15	2	2⅛	×	6	11
22	×	40	"	1.77	5.85	2	2⅛	×	7	3
22	×	42	"	1.87	5 95	2	2⅛	×	7	7
22	×	44	"	1.98	6.65	2	2⅛	×	7	11
22	×	46	"	2.08	6.75	2	2⅛	×	8	3
22	×	48	"	2.19	6 90	2	2⅛	×	8	7
24	×	24	"	1.07	3.40	2	4⅛	×	4	7
24	×	26	"	1.12	3.45	2	4⅛	×	4	11
24	×	28	"	1.17	3.80	2	4⅛	×	5	3
24	×	30	"	1.29	4.20	2	4⅛	×	5	7

Continued on next page.

STORM SASH.

Two-Lighted Windows.

Size of Glass.	Thickness.	Price per Sash, Open.	Price Glazed, Single Strength.	Size of Sash, with 2¼-inch Stiles.			
Inches.	Inches.	$ cts.	$ cts.	Ft.	In.	Ft.	In.
24 × 32	1 1-8	1.35	4.45	2	4⅛	×	5 11
24 × 34	"	1.46	4.90	2	4⅛	×	6 3
24 × 36	" "	1.55	5.00	2	4⅛	×	6 7
24 × 38	"	1.68	5.80	2	4⅛	×	6 11
24 × 40	"	1.77	5.85	2	4⅛	×	7 3
24 × 42	"	1.87	6.55	2	4⅛	×	7 7
24 × 44	"	1.98	6.65	2	4⅛	×	7 11
24 × 46	"	2.08	6.75	2	4⅛	×	8 3
24 × 48	"	2.19	8.30	2	4⅛	×	8 7
26 × 30	"	1.44	4.90	2	6⅛	×	5 7
26 × 32	"	1.51	5.00	2	6⅛	×	5 11
26 × 34	"	1.57	5.45	2	6⅛	×	6 3
26 × 36	"	1.70	5.80	2	6⅛	×	6 7
26 × 38	"	1.84	6.55	2	6⅛	×	6 11
26 × 40	"	1.92	6.60	2	6⅛	×	7 3
26 × 42	"	2.03	6.70	2	6⅛	×	7 7
26 × 44	"	2.13	7.60	2	6⅛	×	7 11
26 × 46	"	2.24	8.35	2	6⅛	×	8 3
26 × 48	"	2.34	8.45	2	6⅛	×	8 7
28 × 30	"	1.44	4.90	2	8⅛	×	5 7
28 × 32	"	1.51	5.40	2	8⅛	×	5 11
28 × 34	"	1.57	5.65	2	8⅛	×	6 3
28 × 36	"	1.70	6.40	2	8⅛	×	6 7
28 × 38	"	1.84	6.55	2	8⅛	×	6 11
28 × 40	"	1.92	6.60	2	8⅛	×	7 3
28 × 42	"	2.03	7.50	2	8⅛	×	7 7
28 × 44	"	2.13	8.25	2	8⅛	×	7 11
28 × 46	"	2.24	8.35	2	8⅛	×	8 3
28 × 48	"	2.34	9.70	2	8⅛	×	8 7
30 × 32	"	1.67	5.75	2	10⅛	×	5 11
30 × 34	"	1.73	6.40	2	10⅛	×	6 3
30 × 36	"	1.86	6.55	2	10⅛	×	6 7
30 × 38	"	2.00	6.70	2	10⅛	×	6 11
30 × 40	"	2.08	7.55	2	10⅛	×	7 3
30 × 42	"	2.19	8.30	2	10⅛	×	7 7
30 × 44	"	2.29	8.40	2	10⅛	×	7 11
30 × 46	"	2.40	9.75	2	10⅛	×	8 3
30 × 48	"	2.50	9.85	2	10⅛	×	8 7
30 × 50	"	2.66	10.00	2	10⅛	×	8 11

Sizes not listed, extra price.
Add for Ventilators in bottom or top rail 10 cents net each.
Add for Swing Light 40 cents net each.
Add for Storm Sash, 1⅜ inches thick, 20 cents net.
Our Storm Sash are made with 2¼ inch Stiles; if 3 inch Stiles are wanted order must so state.
Place your orders for Storm Sash early.

STORM SASH.

Four-Lighted Windows.

Size of Glass.	Thickness	Price per Sash, Open.	Price per Sash, Glazed.	Size of Sash, with 2¼-inch Stiles.			
Inches.	Inches.	$ cts.	$ cts.	Ft.	In.	Ft.	In.
10 × 20	1 1-8	.88	2.10	2	1 ×	3	11
10 × 22	"	.93	2.25	2	1 ×	4	3
10 × 24	"	.99	2.50	2	1 ×	4	7
10 × 26	"	1.04	2.65	2	1 ×	4	11
10 × 28	"	1.09	2.80	2	1 ×	5	3
10 × 30	"	1.15	3.00	2	1 ×	5	7
10 × 32	"	1.22	3.75	2	1 ×	5	11
10 × 34	"	1.28	4.05	2	1 ×	6	3
10 × 36	"	1.36	4.25	2	1 ×	6	7
12 × 20	"	.96	2.45	2	5 ×	3	11
12 × 22	"	1.02	2.65	2	5 ×	4	3
12 × 24	"	1.07	2.85	2	5 ×	4	7
12 × 26	"	1.12	3.05	2	5 ×	4	11
12 × 28	"	1.17	3.20	2	5 ×	5	3
12 × 30	"	1.24	4.05	2	5 ×	5	7
12 × 32	"	1.30	4.25	2	5 ×	5	11
12 × 34	"	1.36	4.50	2	5 ×	6	3
12 × 36	"	1.45	4.75	2	5 ×	6	7
12 × 38	"	1.53	5.05	2	5 ×	6	11
12 × 40	"	1.62	5.50	2	5 ×	7	3
12 × 42	"	1.72	5.85	2	5 ×	7	7
12 × 44	"	1.83	6.45	2	5 ×	7	11
12 × 46	"	1.93	6.75	2	5 ×	8	3
12 × 48	"	2.04	6.85	2	5 ×	8	7
14 × 24	"	1.23	3.25	2	9 ×	4	7
14 × 26	"	1.28	3.50	2	9 ×	4	11
14 × 28	"	1.33	4.30	2	9 ×	5	3
14 × 30	"	1.39	4.70	2	9 ×	5	7
14 × 32	"	1.46	4.95	2	9 ×	5	11
14 × 34	"	1.52	5.25	2	9 ×	6	3
14 × 36	"	1.60	5.60	2	9 ×	6	7
14 × 38	"	1.68	5.80	2	9 ×	6	11
14 × 40	"	1.77	6.20	2	9 ×	7	3
14 × 42	"	1.88	7.10	2	9 ×	7	7
14 × 44	"	1.98	7.20	2	9 ×	7	11
14 × 46	"	2.09	7.75	2	9 ×	8	3
14 × 48	"	2.19	8.15	2	9 ×	8	7
15 × 24	"	1.38	3.70	2	11 ×	4	7
15 × 26	"	1.44	4.50	2	11 ×	4	11

Continued on next Page.

STORM SASH.

Four-Lighted Windows.

Size of Glass.	Thickness.	Price per Sash, Open.	Price per Sash, Glazed.	Size of Sash, with 2¼-inch Stiles.			
Inches.	Inches.	$ cts.	$ cts.	Ft.	In.	Ft.	In.
15 × 28	1 1-8	1.49	4.90	2	11 ×	5	3
15 × 30	"	1.55	5.15	2	11 ×	5	7
15 × 32	"	1.62	5.45	2	11 ×	5	11
15 × 34	"	1.68	5.80	2	11 ×	6	3
15 × 36	"	1.76	6.35	2	11 ×	6	7
15 × 38	"	1.85	6.45	2	11 ×	6	11
15 × 40	"	1.93	7.30	2	11 ×	7	3
15 × 42	"	2.04	7.90	2	11 ×	7	7
15 × 44	"	2.14	8.00	2	11 ×	7	11
15 × 46	"	2.25	9.00	2	11 ×	8	3
15 × 48	"	2.35	9.10	2	11 ×	8	7

Eight-Lighted Windows.

Size of Glass.	Thickness.	Price per Sash, Open.	Price per Sash, Glazed.	Size of Sash, with 2¼-inch Stiles.			
Inches.	Inches.	$ cts.	$ cts.	Ft.	In.	Ft.	In.
9 × 12	1 1-8	.99	2.15	1	11 ×	4	7
9 × 14	"	1.12	2.50	1	11 ×	5	3
9 × 16	"	1.22	2.75	1	11 ×	5	11
9 × 18	"	1.35	3.35	1	11 ×	6	7
10 × 12	"	.99	2.30	2	1 ×	4	7
10 × 14	"	1 12	2.60	2	1 ×	5	3
10 × 16	"	1.22	3.20	2	1 ×	5	11
10 × 18	"	1.35	3.60	2	1 ×	6	7
10 × 20	"	1.51	4.00	2	1 ×	7	3
12 × 14	"	1.17	3.25	2	5 ×	5	3
12 × 16	"	1.30	3.65	2	5 ×	5	11
12 × 18	"	1.45	4.10	2	5 ×	6	7
12 × 20	"	1.62	4.60	2	5 ×	7	3
14 × 16	"	1.47	4.25	2	9 ×	5	11
14 × 18	"	1.60	4.70	2	9 ×	6	7
14 × 20	"	1.77	5.20	2	9 ×	7	3
14 × 22	"	1.98	5.70	2	9 ×	7	11
14 × 24	"	2.19	6.25	2	9 ×	8	7

Sizes not listed, extra price.

Segment and Circle Heads extra price, same as 1⅜ Check Windows.

We make our Storm Sash with 2¼-inch Stiles; if 3-inch are wanted, order must so state, otherwise we will send our regular width.

Add for Ventilator in bottom or top rail 10 cents net; add for Swing Light 40 cents net each; add for Storm Sash, 1⅜ thick, 20 cents net.

If Ventilators are wanted order must so state.

Place your orders early for Storm Sash.

STORM SASH.

Twelve-Lighted Windows.

Size of Glass.	Thickness.	Price per Sash, Open.	Price per Sash, Glazed.	Size of Sash, with 2¼-inch Stiles.			
Inches.	Inches.	$ cts.	$ cts.	Ft.	In.	Ft.	In.
8 × 10	1 1-8	1.07	2.35	2	4½ ×	3	11
8 × 12	"	1.17	2.70	2	4½ ×	4	7
8 × 14	"	1.28	3.10	2	4½ ×	5	3
8 × 16	"	1.41	3.50	2	4½ ×	5	11
9 × 12	"	1.33	3.05	2	7½ ×	4	7
9 × 13	"	1.38	3.25	2	7½ ×	4	11
9 × 14	"	1.44	3.50	2	7½ ×	5	3
9 × 15	"	1.50	3.70	2	7½ ×	5	7
9 × 16	"	1.56	3.90	2	7½ ×	5	11
9 × 18	"	1.71	4.70	2	7½ ×	6	7
10 × 12	"	1.29	3.40	2	10½ ×	4	7
10 × 14	"	1.59	3.85	2	10½ ×	5	3
10 × 15	"	1.66	4.10	2	10½ ×	5	7
10 × 16	"	1.72	4.70	2	10½ ×	5	11
10 × 18	"	1.87	5.20	2	10½ ×	6	7
10 × 20	"	2.04	5.75	2	10½ ×	7	3
10 × 22	"	2.25	6.25	2	10½ ×	7	11
10 × 24	"	2.46	6.90	2	10½ ×	8	7
12 × 14	"	1.91	5.05	3	4½ ×	5	3
12 × 16	"	2.04	5.55	3	4½ ×	5	11
12 × 18	"	2.18	6.10	3	4½ ×	6	7
12 × 20	"	2.35	6.80	3	4½ ×	7	3
12 × 22	"	2.56	7.50	3	4½ ×	7	11
12 × 24	"	2.77	8.15	3	4½ ×	8	7

Sizes not listed, extra price.

Add for Ventilators in top or bottom rail 10 cents net each; add for Swing Light 40 cents net each; add for Storm Sash, 1⅜ thick, 20 cents net.

Segment and Circle Heads extra price, same as 1⅜ Check Windows.

Place your orders early for Storm Sash.

QUEEN ANNE SASH.

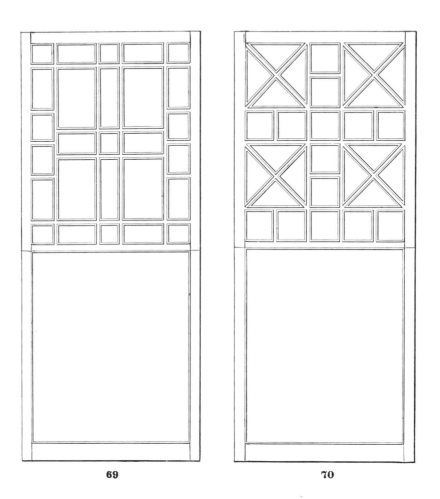

69   70

We make QUEEN ANNE SASH of every description. On the following pages we give a variety of Windows, also a number of Top Sash
in separate cuts. Many of the latter can be utilized as Single Sash by
changing the meeting rail to a wide rail. With Nos. 73 and 74 we
give cuts of the extended Side Stile (or O G Lug) in vogue in some
parts of the country. These cuts are given to facilitate and assist in making orders.

PLEASE BE EXPLICIT IN STATING YOUR WANTS.

WRITE FOR PRICES.

QUEEN ANNE SASH.

71

73

72

74

QUEEN ANNE SASH.

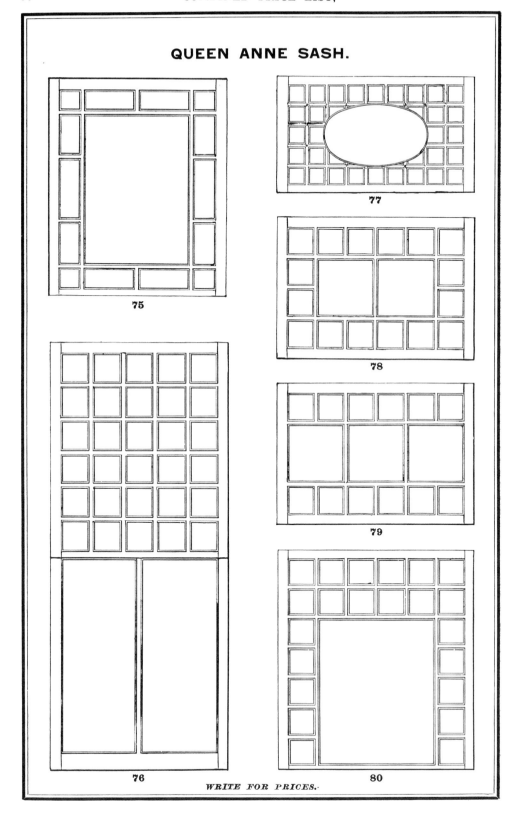

QUEEN ANNE SASH.

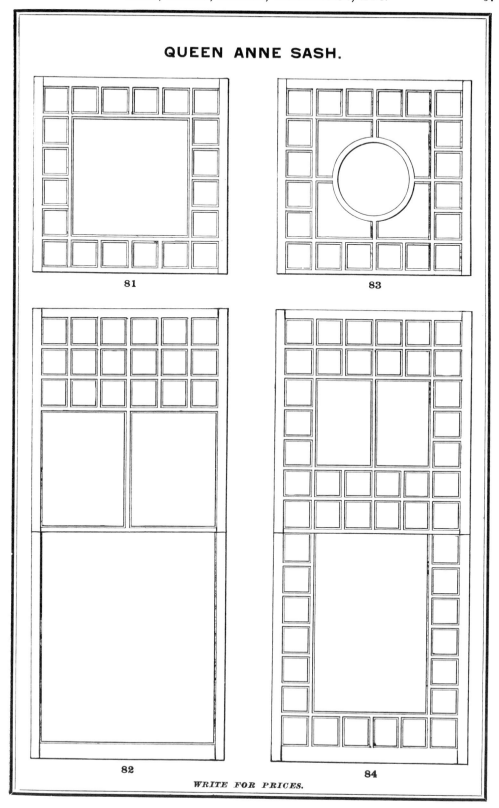

81

83

82

84

QUEEN ANNE SASH.

85

87

86

88

QUEEN ANNE SASH.

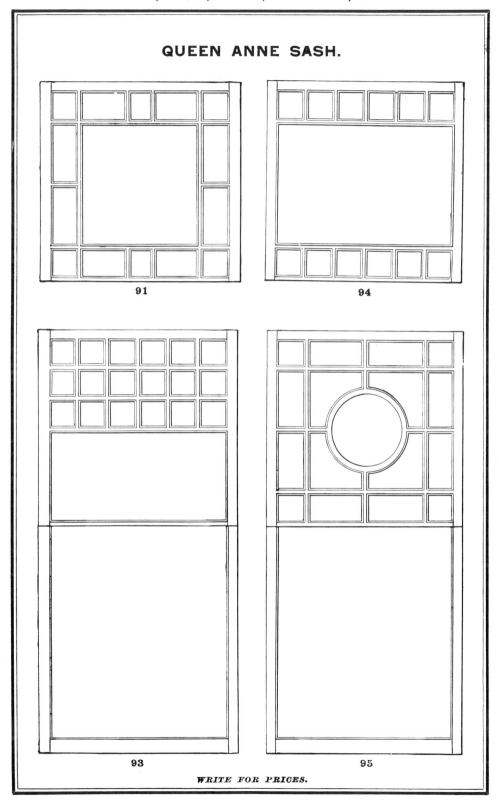

91

94

93

95

WRITE FOR PRICES.

CUTS OF SASH STICKING.

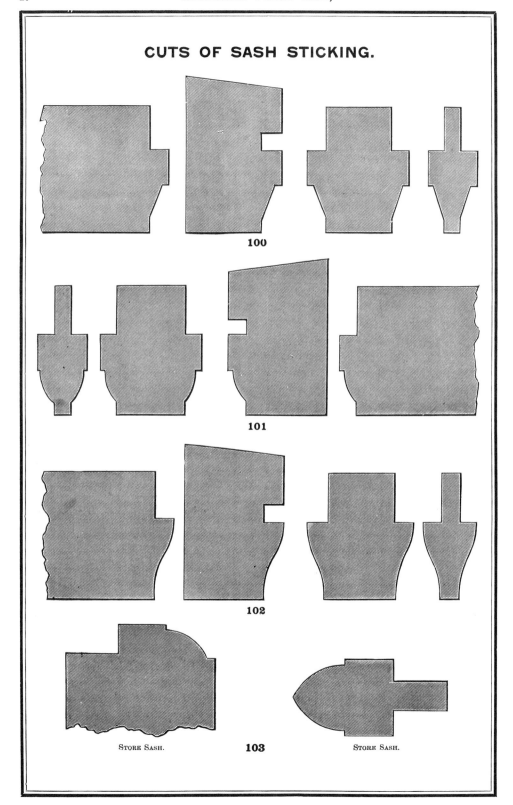

100

101

102

Store Sash.　　　　　**103**　　　　　Store Sash.

CUTS OF SASH STICKING.

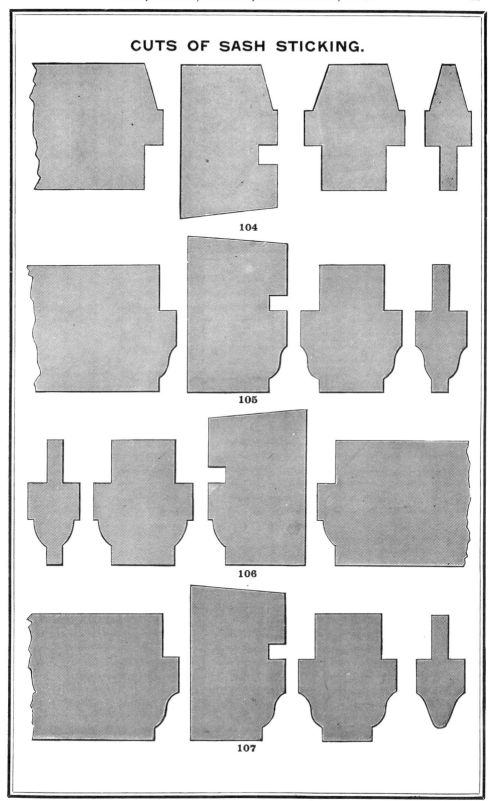

104

105

106

107

GABLE SASH.

Sash No. **116**
Frame No. **598**

Sash No. **117**
Frame No. **590**

Sash No. **118**
Frame No. **591**

Sash No. **119**
Frame No. **592**

Sash No. **120**
Frame No. **594**

Sash No. **121**
Frame No. **593**

Sash No. **122**
Frame No. **595**

Sash No. **123**
Frame No. **596**

Sash No. **124**
Frame No. **597**

WRITE FOR PRICES.

WIRE SCREEN DOORS.

135

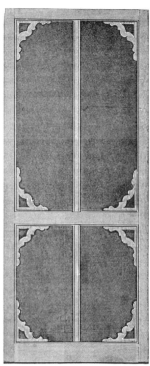

136

Painted in Two Coats of Best Green or Stained in Imitation of Walnut.

Covered with best Wire Cloth. Raised Moulding inside, O G Finish outside.

SIZE.				Thickness.	Discount same as O G Doors.	
					Price Plain.	Price with Brackets.
Ft.	In.	Ft.	In.	Inches.	$ cts.	$ cts.
2	6	× 6	6	7-8	2.15	3.15
2	8	× 6	8	"	2.25	3.25
2	10	× 6	10	"	2.45	3.45
3	0	× 7	0	"	2.70	3.70
2	6	× 6	6	1 1-8	2.30	3.30
2	8	× 6	8	"	2.40	3.40
2	10	× 6	10	"	2.60	3.60
3	0	× 7	0	"	2.90	3.90

With Figured Cloth, add to list 40 cents.

We make all our stock sizes one inch longer and ½-inch wider than list, to allow for fitting. Hardwood frames made to order.

WIRE SCREEN DOORS.

140

141

142

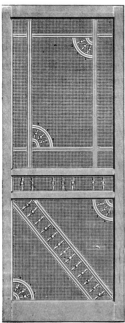

143

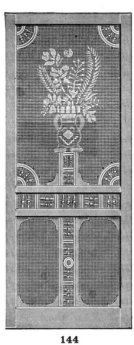

144

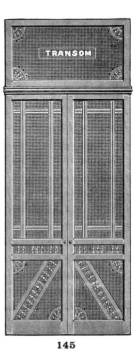

145

SPRING HINGES FOR SCREEN DOORS.

149—(Full Size Cut.)

Price (including Screws), 12½ cents per pair, net.

Having the Spring Hinge for sale, with the necessary Screws for hanging the Doors, enables the retail dealer to furnish the door and trimmings together, at about the same price (or a trifle higher) that the Door alone is usually sold for, besides proving a convenience and saving to purchasers.

O G FOUR-PANEL INCH DOORS.

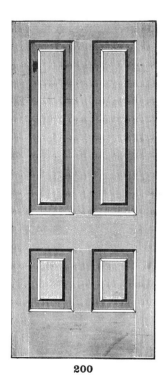

200

200⅛
Section of 1⅜ O G Door.

Raised Panels One Side.

SIZE.				Thickness.	Price, First Quality.	Price, Second Quality.
Ft.	In.	Ft.	In.	Inch.	$ cts.	$ cts.
2	0	× 6	0	1	1.80	1.70
2	4	× 6	4	"	1.90	1.80
2	0	× 6	6	"	2.25	2.15
2	6	× 6	6	"	2.25	2.15
2	8	× 6	8	"	2.45	2.30

Inch Doors are made out of inch lumber, and finish up ⅞ inch thick.
Inch Doors are raised panels on one side; all others are raised on both sides
Doors prepared for Oil Finish, add 75 cents to list.
Sizes not given above, extra price.

O G FOUR-PANEL DOORS.

Raised Panels Both Sides.

Size.				Thickness.	Price, First Quality.	Price, Second Quality.	Price, Third Quality.
Ft.	In.	Ft.	In	Inches.	$ cts.	$ cts.	$ cts.
2	0	× 6	0	1 1-8	2.35	2.20	
2	4	× 6	0	"	2.60	2.40	
2	6	× 6	0	"	2.70	2.50	
2	8	× 6	0	"	2.80	2.60	
3	0	× 6	0	"	2.85	2.65	
2	4	× 6	4	"	2.60	2.40	
2	6	× 6	4	"	2.70	2.50	
2	8	× 6	4	"	2.80	2.60	
2	0	× 6	6	"	2.70	2.50	
2	6	× 6	6	"	2.70	2.50	2 10
2	8	× 6	6	"	2.85	2.65	
2	10	× 6	6	"	3.10	2.90	
3	0	× 6	6	"	3.10	2.90	
2	6	× 6	8	"	2.85	2.65	
2	8	× 6	8	"	2.85	2.65	2.25
2	10	× 6	10	"	3.10	2.90	2.50
3	0	× 7	0	"	3.35	3.15	2.70
2	0	× 6	0	1 3-8	2.90	2.35	
2	6	× 6	0	"	3.15	2.60	
2	8	× 6	0	"	3.35	2.75	
3	0	× 6	0	"	3.80	3.05	
2	4	× 6	4	"	3.15	2.55	
2	6	× 6	4	"	3.30	2.70	
2	0	× 6	6	"	3.30	2.70	
2	4	× 6	6	"	3.30	2.70	
2	6	× 6	6	"	3.30	2.70	2.20
2	8	× 6	6	"	3.55	2.85	
2	10	× 6	6	"	3.90	3.15	
3	0	× 6	6	"	4.05	3.25	
2	0	× 6	8	"	3.55	2.85	
2	4	× 6	8	"	3.55	2.85	
2	6	× 6	8	"	3.55	2.85	

Continued on next Page.

O G FOUR-PANEL DOORS.

Raised Panels Both Sides.

Size.				Thickness.	Price, First Quality.	Price, Second Quality.	Price, Third Quality.
Ft. In.		Ft. In.		Inches.	$ cts.	$ cts.	$ cts.
2 8	×	6 8		1 3-8	3·60	2·90	2·30
2 6	×	6 10		"	3·85	3·10	
2 8	×	6 10		"	3·90	3·15	
2 10	×	6 10		"	4·00	3·25	2·60
2 0	×	7 0		"	3·95	3·20	
2 6	×	7 0		"	4·05	3 25	
2 8	×	7 0			4·10	3·30	
2 10	×	7 0		"	4·20	3·40	
3 0	×	7 0		"	4·40	3·60	2 90
2 6	×	7 6		"	4·80	3·95	
2 8	×	7 6		"	4·80	3·95	
2 10	×	7 6		"	4·90	4·05	
3 0	×	7 6		"	5·05	4·20	
2 6	×	8 0		"	5·70	4·85	
2 8	×	8 0		"	5·70	4·85	
3 0	×	8 0		"	5·70	4·85	
3 0	×	8 6		"	6·60	5·75	
3 0	×	9 0		"	7·50	6·65	
2 6	×	6 6		· 1 3-4	5·50	4·80	
2 8	×	6 8		"	5·90	5·00	
2 10	×	6 10		"	6·30	5·45	
2 6	×	7 0		"	6·40	5·50	
2 8	×	7 0		"	6·45	5 55	
2 10	×	7 0		"	6·55	5·65	
3 0	×	7 0		"	6·75	5·80	
2 6	×	7 6		"	7·25	6·25	
2 8	×	7 6		"	7·25	6·25	
2 10	×	7 6		"	7·35	6·35	
3 0	×	7 6		"	7·50	6·50	
3 0	×	8 0		"	8·20	7·20	
3 0	×	8 6		"	9·20	8·20	
3 0	×	9 0		"	10·25	9·25	

Bevel Panels for Doors are standard.

For Segment Panel O G Doors, add $1.00 to above list price.

For P G Four-Panel Doors, add 15 cents to list.

Sizes not given above, extra price.

Doors prepared for Oil Finish, add 75 cents to list.

FIVE-PANEL O G AND P G DOORS.

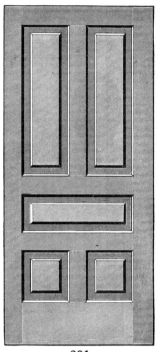

201

202

SIZE.				Price of O G Doors. No. 201.				Price of P G Doors. No. 202.			
				1⅜ Thick.		1¾ Thick.		1⅜ Thick.		1¾ Thick.	
				First Quality.	Second Quality.	First Quality.	Second Quality.	First Quality.	Second Quality.	First Quality.	Second Quality.
Ft.	In.	Ft.	In.	$ cts.	$ cts.	$ cts.	$ cts.	$ cts.	$ cts.	$ cts.	$ cts.
2	6 ×	6	6	3.50	2.90	5.70	5.00	3.65	3.05	5.85	5.15
2	6 ×	6	8	3.75	3.05	6.05	5.20	3.90	3.20	6.20	5.35
2	8 ×	6	8	3.80	3.10	6.10	5.20	3.95	3.25	6.25	5.35
2	6 ×	6	10	4.05	3.30	6.35	5.45	4.20	3.45	6.50	5.60
2	8 ×	6	10	4.10	3.35	6.40	5.50	4.25	3.50	6.55	5.65
2	10 ×	6	10	4.20	3.45	6.50	5.65	4.35	3.60	6.65	5.80
2	0 ×	7	0	4.15	3.40	6.50	5.60	4.30	3.55	6.65	5.75
2	6 ×	7	0	4.25	3.45	6.60	5.70	4.40	3.60	6.75	5.85
2	8 ×	7	0	4.30	3.50	6.65	5.75	4.45	3.65	6.80	5.90
2	10 ×	7	0	4.40	3.60	6.75	5.85	4.55	3.75	6.90	6.00
3	0 ×	7	0	4.60	3.80	6.95	6.00	4.75	3.95	7.10	6.15
2	6 ×	7	6	5.00	4.15	7.45	6.45	5.15	4.30	7.60	6.60
2	8 ×	7	6	5.00	4.15	7.45	6.45	5.15	4.30	7.60	6.60
2	10 ×	7	6	5.10	4.25	7.55	6.55	5.25	4.40	7.70	6.70
3	0 ×	7	6	5.25	4.40	7.70	6.70	5.40	4.55	7.85	6.85
3	0 ×	8	0	5.90	5.05	8.40	7.40	6.05	5.20	8.55	7.55
3	0 ×	8	6	6.80	5.95	9.40	8.40	6.95	6.10	9.55	8.55
3	0 ×	9	0	7.70	6.85	10.45	9.45	7.85	7.00	10.60	9.60

For Doors prepared for Oil Finish, add 75 cents to list.

Sizes not given above, extra price.

FOUR-PANEL FLUSH MOULDED DOORS.

203

Flush (or Sunk) Moulding.

SIZE.				Price, 1⅜ Thick.		Price, 1¾ Thick.	
				Moulded One Side.	Moulded Two Sides.	Moulded One Side.	Moulded Two Sides.
Ft. In.		Ft. In.		$ cts.	$ cts.	$ cts.	$ cts.
2 4	×	6 4		4.20	5.00	6.75	7.60
2 0	×	6 6		4.20	5.00	6.75	7.60
2 6	×	6 6		4.20	5.00	6.75	7.60
2 6	×	6 8		4.55	5.35	7.15	8.00
2 8	×	6 8		4.55	5.35	7.15	8.00
2 10	×	6 10		4.95	5.75	7.65	8.50
2 6	×	7 0		5.20	6.05	7.85	8.70
2 8	×	7 0		5.25	6.10	7.95	8.80
2 10	×	7 0		5.35	6.20	8.05	8.90
3 0	×	7 0		5.55	6.40	8.20	9.10
2 6	×	7 6		6.00	6.85	8.75	9.75
2 8	×	7 6		6.00	6.85	8.75	9.75
2 10	×	7 6		6.10	6.95	8.85	9.85
3 0	×	7 6		6.25	7.10	9.00	10.00
3 0	×	8 0		6.95	7.80	9.80	10.80
3 0	×	8 6		7.70	8.55	10.80	11 80

Add to list Price of Moulded Doors for Circle Top Panels or Segment, $1.45 for each side.
Sizes not given above, extra price.
For Doors prepared for Oil Finish, add 75 cents to list.

FOUR-PANEL RAISED MOULDED DOORS.

204

Raised Moulding.

SIZE.				Price, 1⅜ Thick.		Price, 1¾ Thick.	
				Moulded One Side.	Moulded Two Sides.	Moulded One Side.	Moulded Two Sides.
Ft. In.		Ft. In.		$ cts.	$ cts.	$ cts.	$ cts.
2 0	×	6 6		4.90	6.35		
2 6	×	6 6		4.90	6.35		
2 6	×	6 8		5.30	6.75	8.00	9.45
2 8	×	6 8		5.30	6.75	8.00	9.45
2 10	×	6 10		5.80	7.25	8.50	9.95
2 6	×	7 0		5.95	7.45	8.75	10.25
2 8	×	7 0		6.00	7.50	8.80	10.30
2 10	×	7 0		6.10	7.60	8.90	10.40
3 0	×	7 0		6.30	7.80	9.10	10.60
2 6	×	7 6		6.75	8.25	9.75	11.25
2 8	×	7 6		6.75	8.25	9.75	11.25
2 10	×	7 6		6.85	8.35	9.85	11.35
3 0	×	7 6		7.00	8.50	10.00	11.50
3 0	×	8 0		7.75	9.25	10.80	12.30
3 0	×	8 6		8.65	10.15	11.80	13.30

Add to list price of Moulded Doors for Circle Top Panels or Segment, $1.45 for each side
Sizes not given above, extra price.
For Doors prepared for Oil Finish, add 75 cents to list.

RAISED MOULDED DOORS, CIRCLE TOP PANELS.

205

Raised Moulding.

SIZE.				Price, 1⅜ Thick.		Price, 1¾ Thick.	
				Moulded One Side.	Moulded Two Sides.	Moulded One Side.	Moulded Two Sides.
Ft.	In.	Ft.	In.	$ cts.	$ cts.	$ cts.	$ cts.
2	0	× 6	6	6.35	9.25		
2	6	× 6	6	6.35	9.25		
2	6	× 6	8	6.75	9.65	9.45	12.35
2	8	× 6	8	6.75	9.65	9.45	12.35
2	10	× 6	10	7.25	10.15	9.95	12.85
2	6	× 7	0	7.40	10.35	10.20	13.15
2	8	× 7	0	7.45	10.40	10.25	13.20
2	10	× 7	0	7.55	10.50	10.35	13.30
3	0	× 7	0	7.75	10.70	10.55	13.50
2	6	× 7	6	8.20	11.15	11.20	14.15
2	8	× 7	6	8.20	11.15	11.20	14.15
2	10	× 7	6	8.30	11.25	11.30	14.25
3	0	× 7	6	8.45	11.40	11.45	14.40
3	0	× 8	0	9.20	12.15	12.25	15.20
3	0	× 8	6	10.10	13.05	13.25	16.20

Sizes not given above, extra price.

For Doors prepared for Oil Finish, add 75 cents to list.

FIVE-PANEL MOULDED DOORS.

206

Raised Moulding.

SIZE.				Price, 1¾ Thick.		Price, 1¾ Thick.	
				Moulded One Side.	Moulded Two Sides.	Moulded One Side.	Moulded Two Sides.
Ft. In.		Ft. In.		$ cts.	$ cts.	$ cts.	$ cts.
2 8	×	6 8		6.00	7.95	8.70	10.65
2 10	×	6 10		6.50	8.45	9.20	11.15
2 8	×	7 0		6.70	8.70	9.50	11.50
2 10	×	7 0		6.80	8.80	9.60	11.60
3 0	×	7 0		7.00	9.00	9.80	11.80
2 8	×	7 6		7.45	9.45	10.45	12.45
2 10	×	7 6		7.55	9.55	10.55	12.55
3 0	×	7 6		7.70	9.70	10.70	12.70
2 8	×	8 0		8.45	10.45	11.50	13.50
2 10	×	8 0		8.45	10.45	11.50	13.50
3 0	×	8 0		8.45	10.45	11.50	13.50

For Doors prepared for Oil Finish, add 75 cents to list.
Add to List Price of Moulded Doors for Circle Top Panels or Segment, $1.45 for each side.
Sizes not given above, extra price.

MACHINE CHAMFERED DOORS.

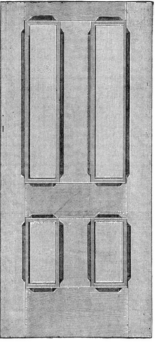

207

SIZE.					Price, 1⅜ Thick.		Price, 1¾ Thick.	
					Chamfered One Side.	Chamfered Two Sides.	Chamfered One Side.	Chamfered Two Sides.
Ft.	In.		Ft.	In.	$ cts.	$ cts.	$ cts.	$ cts.
2	4	×	6	8	4.35	4.85	6.65	7.15
2	6	×	6	8	4.35	4.85	6.65	7.15
2	8	×	6	8	4.40	4.90	6.70	7.20
2	8	×	6	10	4.70	5.20	7.00	7.50
2	10	×	6	10	4.80	5.30	7.10	7.60
2	8	×	7	0	4.90	5.40	7.25	7.75
2	10	×	7	0	5.00	5.50	7.35	7.85
3	0	×	7	0	5.20	5.70	7.55	8.05
2	8	×	7	6	5.60	6.10	8.05	8.55
2	10	×	7	6	5.70	6.20	8.15	8.65
3	0	×	7	6	5.85	6.35	8.30	8.80
3	0	×	8	0	6.50	7.00	9.00	9.50

For Doors prepared for Oil Finish, add 75 cents to list.
Sizes not given above, extra price.

CHAMFERED AND STUB MOULDED DOORS.

208

Four Panel. Beaded Lock Rail.

SIZE.				Price, 1⅜ Thick.		Price, 1¾ Thick.	
				Chamfered and End Moulded One Side.	Chamfered and End Moulded Two Sides.	Chamfered and End Moulded One Side.	Chamfered and End Moulded Two Sides.
Ft.	In.	Ft.	In.	$ cts.	$ cts.	$ cts.	$ cts.
2	6	×	6 6	5.10	5.80	7.30	8.00
2	8	×	6 8	5.40	6.10	7.70	8.40
2	10	×	6 10	5.80	6.50	8.10	8.80
2	8	×	7 0	5.90	6.60	8.25	8.95
2	10	×	7 0	6.00	6.70	8.35	9.05
3	0	×	7 0	6.20	6.90	8.55	9.25
2	8	×	7 6	6.60	7.30	9.05	9.75
2	10	×	7 6	6.70	7.40	9.15	9.85
3	0	×	7 6	6.85	7.55	9.30	10.00
3	0	×	8 0	7.50	8.20	10.05	10.75
3	0	×	8 6	8.40	9.10	11.15	11.85

For Doors prepared for Oil Finish, add 75 cents to list.

Sizes not given above, extra price.

O G SASH DOORS.

210   211

Four and Two Light. Raised Panels Both Sides.

SIZE.				Thickness.	Square Top Glass.		
					Price Unglazed.	Price Glazed, Four Lights.	Price Glazed, Two Lights.
Ft.	In.	Ft.	In.	Inches.	$ cts.	$ cts.	$ cts.
2	6	× 6	6	1 3-8	3.65	5.35	5.85
2	8	× 6	8	"	3.95	5 85	6.30
2	6	× 6	10	"	4 25	6.35	6.75
2	10	× 6	10	"	4.35	6.70	7.60
2	6	× 7	0	"	4.60	6.70	7.30
3	0	× 7	0	"	4.75	7.10	8.00
2	6	× 7	6	"	5.25	7.50	8.65
3	0	× 7	6	"	5.40	7.95	9.50
2	6	× 8	0	"	5.90	8.20	10.25
3	0	× 8	0	"	6.05	9.55	11.20

Sash Doors, 1¼ thick, same price as 1⅜. We make Sash Doors in first quality only.

For prices of 1¾ O G Sash Doors, add the difference between 1⅜ and 1¾ O G Four-Panel Doors, same size. See page 101.

O G SASH DOORS.

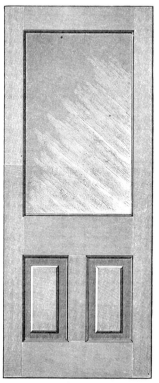

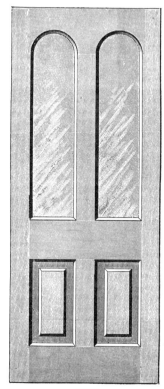

212

213

One and Two Light. Raised Panels Both Sides.

SIZE.				Thickness.	One Light, Square Top Glass.		Two Lights, Circle Top Glass.	
					Unglazed.	Glazed, D'ble Strength.	Unglazed.	Glazed.
Ft.	In.	Ft.	In.	Inches.	$ cts.	$ cts.	$ cts.	$ cts.
2	6	× 6	6	1 3-8	3.65	6.25	4.30	6.50
2	8	× 6	8	"	3.95	7.10	4.60	6.95
2	6	× 6	10	"	4.25	7.40	4.90	7.40
2	10	× 6	10	"	4.35	7.95	5.00	8.25
2	6	× 7	0	"	4.60	8.20	5.25	7.95
3	0	× 7	0	"	4.75	9.30	5.40	8.65
2	6	× 7	6	"	5.25	9.15	5.90	9.30
3	0	× 7	6	"	5.40	10.85	6.05	10.15
2	6	× 8	0	"	5.90	10.65	6.55	10.90
3	0	× 8	0	"	6.05	11.75	6.70	11.85

For prices of 1¾ O G Sash Doors, add the difference between 1⅜ and 1¾ O G Four-Panel Doors, same size. See page 101.

O G SASH DOORS.

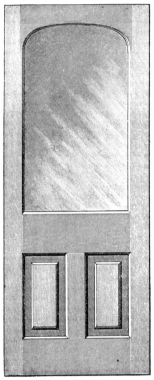

214½—Elliptic.

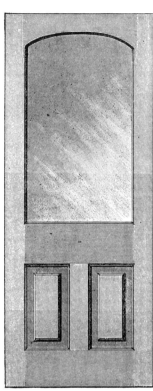

215—Segment.

One Light. Raised Panels Both Sides.

SIZE.				Thickness.	One Light, Elliptic Top Glass.		One Light, Segment Top Glass.	
					Unglazed.	Glazed, D'ble Strength	Unglazed.	Glazed, D'ble Strength
Ft.	In.	Ft.	In.	Inches.	$ cts.	$ cts.	$ cts.	$ cts.
2	6	× 6	6	1 3-8	4.30	7.05	4.30	7.05
2	8	× 6	8	"	4.60	7.90	4.60	7.90
2	6	× 6	10	"	4.85	8.15	4.85	8.15
2	10	× 6	10	"	5.00	8.80	5.00	8.80
2	6	× 7	0	"	5.05	8.85	5.05	8.85
3	0	× 7	0	"	5.40	10.20	5.40	10.20
2	6	× 7	6	"	5.80	9.95	5.80	9.95
3	0	× 7	6	"	6.05	11.80	6.05	11.80
2	6	× 8	0	"	6.70	11.75	6.70	11.75
3	0	× 8	0	"	6.70	12.75	6.70	12.75

For prices of 1¾-inch O G Sash Doors, add the difference between 1⅜ and 1¾ O G Four-Panel Doors, same size. See page 101.

MOULDED SASH DOORS.

216   217

Moulded One Side. Raised Panels Both Sides.

SIZE.				Thickness.	Two Lights, Circle Top Glass.		One Light, Upper Corners Circle.	
					Unglazed.	Glazed.	Unglazed.	Glazed, D'ble Strength.
Ft.	In.	Ft.	In.	Inches.	$ cts.	$ cts.	$ cts.	$ cts.
2	6	× 6	6	1 3-8	6.70	8.90	6.70	9.45
2	8	× 6	8	''	7.10	9.45	7.10	10.40
2	6	× 6	10	''	7.50	10.00	7.50	10.80
2	10	× 6	10	''	7.60	10.85	7.60	11.40
2	6	× 7	0	''	7.95	10.65	7.95	11.75
3	0	× 7	0	''	8.10	11.35	8.10	12.90
2	6	× 7	6	''	8.65	12.05	8.65	12.80
3	0	× 7	6	''	8.80	12.90	8.80	14.55
2	6	× 8	0	''	9.40	13.75	9.40	14.45
3	0	× 8	0	''	9.55	14.70	9.55	15.60

For prices of 1¾-inch Moulded Sash Doors, add the difference between 1⅜ and 1¾ Four-Panel Raised Moulded Doors, same size. See page 101.

MOULDED SASH DOORS.

218

219

Moulded One Side. Raised Panels Both Sides.

SIZE.				Thickness.	One Light, Circle Top Glass.		One Light, Segment Top Glass.	
					Unglazed.	Glazed, D. S.	Unglazed.	Glazed. D. S.
Ft.	In.	Ft.	In.	Inches.	$ cts.	$ cts.	$ cts.	$ cts.
2	6	× 6	6	1 3-8	7.00	9.75	6.70	9.45
2	8	× 6	8	"	7.40	10.70	7.10	10.40
2	6	× 6	10	"	7.85	11.15	7.50	10.80
2	10	× 6	10	"	7.95	11.75	7.60	11.40
2	6	× 7	0	"	8.30	12.10	7.95	11.75
3	0	× 7	0	"	8.45	13.25	8.10	12.90
2	6	× 7	6	"	9.00	13.15	8.65	12.80
3	0	× 7	6	"	9.25	15.00	8.80	14.55
2	6	× 8	0	"	9.80	14.85	9.40	14.45
3	0	× 8	0	"	10.00	16.05	9.55	15.60

For prices of 1¾ Moulded Sash Doors, add the difference between 1⅜ and 1¾ Four-Panel Raised Moulded Doors, same size. See page 101.

CHAMFERED AND STUB MOULDED DOORS.

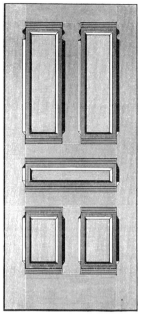

220

Five-Panel.

SIZE.				Price of No. 220, 1⅜ Thick.		Price of No. 220, 1¾ Thick.	
				Chamfered and Moulded on One Side. O G on Other Side.	Chamfered and Moulded on Both Sides.	Chamfered and Moulded on One Side. O G on Other Side.	Chamfered and Moulded on Both Sides.
Ft.	In.	Ft.	In.	$ cts.	$ cts.	$ cts.	$ cts.
2	6 ×	6	8	5.90	6.60	8.10	8.80
2	8 ×	6	8	6.20	6.90	8 50	9.20
2	10 ×	6	10	6.60	7 30	8.90	9.60
2	8 ×	7	0	6.70	7.40	9.05	9.75
2	10 ×	7	0	6.80	7.50	9.15	9.85
3	0 ×	7	0	7.00	7.70	9.35	10.05
2	8 ×	7	6	7.40	8.10	9.85	10.55
2	10 ×	7	6	7.50	8.20	9.95	10.65
3	0 ×	7	6	7.65	8.35	10.10	10.80
3	0 ×	8	0	8.30	9.00	10.85	11.55
3	0 ×	8	6	9.20	9.90	11.95	12.65

For Doors prepared for Oil Finish, add 75 cents to list.
Sizes not given above, extra price.

COTTAGE DOORS.

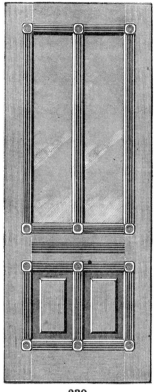

230

GARFIELD, 2-LIGHT.

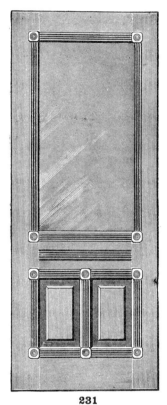

231

GARFIELD, 1-LIGHT.

SIZE.				Thickness.	No. 230.—Garfield. Two-Light, Square Top.		No. 231.—Garfield. One-Light, Square Top.	
					Price Unglazed.	Price Glazed.	Price Unglazed.	Price Glazed, D. S.
Ft.	In.	Ft.	In.	Inches.	$ cts.	$ cts.	$ cts.	$ cts.
2	6	× 6	6	1 3-8	6.20	8.40	5.85	8.45
2	8	× 6	8	"	6.60	8.95	6.20	9.35
2	8	× 6	10	"			6.60	10.20
2	10	× 6	10	"	7.05	10.30	6.65	10.25
2	8	× 7	0	"	7.50	10.40	7.10	10.70
2	10	× 7	0	"	7.55	10.80	7.15	11.35
3	0	× 7	0	"	7.60	10.85	7.20	11.75
2	10	× 7	6	"	8.20	12.30	7.80	12.35
3	0	× 7	6	"	8.25	12.35	7.85	13.30
3	0	× 8	0	"	8.95	14.10	8.55	14.25
3	0	× 8	6	"	9.85	17.30	9.45	16.90

For price of 1¾ Doors, add to above list the difference between 1⅜ and 1¾ Raised Moulded Doors, same size. See page 101.

COTTAGE DOORS.

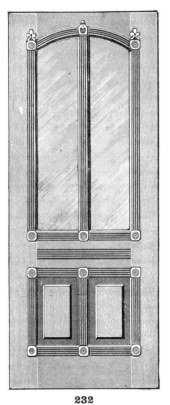

232

JENNY LIND, 2-LIGHT.

233

JENNY LIND, 1-LIGHT.

SIZE.				Thickness.	No. 232.—Jenny Lind. Two-Light.		No. 233.—Jenny Lind. One-Light, Segment Top.	
					Price Unglazed.	Price Glazed.	Price Unglazed.	Price Glazed, D. S.
Ft.	In.	Ft.	In.	Inches.	$ cts.	$ cts.	$ cts.	$ cts.
2	6	× 6	6	1 3-8	7.25	9.45	6.80	9.55
2	8	× 6	8	"	7.65	10.00	7.15	10.45
2	8	× 6	10	"	8.05	11.30	7.55	11.35
2	10	× 6	10	"	8.10	11.35	7.60	11.40
2	8	× 7	0	"	8.55	11.45	8.05	11.85
2	10	× 7	0	"	8.60	11.85	8.10	12.55
3	0	× 7	0	"	8.65	11.90	8.15	12.95
2	10	× 7	6	"	9.25	13.35	8.75	13.55
3	0	× 7	6	"	9.30	13.40	8.80	14.55
3	0	× 8	0	"	10.00	15.15	9.50	15.55
3	0	× 8	6	"	10.90	18.35	10.40	18.30

For price of 1¾ Doors, add to above list the difference between 1⅜ and 1¾ Four-Panel Raised Moulded Doors, same size. See page 101.

COTTAGE DOORS.

234—CONGRESS.

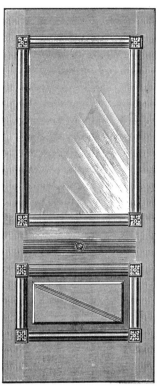

235—LINCOLN.

SIZE.				Thick-ness.	Price, Unglazed.	Price, Glazed, D. S.
Ft.	In.	Ft.	In.	Inches.	$ cts.	$ cts.
2	8 ×	6	8	1 3-8	7·60	10·75
2	8 ×	6	10	"	7·95	11·55
2	10 ×	6	10	"	8·00	11·60
2	8 ×	7	0	"	8·40	12·00
2	10 ×	7	0	"	8·45	12·65
3	0 ×	7	0	"	8 60	13·15
2	10 ×	7	6	"	9·25	13·80
3	0 ×	7	6	"	9·30	14·75
3	0 ×	8	0	"	10·05	15·75

For 1¾ Doors, add to above list the difference between 1⅜ and 1¾ Raised Moulded Doors, same size. See page 101.

COTTAGE DOORS.

236—Bismarck.

Bead Stop and Flush Moulding Opposite.

SIZE.					Price per Door, 1⅜ Inch, Unglazed.	No. of Square Feet of Glass in each Door.
Ft.	In.		Ft.	In.	$ cts.	Feet.
2	8	×	6	8	9.30	4
2	6	×	7	0	10.20	4 1-4
2	8	×	7	0	10 25	4 2-3
2	10	×	7	0	10.30	5 1-12
3	0	×	7	0	10.35	5 5-12
2	6	×	7	6	10.95	5 1-6
2	8	×	7	6	10.95	5 2-3
2	10	×	7	6	11.00	6 1-6
3	0	×	7	6	11.05	6 7-12
3	0	×	8	0	11.80	7 3-4

Doors less than 2 ft. 6 in. wide will be charged same price as the 2 ft. 6 in.

For Doors in pairs (like above cut), add 50 cents to list price of each Door for Astragal.

Prices given above for one Door only.

For price of 1¾ Doors, add the difference between 1⅜ and 1¾ Raised Moulded Doors, same size.   See page 101.

COTTAGE DOORS.

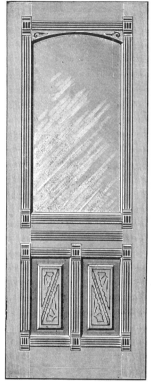

237—GRANT.

238—OSHKOSH.

SIZE.					Thickness.	Prices of No. 237.		Prices of No. 238.	
						Unglazed.	Glazed, D. S.	Unglazed.	Glazed, D. S.
Ft.	In.		Ft.	In.	Inches.	$ cts.	$ cts.	$ cts.	$ cts.
2	6	×	6	6	1 3-8	7.10	9.85	9.20	11.80
2	8	×	6	8	"	7.45	10.75	9.60	12.75
2	8	×	6	10	"	7.85	11.65	10.00	13.60
2	10	×	6	10	"	7.90	11.70	10.05	13.65
2	8	×	7	0	"	8.35	12.15	10.50	14.10
2	10	×	7	0	"	8.40	12.85	10.55	14.75
3	0	×	7	0	"	8.45	13.25	10.60	15.15
2	10	×	7	6	"	9.05	13.85	11.20	15.75
3	0	×	7	6	"	9.10	14.85	11.25	16.70
3	0	×	8	0	"	9.80	15.85	12.15	17.85
3	0	×	8	6	"	10.70	18.60	13.05	20.50

For price of 1¾ Doors, add the difference between 1⅜ and 1¾ Raised Moulded Doors. See page 101.

COTTAGE DOORS.

239—Cream City.

240—Columbus Marginal.

SIZE.				Thickness.	No. **239**	Prices of No. 240.	
						Unglazed.	Glazed, D. S.
Ft.	In.	Ft.	In.	Inches.		$ cts.	$ cts.
2	6	× 6	6	1 3-8		8 85	11.45
2	8	× 6	8	"		9.25	12.40
2	8	× 6	10	"		9.80	13.40
2	10	× 6	10	"		9.85	13.45
2	8	× 7	0	"	*WRITE FOR*	10.35	13.95
2	10	× 7	0	"	*PRICES.*	10.40	14.60
3	0	× 7	0	"		10.45	15.00
2	10	× 7	6	"		11.25	15.80
3	0	× 7	6	"		11.30	16.75
3	0	× 8	0	"		12.20	17.90
3	0	× 8	6	"		13.10	20.55

For price of 1¾ Doors, add to above list the difference between 1⅜ and 1¾ Four-Panel Raised Moulded Doors, same size. See page 101.

For price of Colored and Fancy Glass in Marginal Light Doors, see page 101.

COTTAGE DOORS.

241

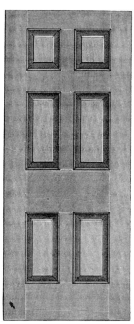

242

WRITE FOR PRICES.

COTTAGE DOORS.

243—Columbus.

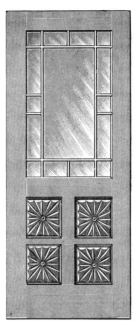

244—Leader.

SIZE.				Thickness.	Prices of No. 243.		Prices of No. 244.	
					Unglazed.	Glazed, D. S.	Unglazed.	Glazed, D. S.
Ft.	In.	Ft.	In.	Inches.	$ cts.	$ cts.	$ cts.	$ cts.
2	6	× 6	6	1 3-8	7 35	9.95	6.85	9.45
2	8	× 6	8	"	7.75	10.90	7.25	10.40
2	8	× 6	10	"	8.15	11.75	7.65	11.25
2	10	× 6	10	"	8.20	11.80	7.70	11.30
2	8	× 7	0	"	8.65	12.25	8.15	11.75
2	10	× 7	0	"	8.70	12.90	8.20	12 40
3	0	× 7	0	"	8.75	13.30	8.25	12.80
2	10	× 7	6	"	9.35	13.90	8.85	13.40
3	0	× 7	6	"	9.40	14.85	8.90	14.35
3	0	× 8	0	"	10.10	15.80	9.60	15.30
3	0	× 8	6	"	11.00	18.45	10.50	17.95

For price of 1¾ Doors No. 243, add to above list the difference between 1⅜ and 1¾ Four-Panel Raised Moulded Doors, same size. See page 101.

For price of 1¾ Doors No. 244, add to above list the difference between 1⅜ and 1¾ O G Doors, same size. See page 101.

For price of Colored and Fancy Glass in Marginal Light Doors, see page 101.

COTTAGE DOORS.

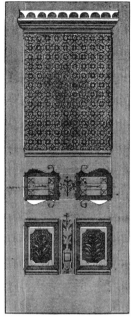

245

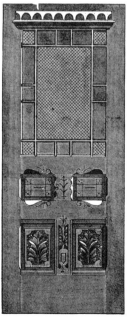

246

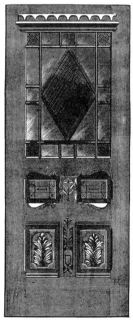

247

WRITE FOR PRICES.

COTTAGE DOORS.

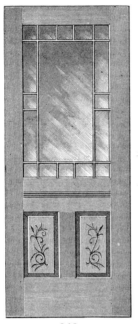

248

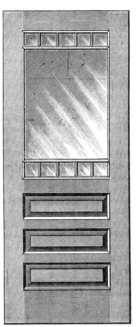

249

SIZE.				Thickness.	Prices of No 248.		Prices of No. 249.	
					Unglazed.	Glazed, D. S.	Unglazed.	Glazed, D. S.
Ft.	In.	Ft.	In.	Inches.	$ cts.	$ cts.	$ cts.	$ cts.
2	6	× 6	6	1 3-8	5.45	8.05	5.10	7.25
2	8	× 6	8	"	5.75	8.90	5.40	8.00
2	8	× 6	10	"	6.05	9.65	5.70	8.30
2	10	× 6	10	"	6.15	9.75	5.80	8.95
2	8	× 7	0	"	6.25	9.85	5.90	9.05
2	10	× 7	0	"	6.35	10.55	6.00	9.60
3	0	× 7	0	"	6.55	11.10	6.20	9.80
2	10	× 7	6	"	7.05	11.60	6.70	10.90
3	0	× 7	6	"	7.20	12.65	6.85	11.40
3	0	× 8	0	"	7.85	13.55	7.50	12.95
3	0	× 8	6	"	8.75	16.20	8.40	14.10

For price of 1¾ Doors, add to above list the difference between 1⅜ and 1¾ O G Doors, same size.   See page 101.

For price of Colored and Fancy Glass in Marginal Light Doors, see page 101.

COTTAGE DOORS.

250

251—Imperial.

SIZE.				Thickness.	Prices of No. 250.		No. **251**
					Unglazed.	Glazed, D. S.	
Ft.	In.	Ft.	In.	Inches.	$ cts.	$ cts.	
2	6	× 6	6	1 3-8	8.60	10.60	
2	8	× 6	8	"	9.00	11.60	
2	8	× 6	10	"	9.40	12.00	
2	10	× 6	10	"	9.45	12.60	
2	8	× 7	0	"	9.90	13.05	*WRITE FOR*
2	10	× 7	0	"	9.95	13.10	*PRICES.*
3	0	× 7	0	"	10.00	13.60	
2	10	× 7	6	"	10.60	14.20	
3	0	× 7	6	"	10.65	15.20	
3	0	× 8	0	"	11.35	16.80	
3	0	× 8	6	"	12.25	17.95	

For price of 1¾ Doors, add to above list the difference between 1⅜ and 1¾ Four-Panel Raised Moulded Doors, same size.   See page 101.

For price of Colored and Fancy Glass in Marginal Light Doors, see page 101.

COTTAGE DOORS.

252—Crown Prince.   253—Cleveland.

SIZE.				Thickness.	No. **252.**	Prices of No. 253.	
---	---	---	---	---	---	Unglazed.	Glazed, D. S.
Ft. In.		Ft. In.		Inches.		$ cts.	$ cts.
2 6	×	6 6		1 3-8		9.70	12.30
2 8	×	6 8		"		10.10	13.25
2 10	×	6 10		"		10.55	14.15
2 8	×	7 0		"		11.00	14.60
2 10	×	7 0		"	*WRITE FOR*	11.05	15.25
3 0	×	7 0		"	*PRICES.*	11.10	15.65
2 8	×	7 6		"		11.65	16.20
2 10	×	7 6		"		11.70	16.25
3 0	×	7 6		"		11.75	17.20
3 0	×	8 0		"		12.65	18.35
3 0	×	8 6		"		13.55	21.00

For price of 1¾ Doors, add to above list the difference between 1⅜ and 1¾ Four-Panel Raised Moulded Doors, same size. See page 101.

For price of Colored and Fancy Glass in Marginal Light Doors, see page 101.

COTTAGE DOORS.

254—Queen Anne.

255—Diagonal.

SIZE.				Thickness.	Prices of No. 254.		No. 255.
					Unglazed.	Glazed, D. S.	
Ft.	In.	Ft.	In.	Inches.	$ cts.	$ cts.	
2	6	× 6	6	1 3-8	10.70	13.30	
2	8	× 6	8	"	11.10	14.25	
2	10	× 6	10	"	11.55	15.15	
2	8	× 7	0	"	12.00	15.60	
2	10	× 7	0	"	12.05	16.25	*WRITE FOR*
3	0	× 7	0	"	12.10	16.65	*PRICES.*
2	8	× 7	6	"	12.65	17.20	
2	10	× 7	6	"	12.70	17.25	
3	0	× 7	6	"	12.75	18.20	
3	0	× 8	0	"	13.65	19.35	
3	0	× 8	6	"	14.55	22.00	

For price of 1¾ Doors, add to above list the difference between 1⅜ and 1¾ Four-Panel Raised Moulded Doors, same size.   See page 101.

For price of Colored and Fancy Glass in Marginal Light Doors, see page 101.

COTTAGE DOORS.

256—Derby.

257—Excelsior.

258—Acme.

WRITE FOR PRICES.

COTTAGE DOORS.

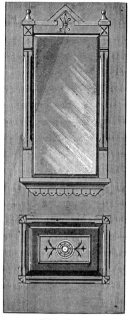

259—Folsom.

260—Winnebago.

SIZE.				Thickness.	Prices of No. 259.		Prices of No. 260.	
					Unglazed.	Glazed, D. S.	Unglazed.	Glazed D. S.
Ft.	In.	Ft.	In.	Inches.	$ cts.	$ cts.	$ cts.	$ cts.
2	6	× 6	6	1 3-8	9.70	12.30	8.60	11 20
2	8	× 6	8	"	10.10	13.25	9.00	12.15
2	8	× 6	10	"	10.50	14 10	9.40	13.00
2	10	× 6	10	"	10.55	14.15	9.45	13.05
2	8	× 7	0	"	11.00	14.60	9.90	13.50
2	10	× 7	0	"	11.05	15.25	9.95	14.15
3	0	× 7	0	"	11.10	15.65	10.00	14.55
2	10	× 7	6	"	11.70	16.25	10.60	15.15
3	0	× 7	6	"	11.75	17.20	10.65	16.10
3	0	× 8	0	"	12.65	18.35	11.55	17.25
3	0	× 8	6	"	13.55	21.00	12.45	19.90

For price of 1¾ Doors, add to above list the difference between 1⅜ and 1¾ Four-Panel Raised Moulded Doors, same size.   See page 101.

For price of Colored and Fancy Glass in Marginal Light Doors, see page 101.

COTTAGE DOORS.

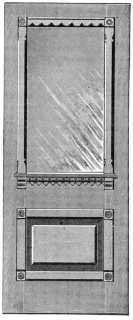 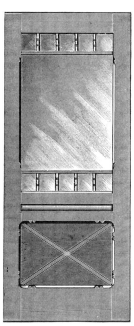

261—NORFOLK.   **262**—PLYMOUTH.

WRITE FOR PRICES.

COTTAGE DOORS.

263—LEE.

264—INDIANA.

SIZE.				Prices of No. 263.		Prices of No. 264.	
				1¾ inch.		1⅜ Inch.	
				Unglazed.	Glazed—D. S.	Unglazed.	Glazed—D. S.
Ft.	In.	Ft.	In.	$ cts.	$ cts.	$ cts.	$ cts.
2	6	× 6	6			5.15	7.75
2	8	× 6	8			5.50	8.65
2	10	× 6	10			5.95	9.55
2	8	× 7	0	19.80	23.40	6.35	9 95
2	10	× 7	0	19.90	24.10	6.40	10.60
3	0	× 7	0	20.00	24.55	6.45	11.00
2	8	× 7	6	20.80	25.35	7.05	11.60
2	10	× 7	6	20.90	25.45	7.10	11.65
3	0	× 7	6	21.00	26.45	7.15	12.60
3	0	× 8	0	22.00	27.70	7.80	13.50
3	0	× 8	6	23.00	30.45	8.70	16.15

For price of No. 264, 1¾ Indiana Doors, add to above list the difference between 1⅜ and 1¾ Four-Panel Raised Moulded Doors, same size. See page 101.

COTTAGE DOORS.

265—CAMBRIDGE.

266—OXFORD.

SIZE.				Thickness.	Prices of No. 265.		Prices of No. 266.	
					Unglazed.	Glazed, D. S.	Unglazed.	Glazed, D. S.
Ft.	In.	Ft.	In.	Inches.	$ cts.	$ cts.	$ cts.	$ cts.
2	6	× 6	6	1 3-8	13.10	15.45	8.60	10.95
2	8	× 6	8	"	13.50	16.10	9.00	11.60
2	8	× 6	10	"	13.90	17.05	9.40	12.55
2	10	× 6	10	"	13.95	17.10	9 45	13.05
2	8	× 7	0	"	14.40	17.55	9.90	13.05
2	10	× 7	0	"	14.45	18.05	9.95	13 55
3	0	× 7	0	"	14.50	18.10	10.00	13.60
2	10	× 7	6	"	15.10	19.65	10.60	15.15
3	0	× 7	6	"	15.15	19.70	10.65	15 20
3	0	× 8	0	"	16.05	21.75	11.55	17.00
3	0	× 8	6	"	16.95	22.90	12.45	19.90

For price of 1¾ Doors, add to above list the difference between 1⅜ and 1¾ Four-Panel Raised Moulded Doors, same size. See page 101.

For price of Colored and Fancy Glass in Marginal Light Doors, see page 101.

COTTAGE DOORS.

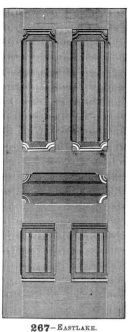

267—Eastlake.

Front Door; the opposite side is
finished like No. 268.

268—Eastlake.

Inside Door; both sides finished
alike.

269—Mikado.

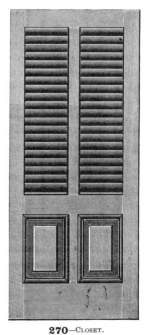

270—Closet.

Stationary Slats.

WRITE FOR PRICES.

COTTAGE DOORS.

271—Washington.

272—Garfield Marginal.

SIZE.				Thick-ness.	Prices of No. 271.—Washington.		Prices of No. 272—Garfield Marginal.	
					Unglazed.	Glazed. D. S.	Unglazed.	Glazed, D. S.
Ft.	In.	Ft.	In.	Inches.	$ cts.	$ cts.	$ cts-	$ cts.
2	6 ×	6	6	1 3 8	22.60	25.20	7 35	9.95
2	8 ×	6	8	"	23.00	26.15	7.70	10.85
2	8 ×	6	10	"	23.40	27.00		
2	10 ×	6	10	"	23.45	27.05	8.30	11.90
2	8 ×	7	0	"	23.90	27.50	8.80	12.40
2	10 ×	7	0	"	23.95	28.15	8.85	13.05
3	0 ×	7	0	"	24.00	28.55	8.90	13.45
2	10 ×	7	6	"	24.60	29.15	9.70	14.25
3	0 ×	7	6	"	24.65	30.10	9.75	15.20
3	0 ×	8	0	"	25.55	31.25	10.65	16.35
3	0 ×	8	6	"	26.45	33.90	11.55	19 00

For price of 1¾ Doors, add to above list the difference between 1⅜ and 1¾ Four-Panel Raised Moulded Doors, same size. See page 101.

For price of Colored and Fancy Glass in **Marginal** Light Doors, see page 101.

COTTAGE DOORS.

273—Jenny Lind Marginal.

274—Grant Marginal.

SIZE.				Thick-ness.	Prices of No. 273.		Prices of No. 274.	
					Unglazed.	Glazed D. S.	Unglazed.	Glazed D. S.
Ft.	In.	Ft.	In.	Inches.	$ cts.	$ cts.	$ cts.	$ cts.
2	6	× 6	6	1 3-8	8.80	11.55	9.10	11.85
2	8	× 6	8	"	9.15	12.45	9.45	12.75
2	8	× 6	10	"	9.65	13.45	10.00	13.80
2	10	× 6	10	"	9.70	13.50	10.05	13.85
2	8	× 7	0	"	10.30	14.10	10.60	14.40
2	10	× 7	0	"	10.35	14.80	10.65	15.10
3	0	× 7	0	"	10.40	15.20	10.70	15.50
2	10	× 7	6	"	11.15	15.95	11.45	16.25
3	0	× 7	6	"	11.20	16.95	11.50	17.25
3	0	× 8	0	"	12.10	18.15	12.40	18.45
3	0	× 8	6	"	13.00	20.90	13.30	21.20

For price of 1¾ Doors, add to above list the difference between 1⅜ and 1¾ Four-Panel Raised Moulded Doors, same size. See page 101.

For price of Colored and Fancy Glass in Marginal Light Doors, see page 101.

COTTAGE DOORS.

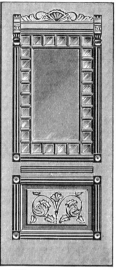

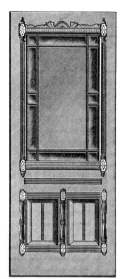

275—Oshkosh Marginal.

276—Nashville.

SIZE.				Thickness.	Prices of No. 275.		Prices of No. 276.	
					Unglazed.	Glazed, D. S.	Unglazed.	Glazed, D. S.
Ft.	In.	Ft.	In.	Inches.	$ cts.	$ cts.	$ cts.	$ cts.
2	6	× 6	6	1 3-8	10.70	13 30	8.65	11.25
2	8	× 6	8	''	11.10	14 25	9.05	12.20
2	10	× 6	10	''	11.70	15.30	9.50	13.10
2	8	× 7	0	''	12.20	15.80	9.90	13.50
2	10	× 7	0	''	12.25	16 45	9.95	14.15
3	0	× 7	0	''	12.30	16.85	10.00	14.55
2	10	× 7	6	''	13.10	17.65	10.60	15.15
3	0	× 7	6	''	13.15	18.60	10.65	16.10
3	0	× 8	0	''	14 25	19.95	11.35	17.05
3	0	× 8	6	''	14.95	22.40	12.25	19.70

For price of 1¾ Doors, add to above list the difference between 1⅜ and 1¾ Four-Panel Raised Moulded Doors, same size. See page 101.

For price of Colored and Fancy Glass in Marginal Light Doors, see page 101.

COTTAGE DOORS.

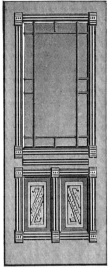

277—Illinois Marginal.

278—Harrison.

SIZE.				Thickness.	Prices of No. 277.		Prices of No. 278.	
					Unglazed.	Glazed, D. S.	Unglazed.	Glazed, D. S.
Ft.	In.	Ft.	In.	Inches.	$ cts.	$ cts.	$ cts.	$ cts.
2	6	× 6	6	1 3-8	7.50	10.10	9.90	12.50
2	8	× 6	8	"	7.85	11.00	10.30	13.45
2	10	× 6	10	"	8.40	12.00	10.75	14.35
2	8	× 7	0	"	8.85	12.45	11.20	14.80
2	10	× 7	0	"	8.90	13.10	11.25	15.45
3	0	× 7	0	"	8.95	13.50	11.30	15.85
2	10	× 7	6	"	9.55	14.10	11.90	16.45
3	0	× 7	6	"	9.60	15.05	11.95	17.40
3	0	× 8	0	"	10.30	16.00	12.85	18.55
3	0	× 8	6	"	11.20	18.65	13.75	21.20

For price of 1¾ Doors, add to above list the difference between 1⅜ and 1¾ Four-Panel Raised Moulded Doors, same size. See page 101.

For price of Colored and Fancy Glass in Marginal Light Doors, see page 101.

COTTAGE DOORS.

279 — MORTON.

280 — CHICAGO.

SIZE.				Thickness.	Prices of No. 279.		Prices of No. 280.	
					Unglazed.	Glazed, D. S.	Unglazed.	Glazed D. S.
Ft.	In.	Ft.	In.	Inches.	$ cts.	$ cts.	$ cts.	$ cts.
2	6	× 6	6	1 3-8	10.40	13.00	10.90	13.50
2	8	× 6	8	"	10.80	13.95	11.30	14.45
2	10	× 6	10	"	11.25	14.85	11.75	15.35
2	8	× 7	0	"	11.70	15.30	12.10	15.70
2	10	× 7	0	"	11.75	15.95	12.20	16.40
3	0	× 7	0	"	11.80	16.35	12.30	16.85
2	10	× 7	6	"	12.40	16.95	12.85	17.40
3	0	× 7	6	"	12.45	17.90	12.95	18.40
3	0	× 8	0	"	13.35	19.05	13.85	19.55
3	0	× 8	6	"	14.25	21.70	14.75	22.20

For price of 1¾ Doors, add to above list the difference between 1⅜ and 1¾ Four-Panel Raised Moulded Doors, same size. See page 101.

For price of Colored and Fancy Glass in Marginal Light Doors, see page 101.

COTTAGE DOORS.

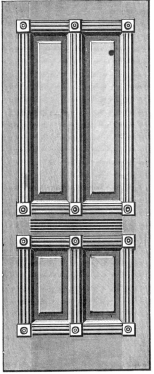

281—Garfield Panel.   **282**—Oshkosh Panel.

		SIZE.			Prices of No. 281.		Prices of No. 282.	
					1⅜ Inch.	1¾ Inch.	1⅜ Inch.	1¾ Inch.
Ft.	In.	Ft.	In.		$ cts.	$ cts.	$ cts.	$ cts.
2	6	×	6	6	6.00	8.70	10.10	12.80
2	8	×	6	8	6.40	9.10	10.50	13.20
2	10	×	6	10	6.85	9.55	10.95	13.65
2	8	×	7	0	7.30	10.10	11.40	14.20
2	10	×	7	0	7.35	10.15	11.45	14.25
3	0	×	7	0	7.40	10.20	11.50	14.30
2	10	×	7	6	8.00	11.00	12.10	15.10
3	0	×	7	6	8.05	11.05	12.15	15.15
3	0	×	8	0	8.75	11.80	13.05	16.10
3	0	×	8	6	9.65	12.80	13.95	17.10

For price of 1¾ Doors, add to above list the difference between 1⅜ and 1¾ Four-Panel Raised Moulded Doors, same size. See page 101.

COTTAGE DOORS.

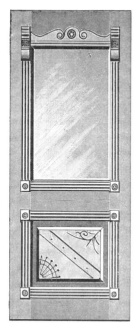

284

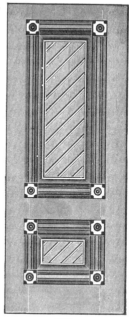

285

286

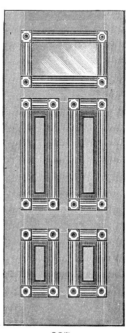

287

WRITE FOR PRICES.

COTTAGE DOORS.

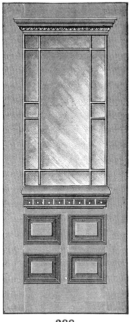

288

289

291

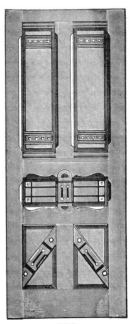

292

WRITE FOR PRICES.

COTTAGE DOORS.

294

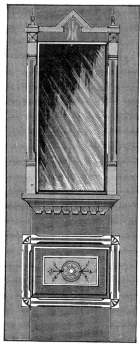

295

296

WRITE FOR PRICES.

COTTAGE DOORS.

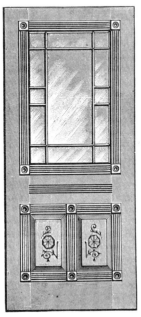

297—GATE CITY.

298

SIZE.				Thickness.	Prices of No. 297.		Prices of 298.	
					Unglazed.	Glazed, D. S.	Unglazed.	Glazed Double Strength.
Ft.	In.	Ft.	In.	Inches.	$ cts.	$ cts.	$ cts.	$ cts.
2	6 ×	6	6	1 3-8	7 35	9.95	5.20	6.85
2	8 ×	6	8	"	7.70	10.85	5.50	7.50
2	8 ×	6	10	"			5 80	8.00
2	10 ×	6	10	"	8.30	11.90	5.90	8.25
2	8 ×	7	0	"	8.80	12.40	6.00	8.35
2	10 ×	7	0	"	8.85	13.05	6.10	8.70
3	0 ×	7	0	"	8.90	13 45	6.30	8.90
2	10 ×	7	6	"	9.70	14.25	6.80	9.95
3	0 ×	7	6	"	9.75	15 20	6.95	10.55
3	0 ×	8	0	"	10.65	16.35	7.60	11.80
3	0 ×	8	6	"	11.55	19 00	8.50	13.95

For price of 1¾ Doors, No. 297, add to above list the difference between 1⅜ and 1¾ Four-Panel Raised Moulded Doors, same size.   See page 101.

For price of 1¾ Doors, No. 298, add to above list the difference between 1⅜ and 1¾ Four-Panel O G Doors, same size.   See page 101.

For price of Colored and Fancy Glass in Marginal Light Doors, see page 101.

COTTAGE DOORS.

301

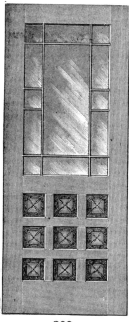

302

303

WRITE FOR PRICES.

COTTAGE DOORS.

304—World's Fair.

305—World's Fair Marginal.

306

307

WRITE FOR PRICES.

INSIDE DOORS.

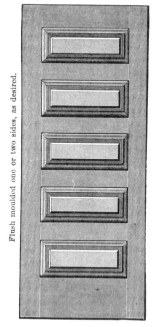

308

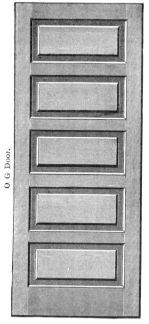

309½

310

311

WRITE FOR PRICES.

FRONT DOORS AND FRAME.

Finish No. **665**

312   313

WRITE FOR PRICES.

FRONT DOORS AND FRAME.

317

INSIDE DOOR AND FRAME.

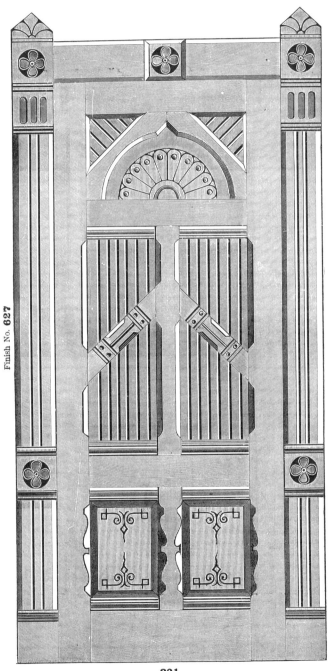

Finish No. **627**

321

WRITE FOR PRICES.

INSIDE DOOR AND FRAME.

Finish No. 628

322

INSIDE DOOR AND FRAME.

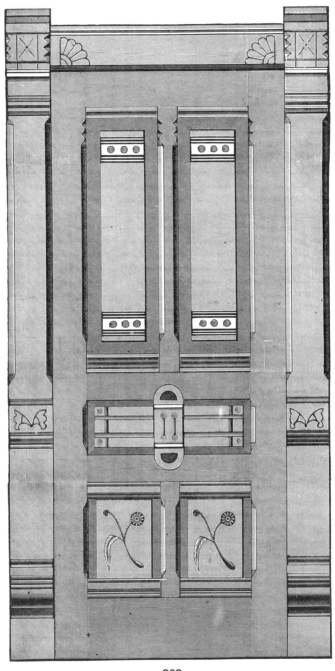

Finish No. **629**

323

WRITE FOR PRICES.

INSIDE DOOR AND FRAME.

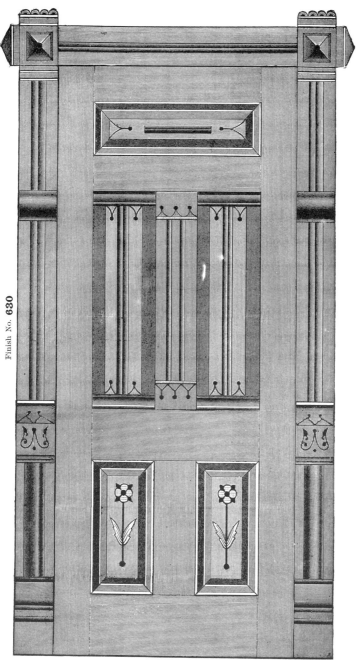

Finish No. **630**

324

WRITE FOR PRICES.

COTTAGE DOORS.

325

SIZE.				Thickness.	Prices of 325.	
					Unglazed.	Glazed Double Strength.
Ft.	In.	Ft.	In.	Inches.	$ cts.	$ cts.
2	6 ×	6	6	1 3-8	5.35	7.50
2	8 ×	6	8	"	5.65	8.25
2	8 ×	6	10	"	6.10	8.70
2	10 ×	6	10	"	6.20	9.35
2	8 ×	7	0	"	6.35	9.50
2	10 ×	7	0	"	6.45	10 05
3	0 ×	7	0	"	6.65	10.25
2	10 ×	7	6	"	7.35	11.55
3	0 ×	7	6	"	7.50	12.05
3	0 ×	8	0	"	8.35	13.80
3	0 ×	8	6	"	9.25	14 95

For prices of 1¾ Doors, add to above list the difference between 1⅜ and 1¾ O G Doors, same size. See page 101.

For price of Colored and Fancy Glass in Marginal Light Doors, see page 101.

MARGINAL LIGHT DOORS.

For Marginal Light Doors, with marginal lights glazed colored, and center light plain D. S., add to Marginal Light open list as follows:

SIZE.				Marginal Lights Four Sides.	Marginal Light Door 249.	Marginal Light Door 250.	Marginal Light Door 266.
Ft. 2	In. 6	Ft. × 6	In. 6	$ cts. 4.30	$ cts. 2.80	$ cts. 2.60	$ cts. 2.90
2	8	× 6	8	4.85	3.15	3.20	3.50
2	8	× 6	10	5.10	3.50	3.40	3.70
2	10	× 6	10	5.55	4.00	3.75	4.25
2	8	× 7	0	5.45	3.70	3.65	3.85
2	10	× 7	0	5.85	4.25	4.00	4.25
3	0	× 7	0	6.35	4.35	4.35	4.70
2	8	× 7	6	6.30			
2	10	× 7	6	6.60	4.80	4.75	5.25
3	0	× 7	6	7.15	5.35	5.10	5.35
3	0	× 8	0	7.90	5.95	5.95	6.30
3	0	× 8	6	9.20	7.20	6.65	7.20

For Marginal Light Doors, with marginal lights glazed colored, and center light plain chipped, ruby or enameled, add to Marginal Light open list as follows:

SIZE.				Marginal Lights Four Sides.	Marginal Light Door 249.	Marginal Light Door 250.	Marginal Light Door 266.
Ft. 2	In. 6	Ft. × 6	In. 6	$ cts. 5.30	$ cts. 4.10	$ cts. 3.85	$ cts. 4.35
2	8	× 6	8	6.00	4.75	4.70	5.00
2	8	× 6	10	6.25	5.00	4.90	5.25
2	10	× 6	10	6.75	5.15	5.25	5.80
2	8	× 7	0	6.55	5.25	5.15	5.50
2	10	× 7	0	7.05	5.75	5.50	6.00
3	0	× 7	0	7.55	6.15	6.00	6.45
2	8	× 7	6	7.45			
2	10	× 7	6	8.00	6.50	6.25	6.75
3	0	× 7	6	8.50	7.00	6.75	7.25
3	0	× 8	0	9.50	7.85	7.60	8.15
3	0	× 8	6	10.50	8.75	8.30	9.05

FOUR-PANEL DOORS.

Difference in list price between 1⅜ and 1¾ inch Four-Panel Doors.

SIZE.				O G Doors.	Raised Moulded Doors.
Ft. 2	In. 6	Ft. × 6	In. 6	$ cts. 2.20	$ cts.
2	8	× 6	8	2.30	2.70
2	8	× 6	10	2.30	2.70
2	10	× 6	10	2.30	2.70
2	8	× 7	0	2.35	2.80
2	10	× 7	0	2.35	2.80
3	0	× 7	0	2.35	2.80
2	8	× 7	6	2.45	3.00
2	10	× 7	6	2.45	3.00
3	0	× 7	6	2.45	3.00
3	0	× 8	0	2.50	3.05
3	0	× 8	6	2.60	3.15

SASH DOOR AND FRAME.

Finish No. **632**

326

WRITE FOR PRICES.

FRONT AND VESTIBULE DOORS.

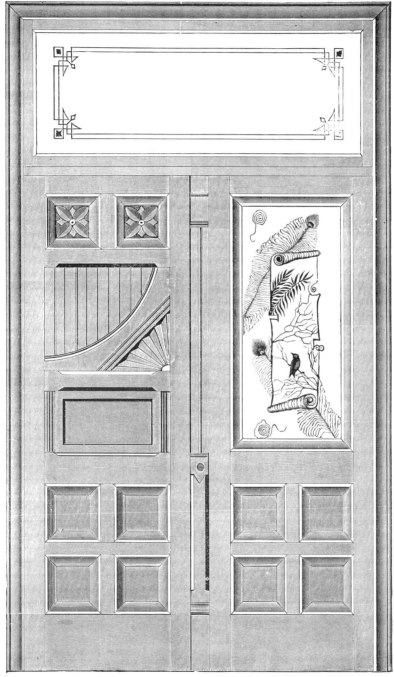

327   328

WRITE FOR PRICES.

FRONT AND VESTIBULE DOORS.

329   330

WRITE FOR PRICES.

FRONT AND VESTIBULE DOORS.

331   332

WRITE FOR PRICES.

FRONT AND VESTIBULE DOORS.

Finish No. **633**

1890

333   334

WRITE FOR PRICES.

FRONT AND VESTIBULE DOORS.

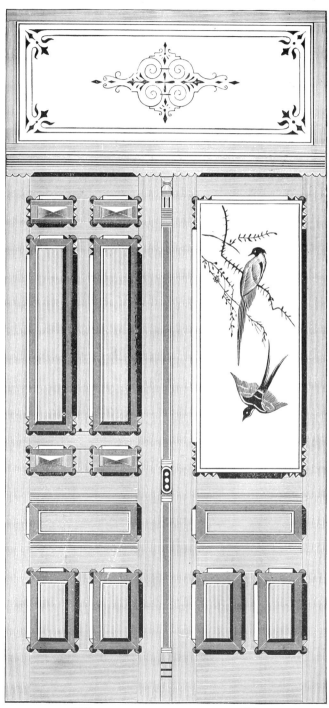

335   336

WRITE FOR PRICES.

FRONT AND VESTIBULE DOORS.

337

338

WRITE FOR PRICES.

339

340

341

FRONT DOORS AND FRAME.

342 343
WRITE FOR PRICES.

FRONT DOORS AND FRAME.

344   *WRITE FOR PRICES.*   345

FRONT AND VESTIBULE DOORS.

| 347 | 348 | 349 | 350 |

WRITE FOR PRICES.

| 351 | 352 | 353 | 354 |

INSIDE AND OUTSIDE DOORS.

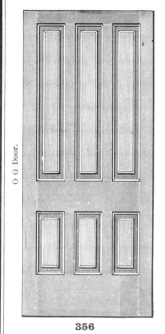

O G Door.

356

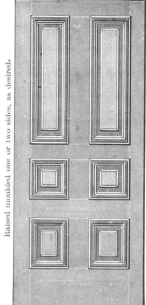

Raised moulded one or two sides, as desired.

357

O G Door.

358

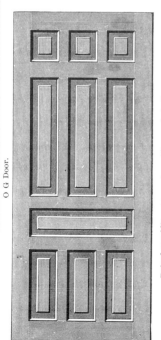

O G Door.

359

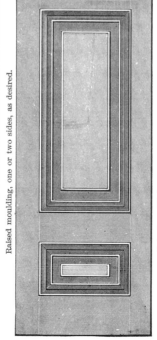

Raised moulding, one or two sides, as desired.

360

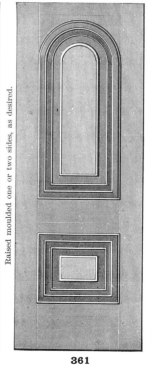

Raised moulded one or two sides, as desired.

361

WRITE FOR PRICES.

FRONT AND VESTIBULE DOORS.

362   363

364   365

366   366½   367   367½

FRONT AND VESTIBULE DOORS.

Flush moulded one or two sides, as desired.

368   369

Flush moulded one or two sides, as desired.

370   371

372

373

374

FRONT AND VESTIBULE DOORS.

375   **375½**

Flush moulded one or two sides, as desired.

Flush moulded one or two sides, as desired.

376   **377**

378

379   **379½**

WRITE FOR PRICES.

FRONT AND VESTIBULE DOORS.

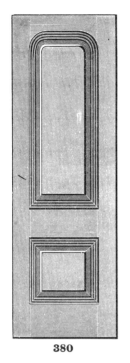

380

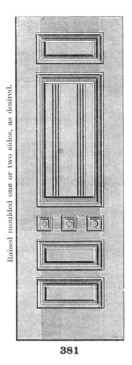

Raised moulded one or two sides, as desired.

381

382

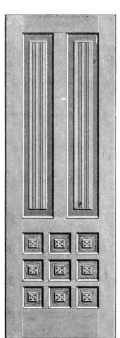

383

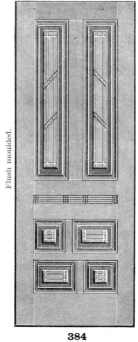

Flush moulded.

384

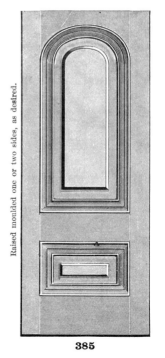

Raised moulded one or two sides, as desired.

385

WRITE FOR PRICES.

FRONT AND VESTIBULE DOORS.

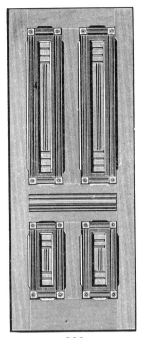

386

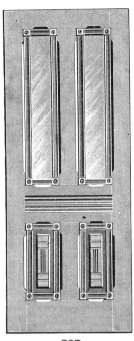

387

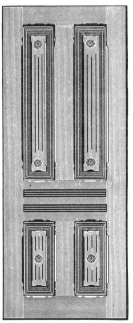

388

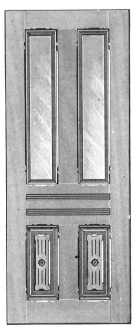

389

WRITE FOR PRICES.

STORE DOORS.

420

Moulded Panel Outside. O G Finish Inside.

SIZE.				Price, 1⅜ inches thick.		Price, 1¾ inches thick.	
				Per Pair, Unglazed.	Per Pair, Glazed S.S.	Per Pair, Unglazed.	Per Pair, Glazed D.S.
Ft. In.		Ft. In.		$ cts.	$ cts.	$ cts.	$ cts.
4 6	×	7 0		9.75	14.45	15.20	20.90
4 6	×	7 6		10.50	16.00	16.90	23.55
4 6	×	8 0		11.40	17.80	18.60	26.50
5 0	×	7 0		10.40	15.50	15.75	21.90
5 0	×	7 6		11.40	17.80	17.50	25.40
5 0	×	8 0		12.50	19.50	19.15	27.80
5 0	×	8 6		13.65	22.35	21.00	31.40

If Double Strength Glass is wanted in 1⅜ Doors, add 10 per cent. to the 1⅜ glazed list.

For Doors made Double Thick, add 50 per cent. to 1¾ list.

Above Doors are not made for Shutters.

STORE DOORS.

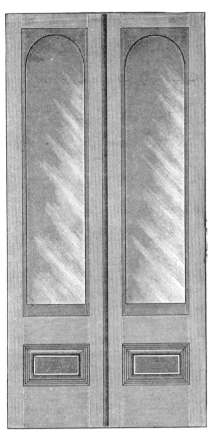

421   422

Heavy Raised Mouldings Around Lower Panels Outside.

SIZE.				Price per Pair, Unglazed, No. 421. 1⅜ inches thick.		Price per Pair, Unglazed, No. 421. 1¾ inches thick.		Amounts to add to List Price of each thickness of Doors for Glazing with Double Strength Glass
				With Sash Rabbeted on for Shutters.	With Shutters Fitted and Trimmed.	With Sash Rabbeted on for Shutters.	With Shutters Fitted and Trimmed.	
Ft.	In.	Ft.	In.	$ cts.	$ cts.	$ cts.	$ cts.	2 lights each door.
4	6 × 7	0		13.30	17.95	18 90	23.60	$5.70
5	0 × 7	0		13.30	17.95	18 90	23.60	6.65
5	0 × 7	6		14.90	19.60	20.80	25.50	7.90
5	0 × 8	0		16 60	21.10	22.70	27.55	6.15
5	0 × 8	6		18 40	22 90	24.60	29.35	7.90
5	0 × 9	0				26.50	31.30	8.65
6	0 × 9	0				27.50	32.30	10.40

For Circle Top Sash, like No. 422, add to above list $2.00 per pair.

Doors made double thick, add 50 per cent. to 1¾ list.

All Store Doors are made without Shutters, unless otherwise ordered. We also make Store Doors and Store Sash, moulded both sides on the glass, either square, circle top, segment, or circle corners, to order. In ordering, always state whether glazed or unglazed, and whether single or double strength glass is wanted, and how many lights in each door.

STORE DOORS.

425   426   427   428

WRITE FOR PRICES.

429   430   431   432

STORE DOORS.

433

441

WRITE FOR PRICES.

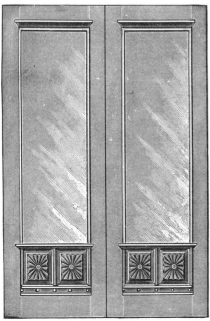

442

443

STORE FRONTS.

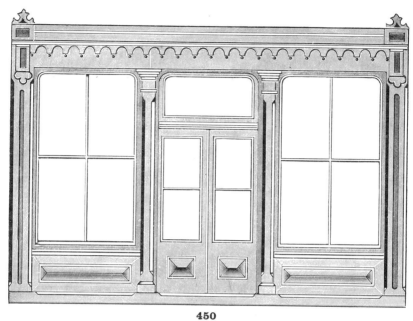

450

N. B.—In ordering Store Fronts be careful to state exact width and height of opening, thickness of Sash, whether Straight or Recess Front, and Double or Single Strength Glass.

☞ If Posts for Store Front are wanted, order must so state.

WRITE FOR PRICES.

451   **452**

STORE FRONTS.

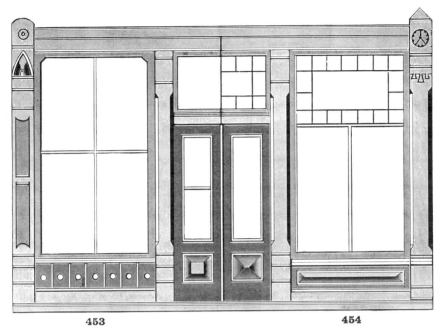

453 454

WRITE FOR PRICES.

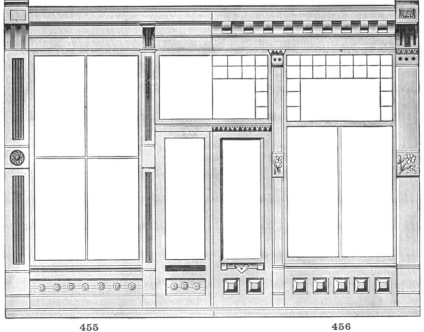

455 456

STORE FRONTS.

457   458

WRITE FOR PRICES.

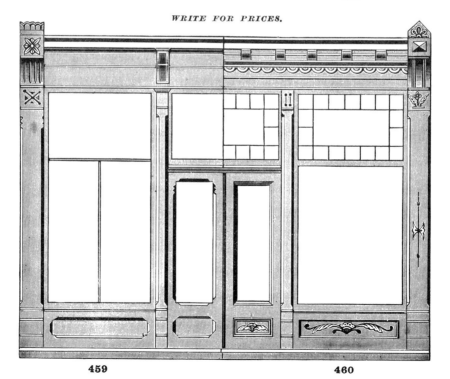

459   460

SECTIONS OF MOULDED DOORS.

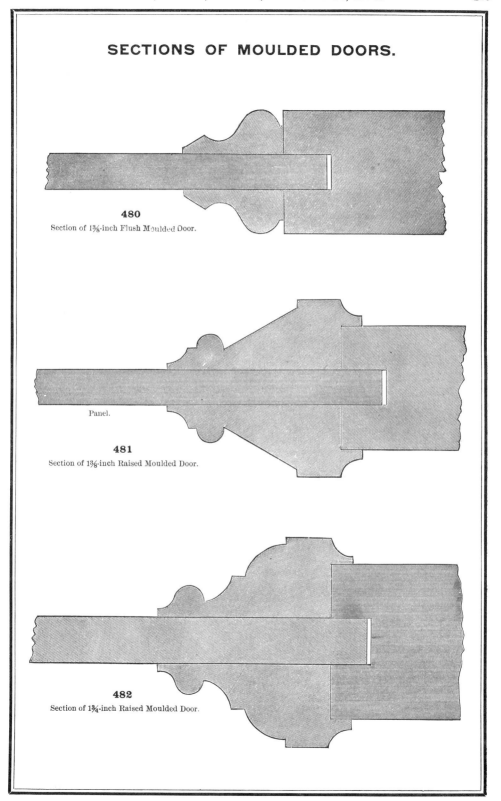

480

Section of 1⅜-inch Flush Moulded Door.

Panel.

481

Section of 1⅜-inch Raised Moulded Door.

482

Section of 1¾-inch Raised Moulded Door.

SECTIONS OF MOULDED DOORS.

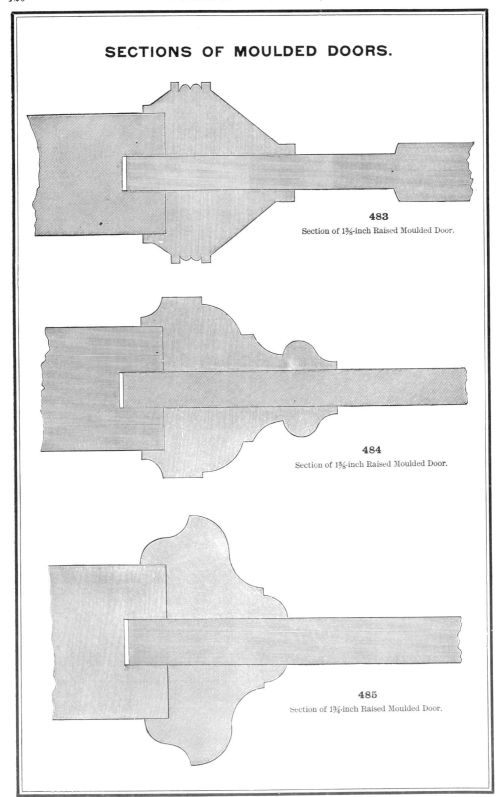

483

Section of 1⅜-inch Raised Moulded Door.

484

Section of 1⅜-inch Raised Moulded Door.

485

Section of 1¾-inch Raised Moulded Door.

SECTIONS OF HARDWOOD DOORS.

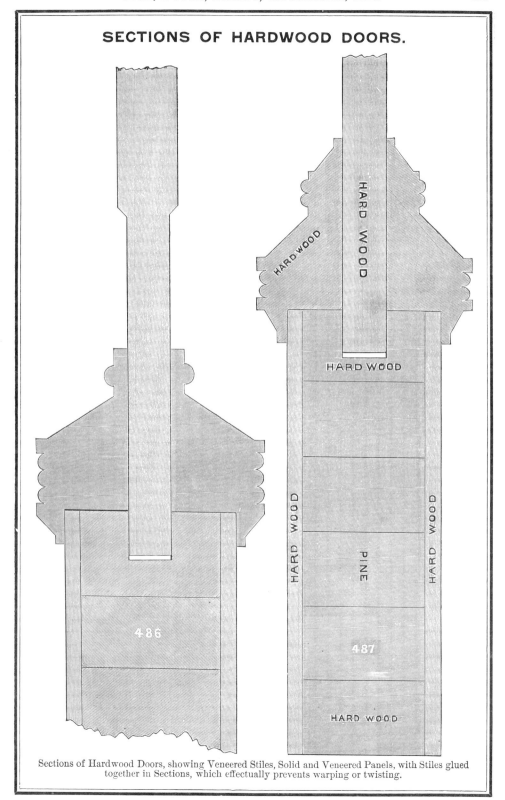

Sections of Hardwood Doors, showing Veneered Stiles, Solid and Veneered Panels, with Stiles glued together in Sections, which effectually prevents warping or twisting.

SECTIONS OF DOORS WITH GLASS PANELS.

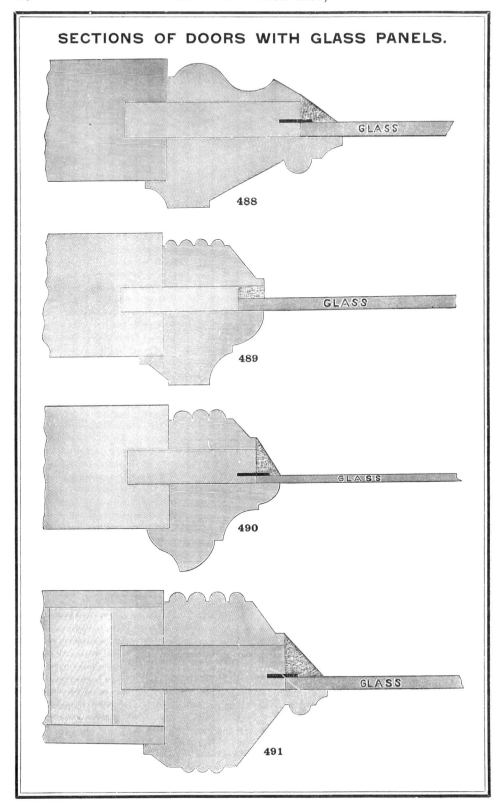

INSIDE BLINDS.

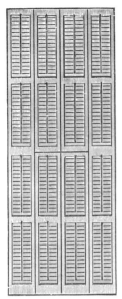

Directions for Ordering.

First—In all cases give the exact outside measure of Blinds wanted.

Second—Give the number of folds.

Third—State if Blinds are to be all slats, or half panels and half slats.

Fourth—State distance from top of window to center of meeting rail of sash, or where Blinds are to be cut.

Fifth—Give thickness of Blinds.

Sixth—If Blinds fold in pockets give size of the pockets.

Seventh—State if Blinds are to be painted or finished in oil.

Eighth—If for oil finish, extra price.

500—All Slats.

501—½ Panels, ½ Slats.

PRICES.

O G Panel or Rolling Slats, measuring height of window, ordinary width, per foot:

Two-fold	$ .65
Three-fold	.80
Four-fold	1.00
Six-fold	1.40

The above prices are for Pine.

If hardwood, such as Cherry, Ash, Maple. or Black Walnut are wanted, we charge extra price.

We make Inside Blinds that are not ex celled, either in workmanship or style.

502—¾ Panel.

503—All Panel.

OUTSIDE BLINDS.

Four-Lighted Windows.

511—Rolling Slats.

SIZE.	Price Rolling Slats.	Price Stationary or Half Stationary Slats.		Size of Blinds.				
	1⅛ thick.	1⅛ thick.	1⅜ thick.					
Inches.	$ cts.	$ cts.	$ cts.	Ft.	In.		Ft.	In.
12 × 20	1.25	1.50	1.90	2	5	×	3	11
12 × 22	1.50	1.75	2.15	2	5	×	4	3
12 × 24	1.50	1.75	2.15	2	5	×	4	7
12 × 26	1.60	1.85	2.25	2	5	×	4	11
12 × 28	1.70	1.95	2.35	2	5	×	5	3
12 × 30	1.80	2.05	2.45	2	5	×	5	7
12 × 32	1.90	2.15	2.55	2	5	×	5	11
12 × 34	2.00	2.25	2.65	2	5	×	6	3
12 × 36	2.10	2.35	2.75	2	5	×	6	7
12 × 38	2.25	2.50	2.90	2	5	×	6	11
12 × 40	2.35	2.60	3.00	2	5	×	7	3
14 × 24	1.65	1.90	2.30	2	9	×	4	7
14 × 26	1.80	2.05	2.45	2	9	×	4	11
14 × 28	1.90	2.15	2.55	2	9	×	5	3
14 × 30	2.00	2.25	2.65	2	9	×	5	7
14 × 32	2.15	2.40	2.80	2	9	×	5	11
14 × 34	2.30	2.55	2.95	2	9	×	6	3
14 × 36	2.40	2.65	3.05	2	9	×	6	7
14 × 38	2.55	2.80	3.20	2	9	×	6	11
14 × 40	2.65	2.90	3.30	2	9	×	7	3
14 × 42	2.80	3.05	3.45	2	9	×	7	7
14 × 44	2.90	3.15	3.55	2	9	×	7	11
14 × 46	3.00	3.25	3.65	2	9	×	8	3
14 × 48	3.15	3.40	3.80	2	9	×	8	7

Two-Lighted Windows.

Blinds for Two-Lighted Windows, with glass 20, 22 or 24 inches wide, same price as Blinds for Four-Lighted Windows with 12-inch glass, same height.

Blinds for Two-Lighted Windows, with glass 26 or 28 inches wide, same price as Blinds for Four-Lighted Windows with 14-inch glass, same height.

Blinds for Two-Lighted Windows, with glass 30 inches wide, same price as Blinds for Four-Lighted Windows with 15-inch glass, same height.

Blinds for 34-inch glass and longer made three panels, unless otherwise ordered.

Eight-Lighted Windows.

512—Stationary Slats.

SIZE.	Price, Rolling Slats.	Price, Stationary or Half Stationary Slats.		Size of Blinds.				
	1⅛ thick.	1⅛ thick.	1⅜ thick.					
Inches.	$ cts.	$ cts.	$ cts.	Ft.	In.		Ft.	In.
9 × 12	1.50	1.75	2.15	1	11	×	4	7
9 × 14	1.60	1.85	2.25	1	11	×	5	3
9 × 16	1.80	2.05	2.45	1	11	×	5	11
9 × 18	2.00	2.25	2.65	1	11	×	6	7
10 × 12	1.50	1.75	2.15	2	1	×	4	7
10 × 14	1.60	1.85	2.25	2	1	×	5	3
10 × 16	1.80	2.05	2.45	2	1	×	5	11
10 × 18	2.00	2.25	2.65	2	1	×	6	7
10 × 20	2.20	2.45	2.85	2	1	×	7	3
12 × 14	1.70	1.95	2.35	2	5	×	5	3
12 × 16	1.90	2.15	2.55	2	5	×	5	11
12 × 18	2.10	2.35	2.75	2	5	×	6	7
12 × 20	2.35	2.60	3.00	2	5	×	7	3

For 15-inch glass add 15 cents to price of 14-inch.
For Blinds 1⅜ thick add to price of 1⅛ 40 cents.
Sizes not given, extra price.
☞ Our Regular Stock Blinds are made with O G Stiles.
We make Square Stiles only on Special orders.

OUTSIDE BLINDS.

Twelve-Lighted Windows.

513
Half Stationary and Half Rolling Slats.

SIZE OF GLASS.	Price, Rolling Slats. 1⅛ thick.	Price, Stationary or Half Stationary Slats.		Size of Blinds.	
		1⅛ thick.	1⅜ thick.		
Inches.	$ cts.	$ cts.	$ cts.	Ft. In.	Ft. In.
8 × 10	1.25	1.50	1.90	2 4½ ×	3 11
8 × 12	1.50	1.75	2.15	2 4½ ×	4 7
8 × 14	1.60	1.85	2.25	2 4½ ×	5 3
9 × 12	1.50	1.75	2.15	2 7½ ×	4 7
9 × 13	1.60	1.85	2.25	2 7½ ×	4 11
9 × 14	1.70	1.95	2.35	2 7½ ×	5 3
9 × 15	1.80	2.05	2.45	2 7½ ×	5 7
9 × 16	1.90	2.15	2.55	2 7½ ×	5 11
9 × 18	2.10	2.35	2.75	2 7½ ×	6 7
10 × 12	1.65	1.90	2.30	2 10½ ×	4 7
10 × 14	1.90	2.15	2.55	2 10½ ×	5 3
10 × 15	2.00	2.25	2.65	2 10½ ×	5 7
10 × 16	2.15	2.40	2.80	2 10½ ×	5 11
10 × 18	2.40	2.65	3.05	2 10½ ×	6 7
10 × 20	2.65	2.90	3.30	2 10½ ×	7 3
10 × 22	2.90	3.15	3.55	2 10½ ×	7 11
10 × 24	3.15	3.40	3.80	2 10½ ×	8 7

For 12-inch Twelve-Light Blinds, add 30c to list price of 10-inch.

1⅜ thick, add to list price of 1⅛, per pair, 40c. Segment Head Blinds, add 75c per pair. Half Circle Head Blinds, add $1.50 per pair.

Size of Blinds measure same as Check Rail Windows, with the addition of 1 inch to bottom rail for sub-sill frame, which can be cut off if necessary.

DOOR BLINDS.

514
Three Panel Blinds.

SIZE.				Thickness.	Price.
Ft.	In.	Ft.	In.	Inches.	$ cts.
2	6 ×	6	6	1 1-8	2.50
2	8 ×	6	8	"	2.70
2	10 ×	6	10	"	2.90
3	0 ×	7	0	"	3.15

1⅜ thick, add to list price of 1⅛ 40c per pair.

In ordering, state if Blinds are to be a pair or single piece, to each opening.

Sizes not given, extra price.

All Door Blinds made in pairs are rabbeted same as Window Blinds, unless otherwise ordered.

OUTSIDE BLINDS.

Two-Lighted Pantry Windows.

Size of Glass.			Thickness.	Price, Single Blind.	Size of Blind.				
Inches.			Inches.	$ cts.	Ft.	In.		Ft.	In.
12	×	24	1 1-8	1.00	1	4⅛	×	4	7
12	×	26	"	1.10	1	4⅛	×	4	11
12	×	28	"	1.15	1	4⅛	×	5	3
12	×	30	"	1.20	1	4⅛	×	5	7
12	×	32	"	1.25	1	4⅛	×	5	11
12	×	34	"	1.35	1	4⅛	×	6	3
12	×	36	"	1.40	1	4⅛	×	6	7
14	×	24	"	1.10	1	6⅛	×	4	7
14	×	26	"	1.20	1	6⅛	×	4	11
14	×	28	"	1.25	1	6⅛	×	5	3
14	×	30	"	1.35	1	6⅛	×	5	7
14	×	32	"	1.45	1	6⅛	×	5	11
14	×	34	"	1.55	1	6⅛	×	6	3
14	×	36	"	1.60	1	6⅛	×	6	7
14	×	40	"	1.75	1	6⅛	×	7	3

Four-Lighted Pantry Windows.

Size of Glass.			Thickness.	Price, Single Blind.	Size of Blind.				
Inches.			Inches.	$ cts.	Ft.	In.		Ft.	In.
8	×	10	1 1-8	.85	1	0⅛	×	3	11
9	×	12	"	1.00	1	1⅛	×	4	7
9	×	14	"	1.15	1	1⅛	×	5	3
9	×	16	"	1.25	1	1⅛	×	5	11
9	×	18	"	1.40	1	1⅛	×	6	7
10	×	12	"	1.00	1	2⅛	×	4	7
10	×	14	"	1.15	1	2⅛	×	5	3
10	×	16	"	1.25	1	2⅛	×	5	11
10	×	18	"	1.40	1	2⅛	×	6	7

For 12 and 14 inch, see Two-Light List above, same height.

SHUTTERS.

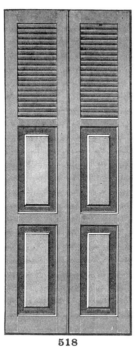

518
6-Panel Shutters,
Upper Panels Stationary Slats.

519
O G 4-Panel Shutters,
Raised Panel.

520
4-Panel Shutters,
Flush Moulded.

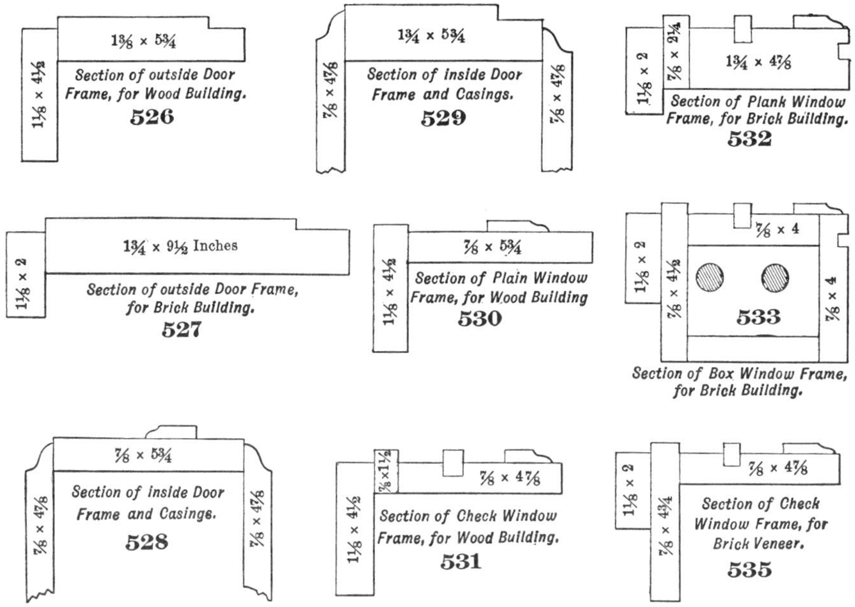

OUTSIDE DOOR FRAMES.

Size.	For Wood Building. Like Fig. 526 Above. With Plain Outside Casings 4½ × 1⅛ in. Rabbeted Jambs for 4-in. Stud.		For Wood Building. For Transoms Add.	For Brick Building. Like Fig. 527 Above. With 1¾ inch Rabbeted Jambs and Hanging Stile, 1⅛ × 2 in.	For Brick Building. For Transoms Add.
Ft. In. Ft. In.	1⅜ Jambs.	1¾ Jambs.	cts.	$ cts.	cts.
2 6 × 6 6	$1.70	$2.00	.65	2.40	.80
2 8 × 6 8	1.75	2.10	.70	2.50	.85
2 10 × 6 10	1.85	2.25	.75	2.60	.90
3 0 × 7 0	2.00	2.40	.80	2.70	.95

INSIDE DOOR FRAMES.

Size.	With 5¾ × ⅞ inch Jambs and 4⅞ inch O G Casings both sides, Like Fig. 528 Above. Price Without Transoms.	For Transoms Add.	With 5¾ × 1⅛ or 1⅜ inch Jambs and 4⅞ inch O G Casings both sides, Like Fig. 529 Above. Price Without Transoms.	For Transoms Add.
Ft. In. Ft. In.	$ cts.	cts.	$ cts.	cts.
2 6 × 6 6	1.85	.55	2.15	.65
2 8 × 6 8	1.90	.55	2.20	.70
2 10 × 6 10	1.95	.60	2.30	.80
3 0 × 7 0	2.00	.65	2.35	.85

For Circle Top or Circle Corner Door Frames, add to List Prices of Square Top $2.25.
Frames for Wood Building, with Moulded Cap, add 45 cents.
For Segment Frames for Brick Buildings, add $1.25.
Orders for Frames should give width of Jambs wanted.
Orders for Outside Door Frames should give width of Rabbet to receive Door.
Extra price for wider Jambs.

WINDOW FRAMES.

For Four-Light Windows.

Wood Building.		Brick Building.	
For Check Rail Sash, Outside Casing, 1⅛x4½ inches, like No. 531.		With 1¾ inch Plank Jambs, and Hanging Stile, like No. 532.	Box Frames with Pulleys and Hanging Stile, like No. 533.
Size of Glass.	Price.		

Size of Glass	Price $ cts.	With 1¾ inch Plank Jambs $ cts.	Box Frames $ cts.
10, 12 or 14 × 20	1.70	1.80	2.45
10, 12 or 14 × 22	1.75	1.85	2.50
10, 12 or 14 × 24	1.80	1.90	2.55
10, 12 or 14 × 26	1.85	1.95	2.60
10, 12 or 14 × 28	1.90	2.00	2.65
10, 12 or 14 × 30	1.95	2.05	2.70
10, 12 or 14 × 32	2.00	2.10	2.80
10, 12 or 14 × 34	2.10	2.20	2.85
10, 12 or 14 × 36	2.15	2.25	2.95
10, 12 or 14 × 40	2.25	2.35	3.10
10, 12 or 14 × 44	2.35	2.45	3.25
10, 12 or 14 × 48	2.50	2.60	3.40

For Eight-Light Windows.

Size of Glass	Wood Building		Brick Building	
	For Plain Rail Sash, with Casings 4½x1⅛ inch, like No. 530.	For Check Rail Sash, with Casings 4½x1⅛ inch, like No. 531.	With 1¾ inch Plank Jambs, and Hanging Stile, like No. 532.	Box Frames with Pulleys and Hanging Stile, like No. 533.
Inches	$ cts.	$ cts.	$ cts.	$ cts.
12 × 14	1.40	1.90	2.00	2.65
12 × 16	1.45	2.00	2.10	2.80
12 × 18	1.55	2.15	2.25	2.95
12 × 20	1.65	2.25	2.35	3.10
12 × 22	1.80	2.35	2.45	3.25
12 × 24	1.90	2.50	2.60	3.40

For Twelve-Light Windows.

Size of Glass				
8 × 10	1.20	1.70	1.80	2.45
9 × 12	1.30	1.80	1.90	2.55
9 × 14	1.40	1.90	2.00	2.65
9 × 15	1.45	1.95	2.05	2.70
9 × 16	1.45	2.00	2.10	2.80
9 × 18	1.55	2.15	2.25	2.95
10 × 12	1.35	1.80	1.90	2.55
10 × 14	1.45	1.90	2.00	2.65
10 × 16	1.50	2.00	2.10	2.80
10 × 18	1.60	2.15	2.25	2.95
10 × 20	1.70	2.25	2.35	3.10

For Circle Top outside, square inside, Window Frames, add to List of Square Top $1.00.
For Frames for Wood Building, with Pulleys for Weights, add to List Price 45 cents.
For Segment outside, square inside, add to List Price 50 cents.
Frames for Wood Building with Moulded Cap, add 45 cents.
Frames for Two-Light Windows, same price as Four-Light, same height.
Write for Special Prices.

GOTHIC WINDOW FRAMES.

557

WRITE FOR PRICES.

559

558

Gothic Window Frames made any styles desired,
with or without Stained Glass.

When ordering Gothic Windows, Doors, or
Frames, give radius and size of opening.

DESIGN FOR WINDOW FRAME.

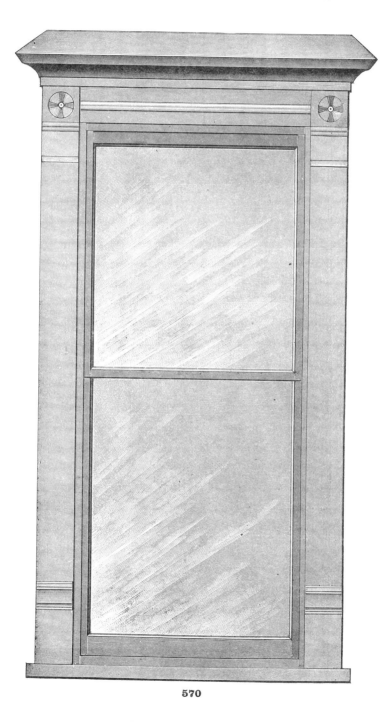

570

WRITE FOR PRICES.

DESIGN FOR WINDOW FRAME.

571

DESIGNS FOR WINDOW FRAMES.

572

573

WRITE FOR PRICES.

574

575

DESIGNS FOR WINDOW FRAMES.

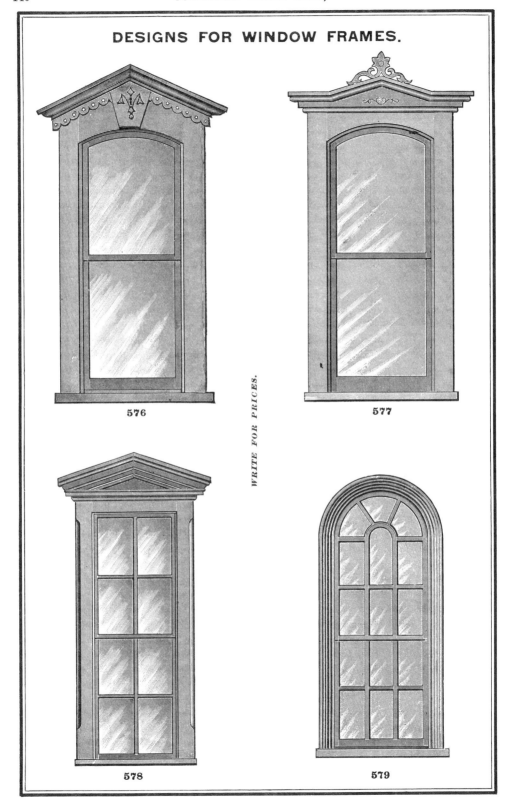

WRITE FOR PRICES.

576

577

578

579

DESIGNS FOR WINDOW FRAMES.

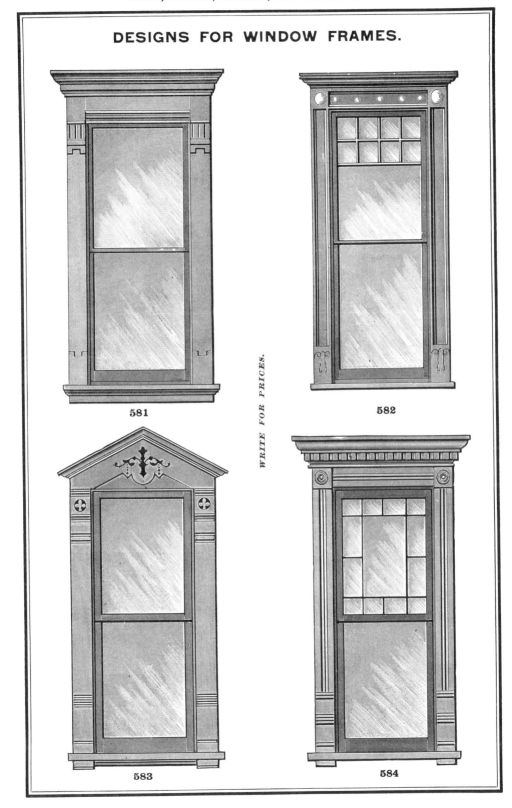

WRITE FOR PRICES.

581

582

583

584

DESIGN FOR WINDOW FRAME.

586

DESIGN FOR WINDOW FRAME.

587

GABLE WINDOW FINISH.

Number **590**　　　　　　Number **593**　　　　　　Number **596**
*　**591**　　　　　　　"　**594**　　　　　　　"　**597**
"　**592**　　　　　　　"　**595**　　　　　　　"　·**598**

SEE CUTS ON PAGE 42.

WOOD VENTILATORS.

610　　　　　　　　611　　　　　　　　612

FINISH FOR INSIDE DOORS.

Number **625** Finish.. ....See Door Cut Number **208**	Number **630** Finish.......See Door Cut Number **324**
" **627** " ...." " " " **321**	" **632** " ....." " " " **326**
" **628** " .. ..." " " " **322**	" **633** " ...." " " " **333**
" **629** " ...." " " " **323**	" **660** " ...." " " " **390**

INTERIOR FINISHING

Done in Maple, Ash, Red Oak, White Oak, Birch, Cherry, Sycamore, Mahogany, and all other Woods, in the best style of workmanship and of thoroughly kiln-dried material.

ESTIMATES FURNISHED IF DESIRED.

INSIDE FINISH.

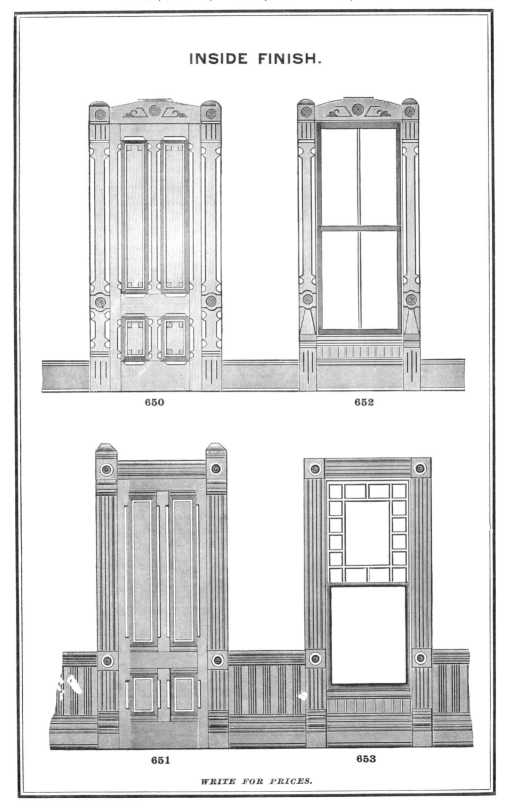

650

652

651

653

WRITE FOR PRICES.

INSIDE FINISH.

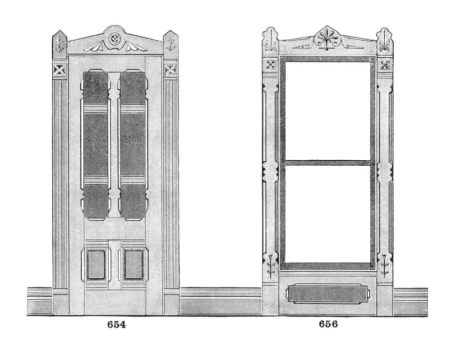

654   656

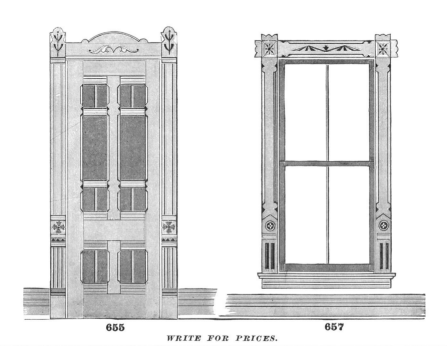

655   657

WRITE FOR PRICES.

INSIDE FINISH.

658

659

WRITE FOR PRICES.

INSIDE FINISH.

Door No. **390**
Finish No. **660**

WRITE FOR PRICES.

PORTIERE WORK.

675
Made any Size.

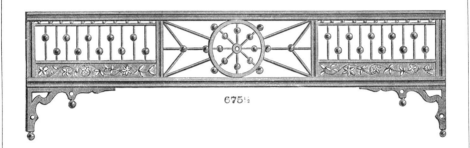

675½

676
Made any Size.

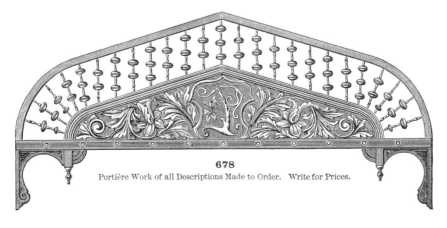

678
Portière Work of all Descriptions Made to Order. Write for Prices.

CORNER BEADS.

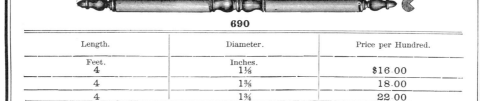

690

Length.	Diameter.	Price per Hundred.
Feet. 4	Inches. 1⅛	$16.00
4	1⅜	18.00
4	1¾	22.00

CORNER, PLINTH, AND HEAD BLOCKS.

We manufacture *CORNER AND PLINTH BLOCKS* in a great variety of patterns, and give following a few cuts of styles with prices. The prices given are for *White Pine* by the hundred. Red Oak or Birch are 50 per cent. higher and Walnut 100 per cent. higher than marked prices. We also furnish *Carved* Corner or Plinth Blocks in endless varieties, at a small additional cost over those turned.

☞ *We sell Blocks in quantity desired. A liberal Discount to Dealers.*

856
5½ × 10 × 1⅛, $15.00

780
5½ × 5½, $5.00

855
5½ × 11 × 1⅜, $50.00

935
5½ × 10 × 1⅜, $8.00

936
5½ × 12 × 1⅜, $20.00

937
5½ × 10 × 1⅜, $9.00

WOOD CORNER BLOCKS.

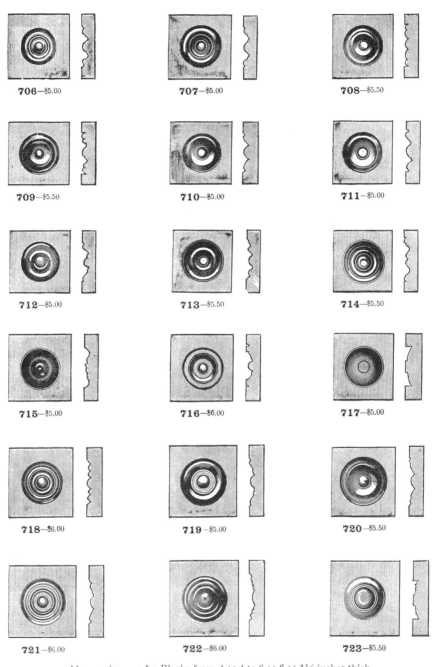

706—$5.00

707—$5.00

708—$5.50

709—$5.50

710—$5.00

711—$5.00

712—$5.00

713—$5.50

714—$5.50

715—$5.00

716—$6.00

717—$5.00

718—$6.00

719—$5.00

720—$5.50

721—$6.00

722—$6.00

723—$5.50

Above prices are for Blocks from 4×4 to $6 \times 6 \times 1\frac{1}{8}$ inches thick.
Prices are for White Pine by the hundred.

WOOD CORNER BLOCKS.

724

4½ to 6 in. $10.00

725

4½ to 6 in. $10.00

726

4½ to 6 in. $7.00

727

4½ to 6 in. $7.00

728

4½ to 6 in. $20.00

729

4½ to 6 in. $20.00

730

4½ to 6 in. $7.00

731

4½ to 6 in. $6.50

732

4½ to 6 in. $5.50

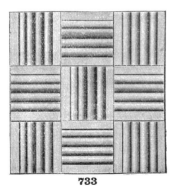

733

4½ to 6 in. $20 00

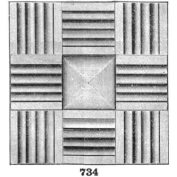

734

4½ to 6 in. $20.00

Prices are for White Pine by the hundred for Blocks 1⅛ inches thick.

WOOD CORNER BLOCKS.

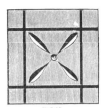

735
4½ to 6 in. × 1⅛, $5.50

736
4½ to 6 in. × 1⅛, $6.50

736½
4½ to 6 in. × 1⅛, $6.00

737
4½ to 6 in. × 1⅛, $6.50

738
4½ to 6 in. × 1⅛, $5.50

739
4½ to 6 in. × 1⅛, $6.50

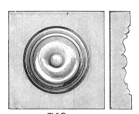

740
4½ to 6 in. × 1⅛, $5.50

741
4½ to 6 in. × 1⅛, $25.00

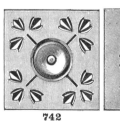

742
4½ to 6 in. × 1⅛, $8.50

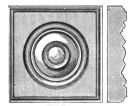

743
4½ to 6 in. × 1⅛, $7.00

744
4½ to 6 in. × 1⅛, Hand Carved, $110.00

745
4½ to 6 in. × 1⅛, $6.50

WOOD CORNER BLOCKS.

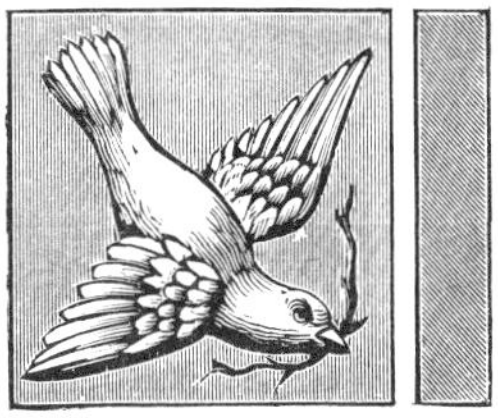

747

4½ to 6 × 1⅛, $25.00

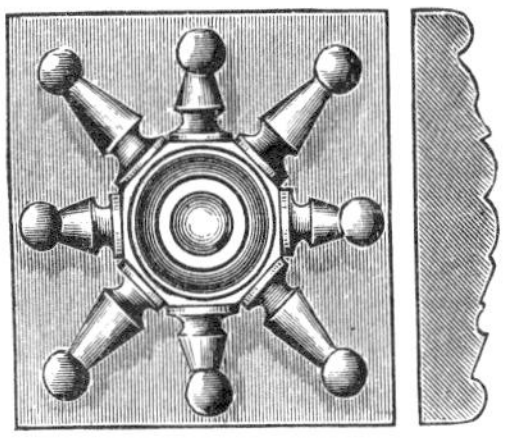

748

4½ to 6 × 1⅛, $18.00

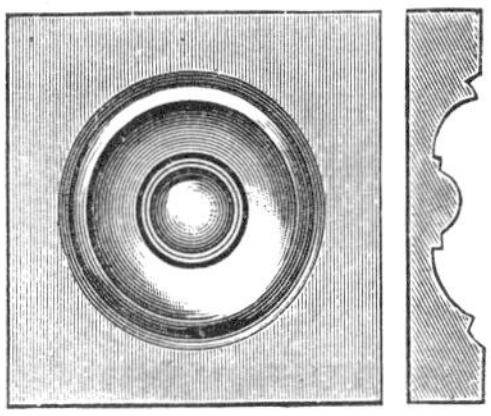

749

4½ to 6 × 1⅛, $5.00

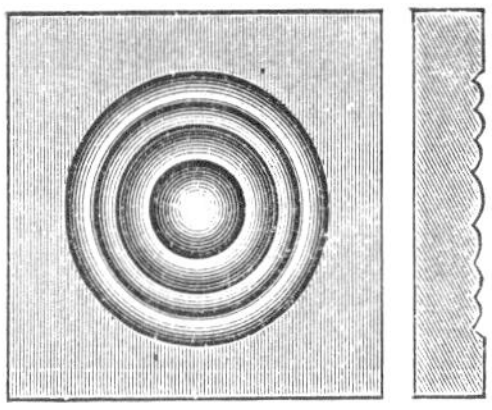

750

4½ to 6 × 1⅛, $5.50

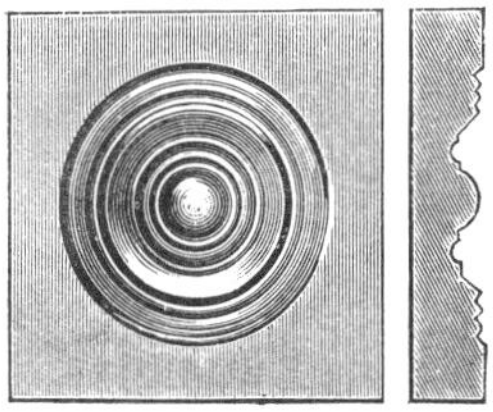

751

4½ to 6 × 1⅛, $6.00

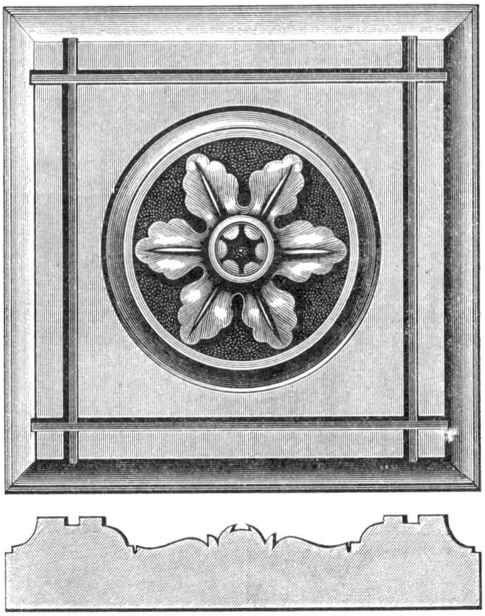

752

SIZE.	Thickness.	Price per 100.
4½ to 5¾ In. Square.	1⅛	$15.00
6 to 6¾ " "	"	18.00
5 to 5¾ " "	1⅜	18.00
6 to 6¾ " "	"	20.00

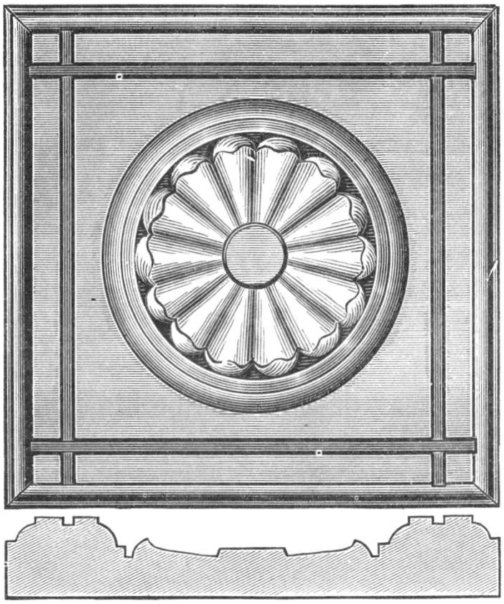

753

Prices same as No. 752 above.

WOOD CORNER BLOCKS AND ORNAMENTS.

754

1⅝ × 8, $12.50 per 100

756

SIZE.	Thickness.	Price per 100.
4½ to 5¾ In. Square.	1⅛	$15.00
6 to 6¾ " "	"	18.00
5 to 5¾ " "	1⅜	18.00
6 to 6¾ " "	"	20.00

755

3⅛ × 2½, $8.00 per 100
2¾ × 4½, $13.00 per 100

757

Sizes and prices same as No. 756.

WOOD CORNER BLOCKS AND ORNAMENTS.

758

Price same as No. 756.

760

4 In. Diameter. $18.00 per 100

761

3¾ In. Square. $18.00 per 100
4¾ In. Square.   25.00 per 100

759

SIZE.	Thickness.	Price per 100.
5 to 6 In. Square	1⅛	$25.00
6 to 6¾ " "	1⅜	30.00
7 to 8½ " "	"	35.00
6 to 6¾ " "	1¾	35.00
7 to 8¼ " "	"	38.00

762

2¾ × 6 In. $25.00 per 100
3¾ × 8 In.   30.00 per 100

WOOD ORNAMENTS.

763

764

765

766

767

768

769

770

771

PRICES OF ABOVE ORNAMENTS.

No.	Size.			Per 100.	No.	Size.			Per 100.
763	1	inches	diameter.	$1.50	765	2⅜	inches	square.	$ 5 50
763	1¼	"	"	2.00	766	1⅞	"	"	4.25
763	1½	"	"	2 50	767	1¾	"	diameter.	3.00
763	1¾	"	"	3.00	768	1⅞	"	square.	4.25
763	2	"	"	3.75	768	2⅜	"	"	6.00
763	2¼	"	"	4.50	768	3¼	"	"	15.00
763	2½	"	"	5.50	769	1¾	"	"	3.75
763	2¾	"	"	6.50	770	1¾	"	diameter.	3.00
763	3¼	"	"	7.50	770	2½	"	"	6.50
764	1	"	"	2.00	771	1⅛	"	"	2.00
764	1¼	"	"	3.00	771	1⅜	"	"	2.50
764	1½	"	"	3.75	771	1⅝	"	"	3 00
764	1¾	"	"	4.25	771	2¼	"	"	4.50
764	2	"	"	4.50					

WOOD CORNER BLOCKS.

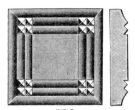

776

4½ to 6 in. sq. × 1⅜ $9.00 per 100

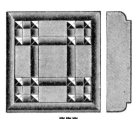

777

4½ to 6 in. sq. × 1⅜ $15.00 per 100

778

4½ to 6 in. sq. × 1⅛ $10.00 per 100

779

4½ to 6 in. sq. × 1⅛ $20.00 per 100

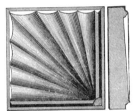

787

5 to 6 in. sq. × 1⅛ $15.00 per 100

788

5 to 6 in. sq. × 1⅛ $25.00 per 100

791

5 to 6 in. sq. × 1⅛ $10.00 per 100

792

5 to 6 in. sq. × 1⅛ $7.00 per 100

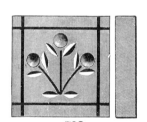

793

5 to 6 in. sq. × 1⅛ $7.00 per 100

794

5 to 6 in. sq. × 1⅛ $6.50 per 100

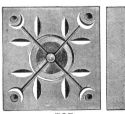

795

5 to 6 in. sq. × 1⅛ $7.50 per 100

796

5 to 6 in. sq. × 1⅛ $6.00 per 100

WOOD CORNER BLOCKS.

798—A
5⅜ inches square, $42.00 per 100

798—B
5⅜ and 5¾ inches square, $42.00 per 100

798—C
5⅜ and 5¾ inches square, $42.00 per 100

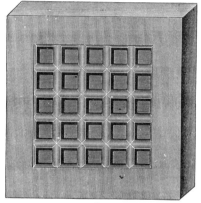

798—D
5⅜ and 5¾ inches square, $42.00 per 100

798—E
5¾ and 5¾ inches square, $42.00 per 100

798—F
5¾ and 5¾ inches square, $42.00 per 100

WOOD HEAD BLOCKS.

802

5½×10, $10.00 per 100

803

5½×10, $18.00 per 100

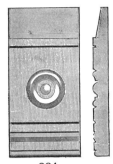

804

5½×10, $10.00 per 100

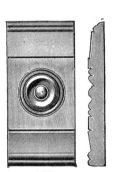

805

5½×10, $11.00 per 100

806

5½×11, $15.00 per 100

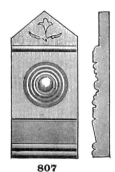

807

5½×11, $16.00 per 100

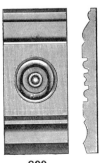

809

5½×10, $10.00 per 100

810

5½×10, $10.00 per 100

811

5½×12, $14.00 per 100

812

5½×12, $16.00 per 100

Above Blocks are 1⅛ inches thick.

WOOD HEAD BLOCKS.

814
5½×11, $13.00 per 100

815
5½×11, $11.00 per 100

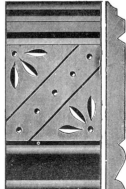

816
5½×11, $11.00 per 100

817
5½×10, $12.00 per 100

818
5½×10, $11.00 per 100

819
5½×12, $12.00 per 100

820
5½×12, $15.00 per 100

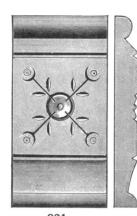

821
5½×9½, $12.00 per 100

822
5½×10, $30.00 per 100

Above Blocks are 1⅛ inches thick.

WOOD HEAD BLOCKS.

823
5½ × 10, $17.00 per 100

824
5½ × 10, $12.00 per 100

825
5½ × 11, hand carved, $120.00 per 100

825—A
3 inches Square, $16.00 per 100

825—B
3½ inches Square, $17.00 per 100

825—C
3 inches Square, $17.00 per 100

825—A, B, and C are Pressed Wood Ornaments, which can be used for center pieces of Corner or Head Blocks, at greatly reduced price over hand carving, and equally as effective.

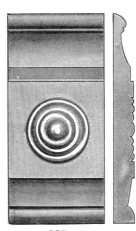

826
5½ × 10, $12.00 per 100

827
5½ × 10½, $11.00 per 100

828
5½ × 10, $11.00 per 100

WOOD HEAD BLOCKS.

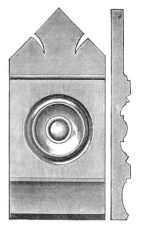

829
5½ × 10½ × 1⅛, $30.00 per 100

830
5½ × 11 × 1⅛, $20.00 per 100

831
5½ × 10½ × 1⅛, $14.00 per 100

832
5 to 5¾ × 9 × 1¾ thick, $40.00
6 to 6¾ × 10 × 1¾ "   45.00

832—A
2½ in. Square, $9.00 per 100
Can be used as Center for
Head Blocks.

833
5 to 5¾ × 13 × 1¾ thick, $50.00
6 to 6¾ × 13 × 1¾ "   60.00
7 to 8 × 13 × 1¾ "   75.00

WOOD HEAD BLOCKS.

834

5½ × 12½, $60.00 per 100

835

5½ × 11½, $13 00 per 100

836

5½ × 12, $24 00 per 100

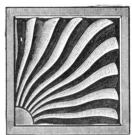

836—A

836—B

836—C

836—A, B, and C are Wood Ornaments, which can be used with good effect for centers of Corners and Head Blocks.

837

5½ × 12, $50.00 per 100

839

5½ × 12½, $25.00 per 100

844

5½ × 12, $55.00 per 100

WOOD BASE OR PLINTH BLOCKS.

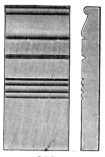

900
5½ × 10 × 1⅜, $11.00 per 100

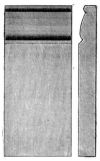

901
5½ × 9 × 1⅜, $8.00 per 100

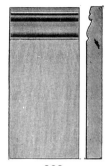

902
5½ × 9 × 1⅜, $9.00 per 100

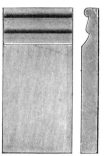

903
5⅝ × 8 × 1⅜, $8.00 per 100

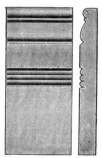

904
5½ × 10 × 1⅜, $11.00 per 100

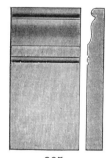

905
5½ × 10 × 1⅜, $9.00 per 100

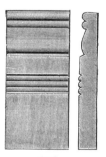

906
5½ × 10 × 1⅜, $11.00 per 100

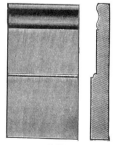

907
5½ × 10 × 1⅜, $10.00 per 100

908
5½ × 10 × 1⅜, $10.00 per 100

WOOD BASE OR PLINTH BLOCKS.

909
5½ × 12 × 1⅜, $12.00 per 100

910
5½ × 10 × 1⅜, $10.00 per 100

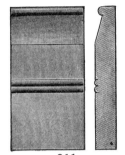

911
5½ × 10 × 1⅜, $10.00 per 100

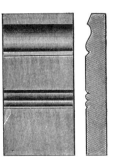

912
5½ × 10 × 1⅜, $10.00 per 100

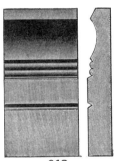

913
5½ × 10 × 1⅜, $11.00 per 100

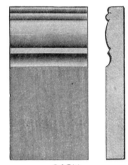

913½
5¼ × 10 × 1⅜, $9.50 per 100

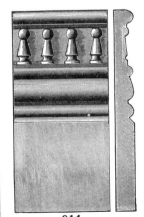

914
5½×12×1⅜, $20.00 per 100

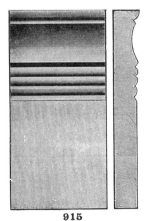

915
5½×11×1⅜, $11.00 per 100

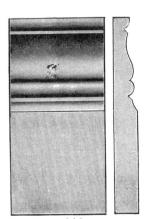

916
5½×11×1⅜, $11.00 per 100

WOOD BASE OR PLINTH BLOCKS.

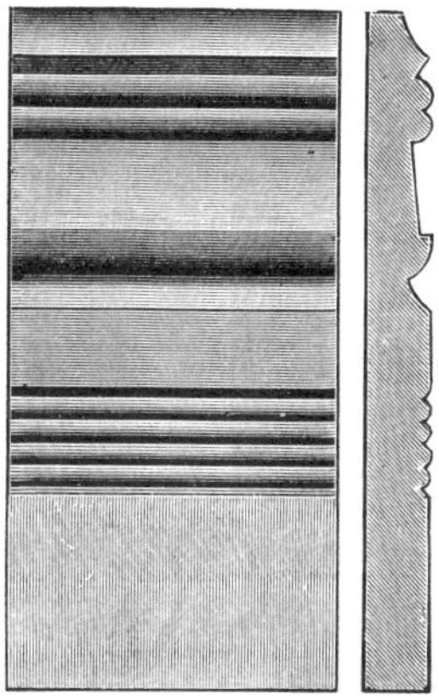

917
5½×11×1⅜, $13.00 per 100

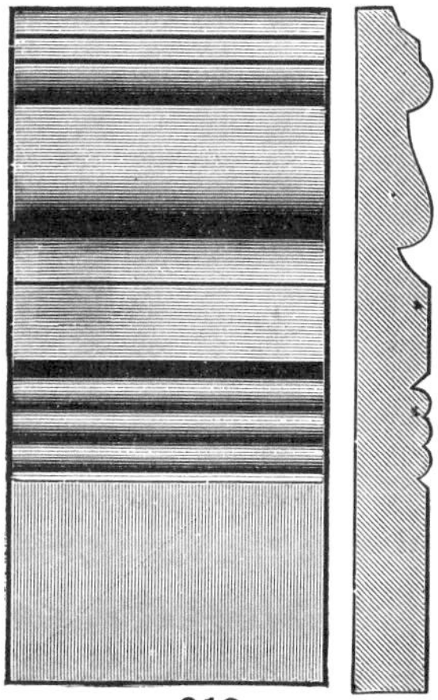

918
5½×12×1⅜, $13.00 per 100

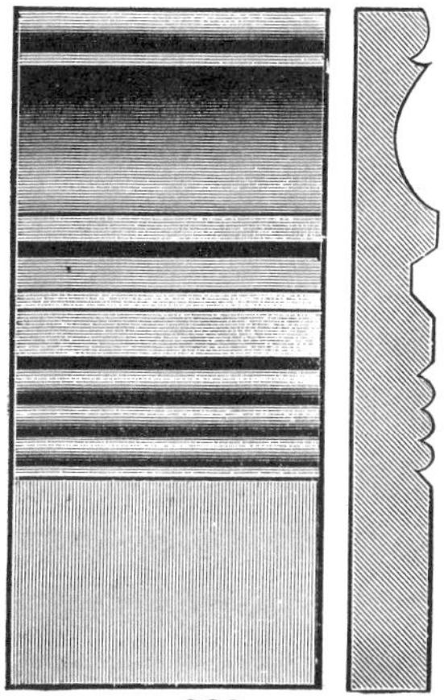

929
5½×12×1⅜, $13.00 per 100

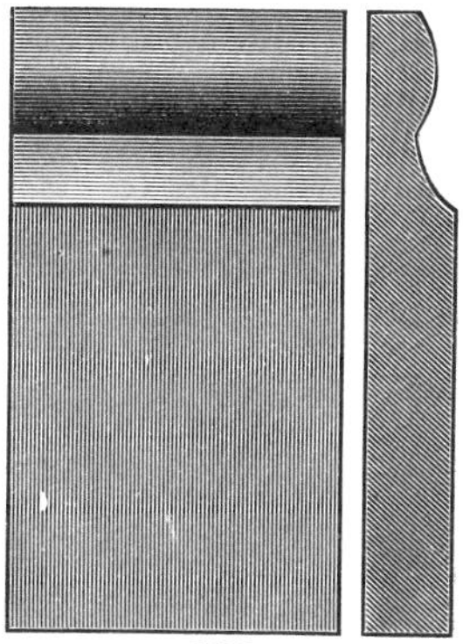

938
5½×10×1⅜, $8.00 per 100

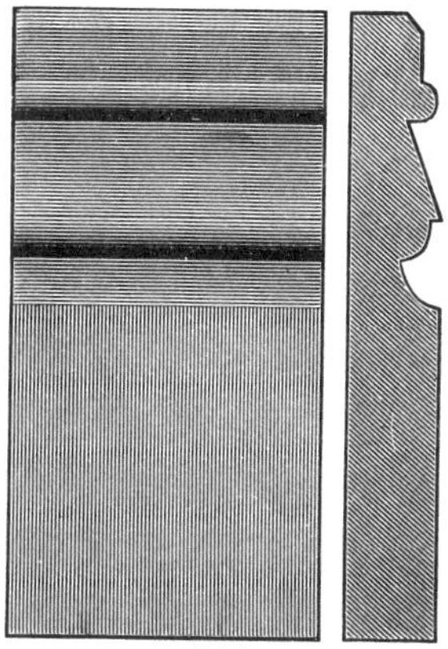

940
5½×11×1⅜, $9.50 per 100

941
5½×10×1⅜, $8.00 per 100

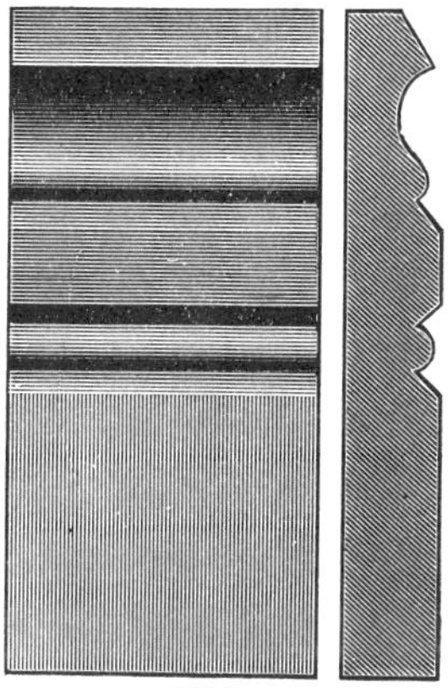

944
5½×11×1⅜, $9.00 per 100

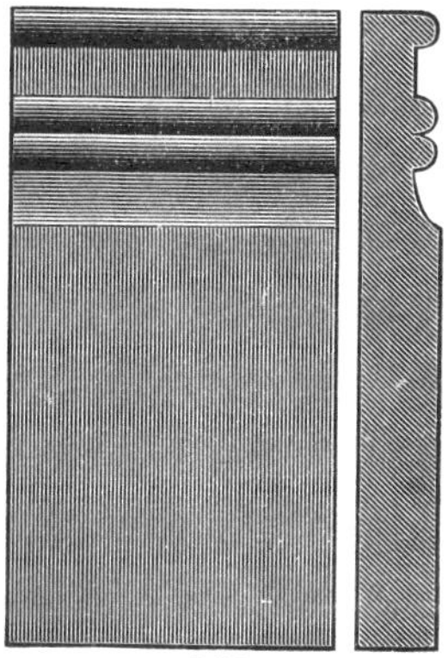

949
5½×10×1⅜, $8.00 per 100

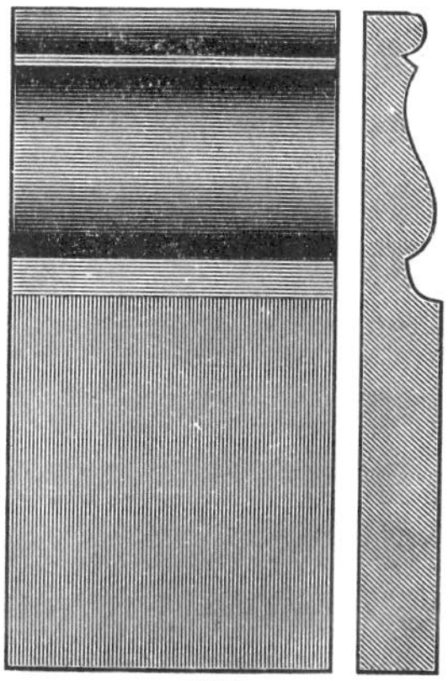

950
5½×12×1¾, $9.50 per 100

STAIRS

STAIR RAILING,

Balusters, Newel Posts, Mantels

PEW ENDS, Etc.

ALSO

Interior Finish

OF EVERY DESCRIPTION

IN ALL KINDS OF

HARD AND SOFT WOODS.

Brackets, Corner and Plinth Blocks, Corner
Beads, Etc.,

A SPECIALTY.

STAIRS, NEWEL POSTS, BALUSTERS, STAIR RAILING, ETC.

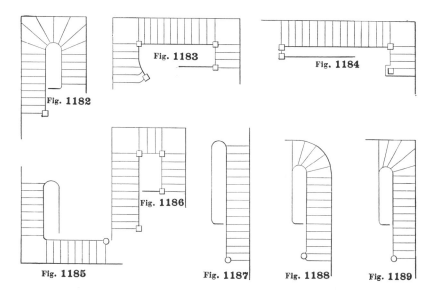

Fig. 1182

Fig. 1183

Fig. 1184

Fig. 1185

Fig. 1186

Fig. 1187

Fig. 1188

Fig. 1189

DIRECTIONS NECESSARY FOR ORDERING STAIRS AND STAIR RAILING.

When a flight of stairs is wanted, we should know the height of story from floor to floor, width of joists in second story, width and run of stairs, the size of cylinder, style of base used in the hall, with rough sketch showing about the shape of stairs wanted.

FOR STAIR RAILING, STRAIGHT FLIGHT,

We require the width of rise and step as sawed out on string board, the number of risers, the size of cylinder from face to face of string or face board, which way it turns at head of stairs, and the number of feet of straight rail required at landing. Unless we receive plan showing otherwise, we always suppose the top riser for a straight flight of stairs to be placed at the edge or spring of cylinder.

FOR CIRCULAR OR WINDING STAIRS,

We should have an exact plan of stairs as built, giving the width of rise and step, the location of risers in cylinder, etc.; and, when there are straight steps below or above the cylinder, always give the distance from the first square riser to the edge or spring line of cylinder, on the face of string or face board. *Always write your address in full on the plans.*

PRICE LIST OF STAIR WORK.

Outside Posts, Newels, Balusters, Etc.

BALUSTERS.

We turn all our Stair Balusters 2 ft. 4 in. and 2 ft. 8 in. long, unless otherwise ordered. Are prepared to furnish, on short notice, any length or style desired. Odd lengths cost extra.

Fancy Turned Balusters.

Nos. 1200 and 1201.

Sizes.	1½ in.	1¾ in.	2 in.	2¼ in.	2½ in.
	Cts.	Cts.	Cts.	Cts.	Cts.
Oak or Ash...	9	12	12	15	17
Wal't or Ch'ry,	11	17	17	21	23

Nos. 1202 and 1203.

Sizes.	1½ in.	1¾ in.	2 in.	2¼ in.	2½ in.
	Cts.	Cts.	Cts.	Cts.	Cts.
Oak or Ash...	11	14	14	17	19
Wal't or Ch'ry,	13	19	19	23	25

Nos. 1206 to 1214 inclusive.

Sizes.	1¾ in.	2 in.	2¼ in.	2½ in.	2¾ in.
	Cts.	Cts.	Cts.	Cts.	Cts.
Oak or Ash....	17	17	20	22	30
Wal't or Ch'ry,	22	22	26	28	43

Octagon Balusters.

No. 1205.

Sizes.	1¾ in.	2 in.	2¼ in.	2½ in.	2¾ in.
	Cts.	Cts.	Cts.	Cts.	Cts.
Oak or Ash....	19	19	23	25	35
Wal't or Ch'ry,	24	24	29	31	48

For No. 1204, Fluted, add to list of No. 1205 1c. Mahogany costs about double price.

NEWELS.

Fancy Turned Newel Posts.

Nos. 1300 and 1301.

Sizes.	4 in.	5 in.	6 in.	7 in.
Pine..................	$ .90	$1.25	$1.50	
Oak or Ash.............	3.00	3.50	4.00	$4.50
Walnut or Cherry......	3.50	4.00	4.50	5 00

Plain Octagon Staved Newel Posts.

No. 1302, Walnut, Cherry, Oak, or Ash.

Sizes.	8 in.	9 in.	10 in.	11 in.	12 in.
Prices.........	$5.75	$6.00	$6.25	$6.50	$7.00

For Raised O G Panels, add to above prices $1.50 each.

For Mahogany Posts, add to above prices $4.00 each.

Octagon Sunk Panel Newel Posts.

FANCY MOULDED.

No. 1303, Walnut, Cherry, Oak, or Ash.

Sizes.	8 in.	9 in.	10 in.	11 in.	12 in.
Prices......	$8.50	$9.00	$9.50	$10.00	$10.50

For Circle Top Panels, add $1.25
For Posts like No. 1304, add $3.00
For Posts like No. 1305, add $4.50

PLATFORM OR ANGLE NEWELS.

Sizes.	Oak or Ash.	Walnut or Cherry.
No. 1501, 5 inch..........	$4.50	$5.00
No. 1502, 5 inch..........	5.00	5.50
No. 1503, 5 inch..........	6.50	7.00
No. 1504, 5 inch..........	5.00	5.50
No. 1505, 5 inch..........	6.50	7.00
No. 1506, 5 inch..........	7.00	7.50

POSTS FOR OUTSIDE BALUSTRADE.

Pine, ordinary lengths (see page 199).

Numbers.	Price, 3¾ inches.	Price, 4¾ inches.	Price, 5¾ inches.
1630	$ .75	$1.00	$1.25
1631	.75	1 00	1.25
1632	1.00	1.25	1.50
1634	1.50	1.75	2.00
1635		1.75	2.00
1639	2.00	2.25	2.50
1640	1.00	1.25	1.50

TURNED BALUSTERS.

For Outside Balustrade see pages 201 and 202.

Prices in Pine or Whitewood.

Length. inches.	8	10	12	14	16	18	20	22	24
	Cts.	Cts.	Cts.	Cts.	Cts.	Cts.	Cts	Cts.	Cts.
Size, 1¾ x 1¾ in.	6	6	6	7	8	9	11		
Size, 2¾ x 2¾ in.		8	9	10	11	12	13		
Size, 3¾ x 3¾ in.		12	13	14	15	16	17	19	21

SAWED PINE BALUSTERS.

For any of the Patterns on page 202, size 5¾ × ⅞ 18 or 20 inches long, price 16 cents each.

PORCH AND VERANDA COLUMNS.

Basswood or Whitewood.

4¾ to 5¾ inches square (pages 200 and 201).

Numbers.	Price, 8 ft. long.	Price, 10 ft. long.
1645	$3.00	$3.50
1646	3.00	3.50
1647	3.00	3.50
1648	3.00	3 75
1648½	4.50	5.50
1649	3.00	3.50
1650	3.00	3.50
1651	3.00	3.50
1652	3.00	3.50
1653	3.00	3.50
1654	3.00	3.50

Discounts to Dealers.

BALUSTERS.

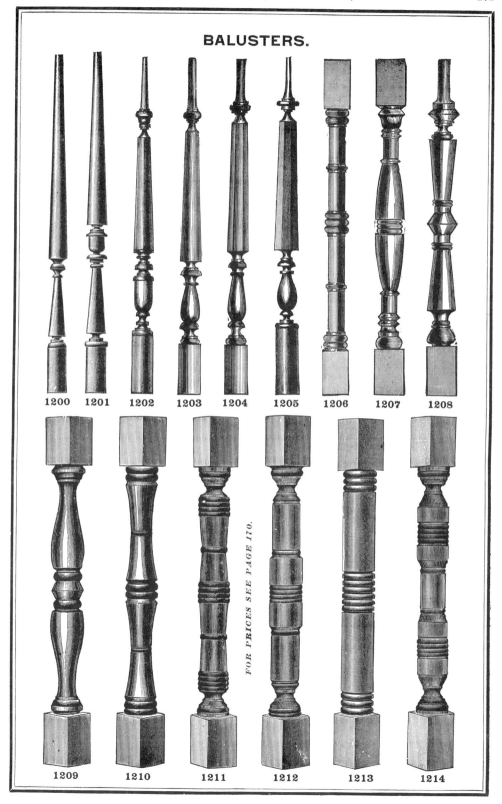

FOR PRICES SEE PAGE 170.

1200 1201 1202 1203 1204 1205 1206 1207 1208

1209 1210 1211 1212 1213 1214

BALUSTERS.

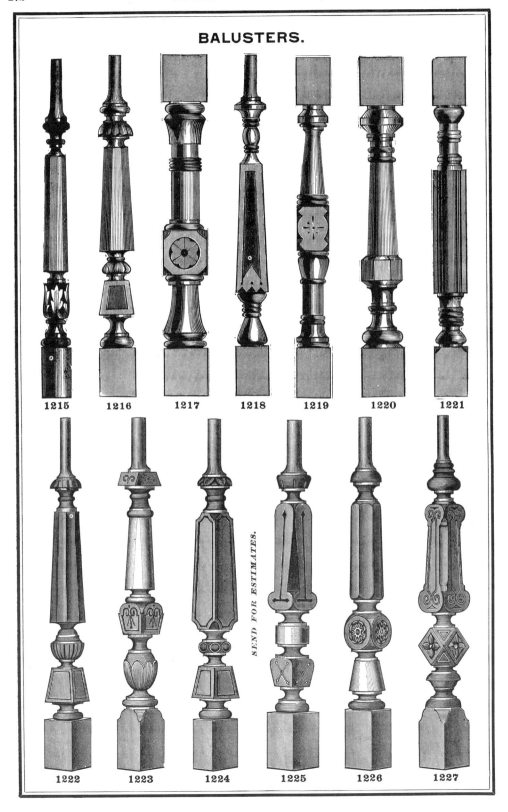

1215   1216   1217   1218   1219   1220   1221

SEND FOR ESTIMATES.

1222   1223   1224   1225   1226   1227

NEWEL POSTS.

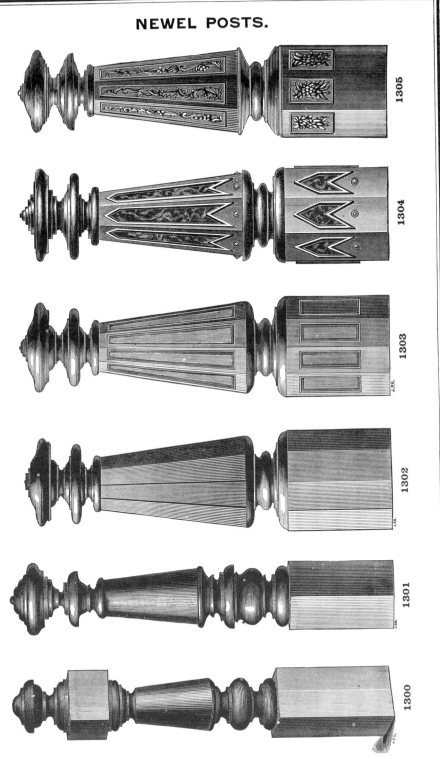

1305

1304

1303

1302

1301

1300

FOR PRICES SEE PAGE 170.

NEWEL POSTS.

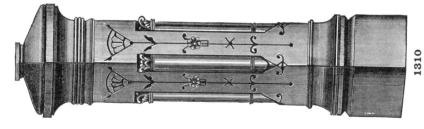

1310

1309

1308

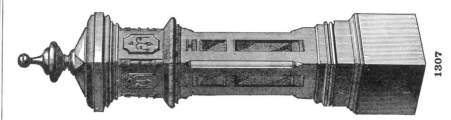

1307

1306

SEND FOR ESTIMATES.

NEWEL POSTS.

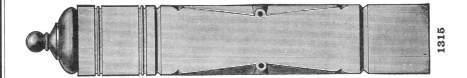

1315

1314

1313

1312

1311

SEND FOR ESTIMATES.

NEWEL POSTS.

1320

1319

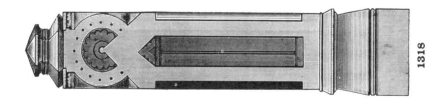

1318

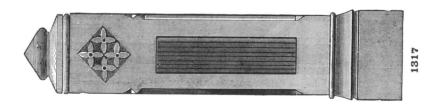

1317

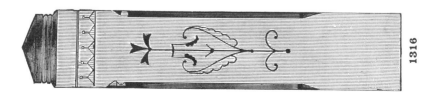

1316

SEND FOR ESTIMATE

NEWEL POSTS.

1371

1370

1344

1340

1336

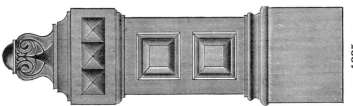

1335

SEND FOR ESTIMATES.

STAIR RAILS.

Thickness of Rails varies from 1¾ to 2¾, proportionate to width.

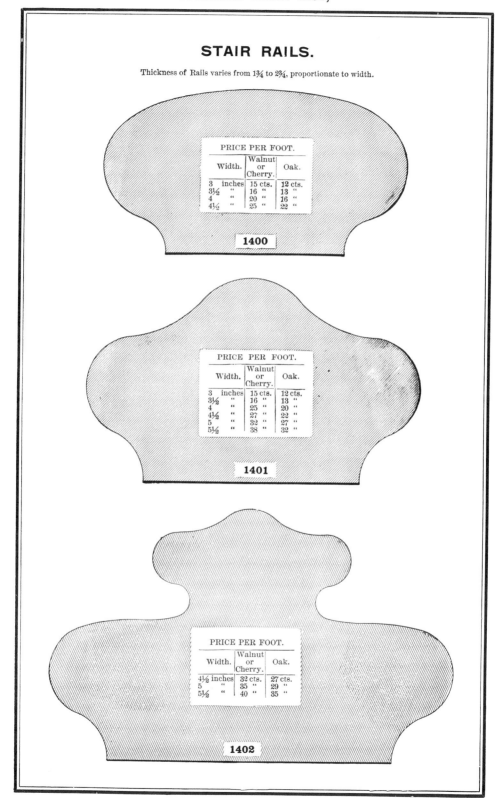

PRICE PER FOOT.

Width.	Walnut or Cherry.	Oak.
3 inches	15 cts.	12 cts.
3½ "	16 "	13 "
4 "	20 "	16 "
4½ "	25 "	22 "

1400

PRICE PER FOOT.

Width.	Walnut or Cherry.	Oak.
3 inches	15 cts.	12 cts.
3½ "	16 "	13 "
4 "	25 "	20 "
4½ "	27 "	22 "
5 "	32 "	27 "
5½ "	38 "	32 "

1401

PRICE PER FOOT.

Width.	Walnut or Cherry.	Oak.
4½ inches	32 cts.	27 cts.
5 "	35 "	29 "
5½ "	40 "	35 "

1402

STAIR RAILS.

Thickness of Rails varies from 1¾ to 2¾, proportionate to width.

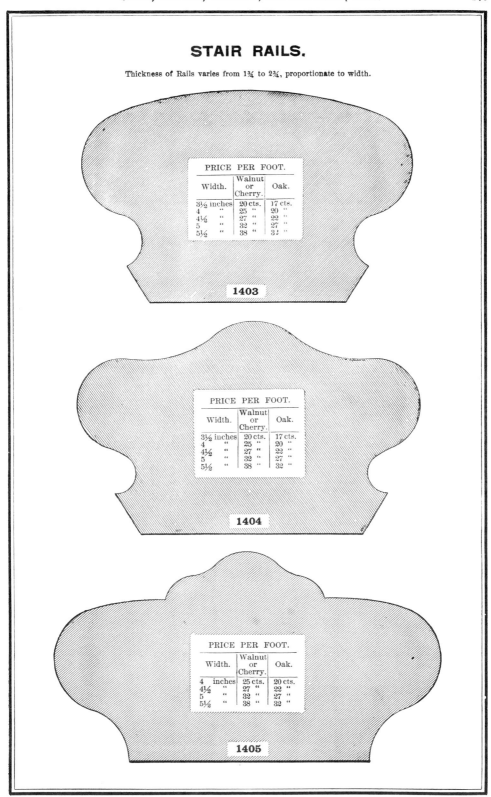

PRICE PER FOOT.

Width.	Walnut or Cherry.	Oak.
3½ inches	20 cts.	17 cts.
4 "	25 "	20 "
4½ "	27 "	22 "
5 "	32 "	27 "
5½ "	38 "	32 "

1403

PRICE PER FOOT.

Width.	Walnut or Cherry.	Oak.
3½ inches	20 cts.	17 cts.
4 "	25 "	20 "
4½ "	27 "	22 "
5 "	32 "	27 "
5½ "	38 "	32 "

1404

PRICE PER FOOT.

Width.	Walnut or Cherry.	Oak.
4 inches	25 cts.	20 cts.
4½ "	27 "	22 "
5 "	32 "	27 "
5½ "	38 "	32 "

1405

STAIR RAILS.

Thickness of Rails varies from 1¾ to 2¾, proportionate to width.

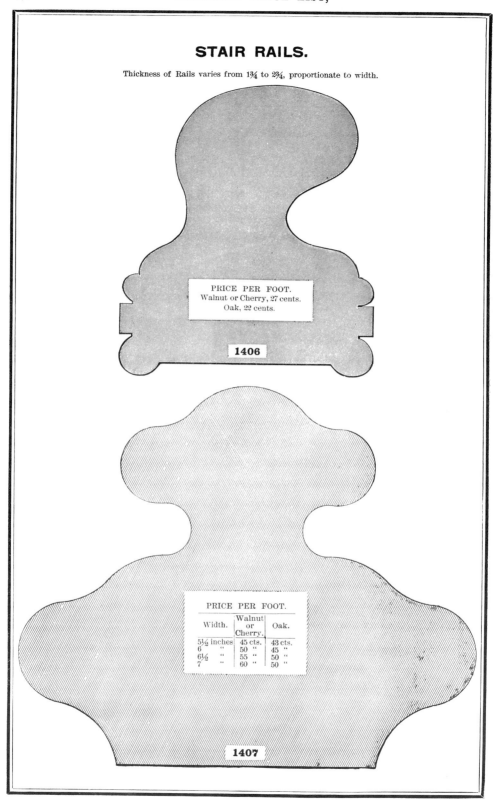

PRICE PER FOOT.
Walnut or Cherry, 27 cents.
Oak, 22 cents.

1406

PRICE PER FOOT.

Width.	Walnut or Cherry.	Oak.
5½ inches	45 cts.	43 cts.
6 "	50 "	45 "
6½ "	55 "	50 "
7 "	60 "	50 "

1407

STAIR RAILS.

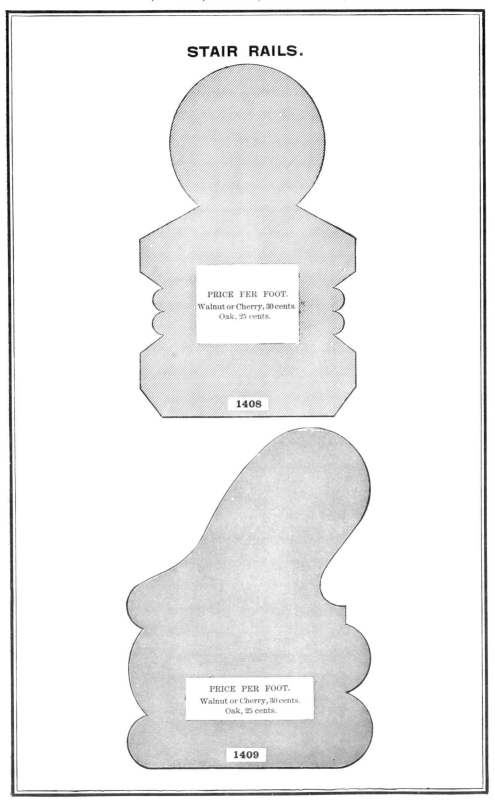

PRICE PER FOOT.
Walnut or Cherry, 30 cents.
Oak, 25 cents.

1408

PRICE PER FOOT.
Walnut or Cherry, 30 cents.
Oak, 25 cents.

1409

STAIR RAILS.

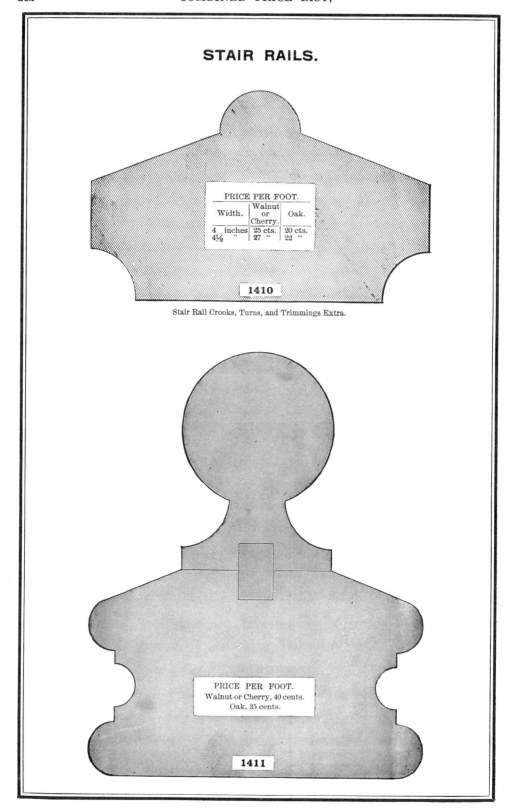

PRICE PER FOOT.

Width.	Walnut or Cherry.	Oak.
4 inches	25 cts.	20 cts.
4½ "	27 "	22 "

1410

Stair Rail Crooks, Turns, and Trimmings Extra.

PRICE PER FOOT.
Walnut or Cherry, 40 cents.
Oak, 35 cents.

1411

STAIR RAILS.

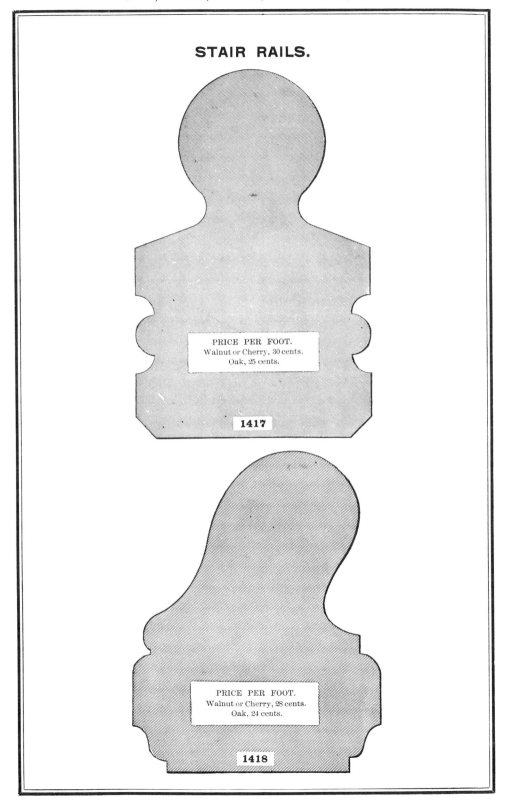

PRICE PER FOOT.
Walnut or Cherry, 30 cents.
Oak, 25 cents.

1417

PRICE PER FOOT.
Walnut or Cherry, 28 cents.
Oak, 24 cents.

1418

STAIR RAILS.

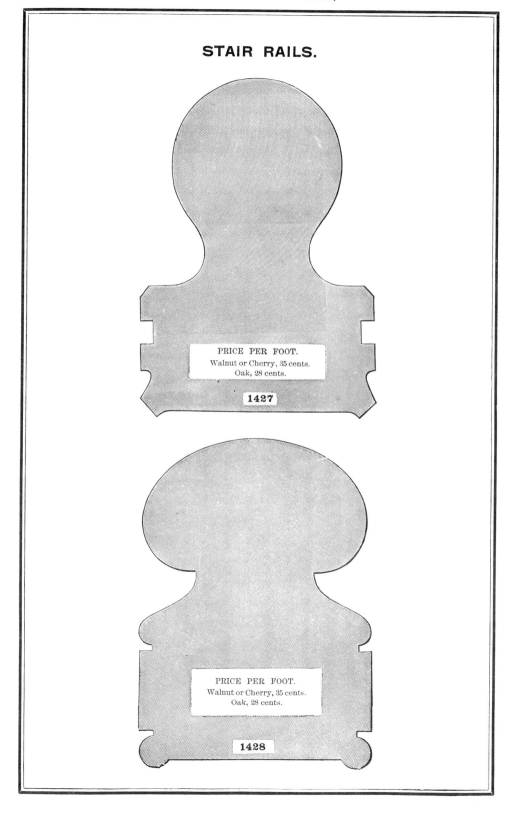

PRICE PER FOOT.
Walnut or Cherry, 35 cents.
Oak, 28 cents.

1427

PRICE PER FOOT.
Walnut or Cherry, 35 cents.
Oak, 28 cents.

1428

PLATFORM NEWELS.

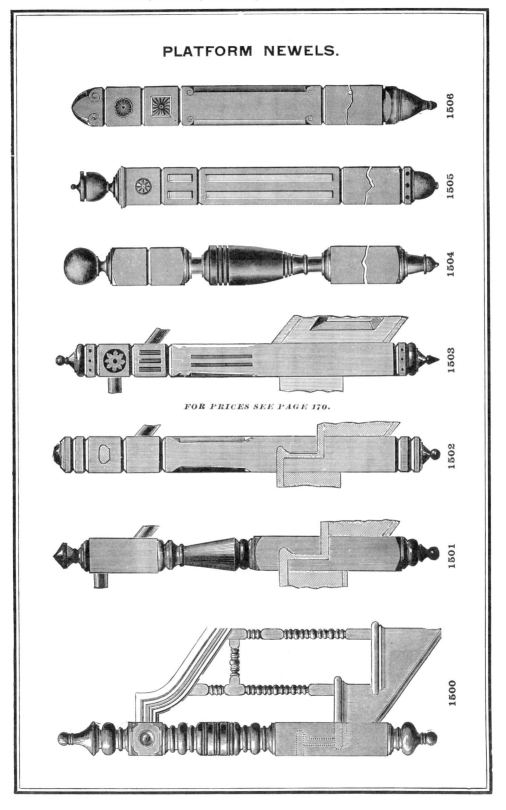

FOR PRICES SEE PAGE 170.

1506
1505
1504
1503
1502
1501
1500

DESIGNS FOR STAIRS.

1520

1521

1522

1523

WRITE FOR PRICES.

DESIGNS FOR STAIRS.

1524

1525   1526   1527

WRITE FOR PRICES.

DESIGN FOR STAIRS.

1528

DESIGN FOR STAIRS.

1529

DESIGN FOR STAIRS.

1530

DESIGN FOR STAIRS.

1531

WRITE FOR PRICES.

DESIGN FOR STAIRS.

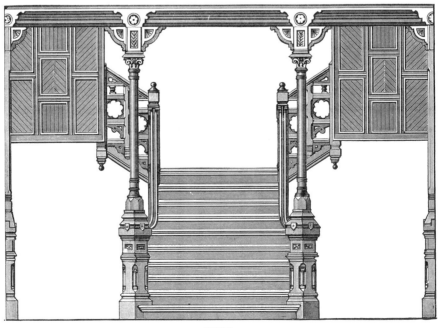

1532

WRITE FOR PRICES.

DESIGNS FOR STAIRS.

1533

1534

1535

1536

WRITE FOR PRICES.

DESIGNS FOR STAIRS.

1543

1542

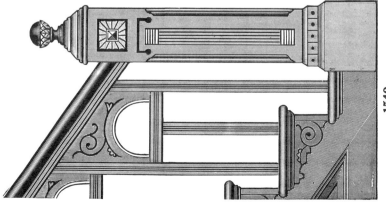

1540

WRITE FOR PRICES.

DESIGNS FOR STAIRS.

1551

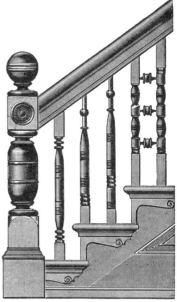

1552

1553

1554

WRITE FOR PRICES.

STAIR BRACKETS.

Level Brackets for Stairs, 4 inches wide, ¼ inch thick.   Price per foot: Pine, 6 cents;
Black Walnut, 10 cents.

Stair Brackets, 8
to 10 inches long.
Walnut, 10 cents;
Pine, 6 cents each;

OUTSIDE RAILS.

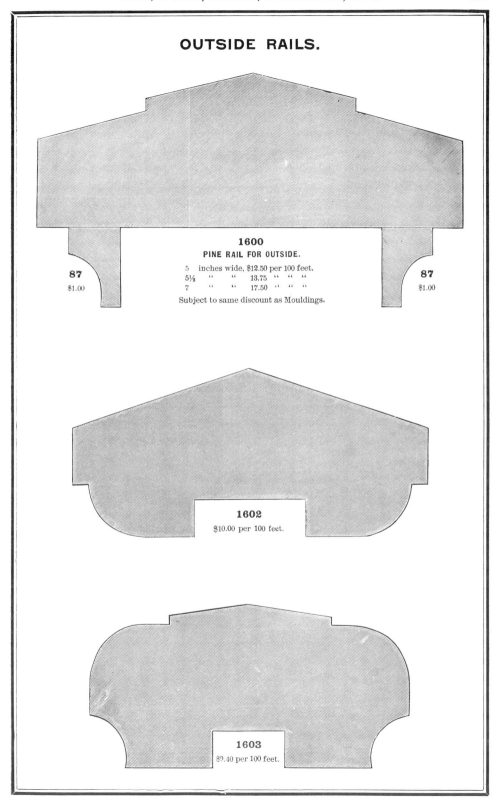

1600

PINE RAIL FOR OUTSIDE.

5 inches wide, $12.50 per 100 feet.
5½   "   "   13.75 " " "
7   "   "   17.50 " " "

Subject to same discount as Mouldings.

87

$1.00

87

$1.00

1602

$10.00 per 100 feet.

1603

$9.40 per 100 feet.

RAILS AND BASE FOR OUTSIDE.

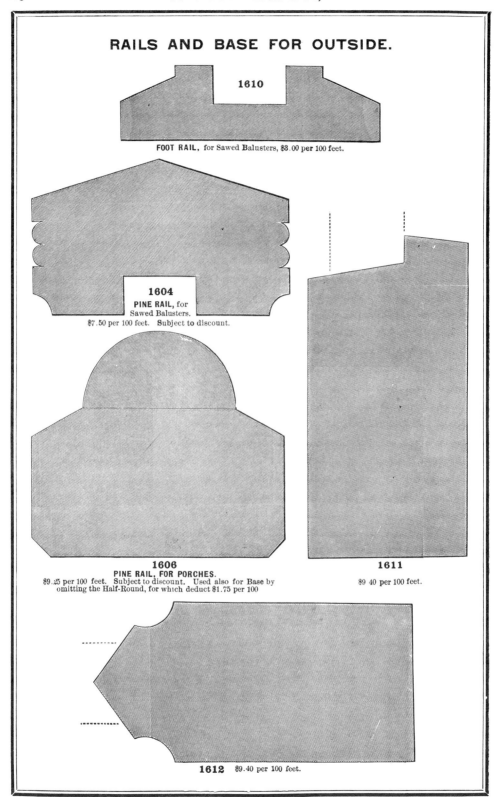

1610

FOOT RAIL, for Sawed Balusters, $3.00 per 100 feet.

1604
PINE RAIL, for
Sawed Balusters.
$7.50 per 100 feet. Subject to discount.

1606
PINE RAIL, FOR PORCHES.
$9.25 per 100 feet. Subject to discount. Used also for Base by
omitting the Half-Round, for which deduct $1.75 per 100

1611
$9 40 per 100 feet.

1612 $9.40 per 100 feet.

NEWELS FOR BALUSTRADE AND PORCH WORK.

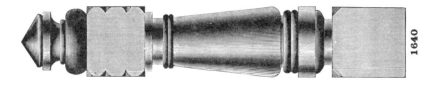

1640

1639

FOR PRICES SEE PAGE 170.

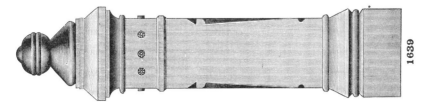

1635

1634

1632

1631

1630

VERANDA POSTS.

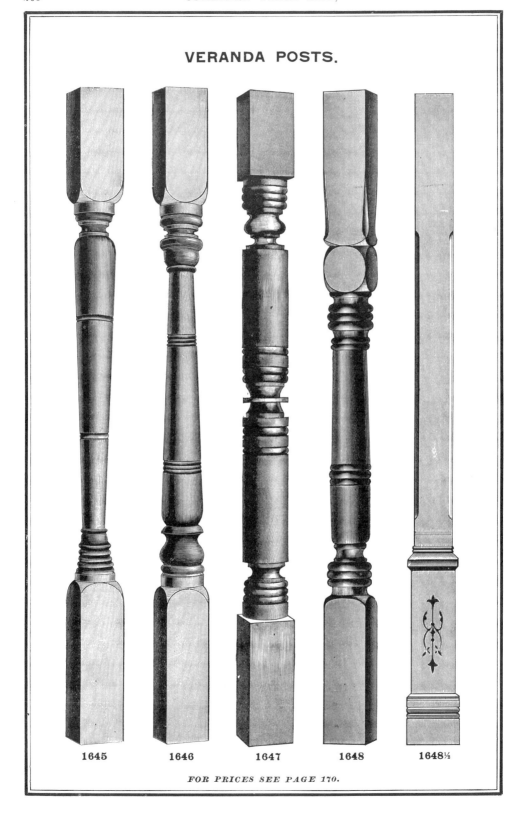

1645   1646   1647   1648   1648½

FOR PRICES SEE PAGE 170.

VERANDA POSTS.

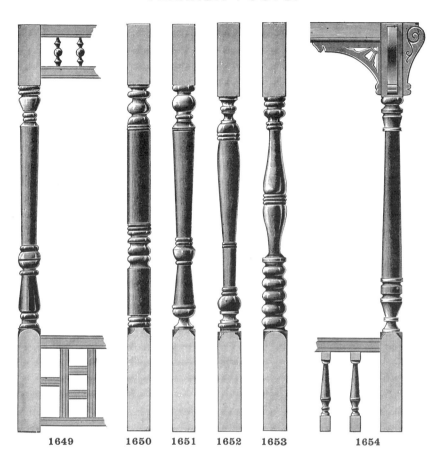

1649   1650   1651   1652   1653   1654

OUTSIDE BALUSTERS.

1660   1661   1662   1663   1664   1665

FOR PRICES SEE PAGE 170.

TURNED AND SAWED OUTSIDE BALUSTERS.

1666	1667	1668	1676	1677	1678

1700	1701	1702	1703

1704	1705	1706	1707

1730	1731	1732	1733	1734

FOR PRICES SEE PAGE 170.

VERANDAS.

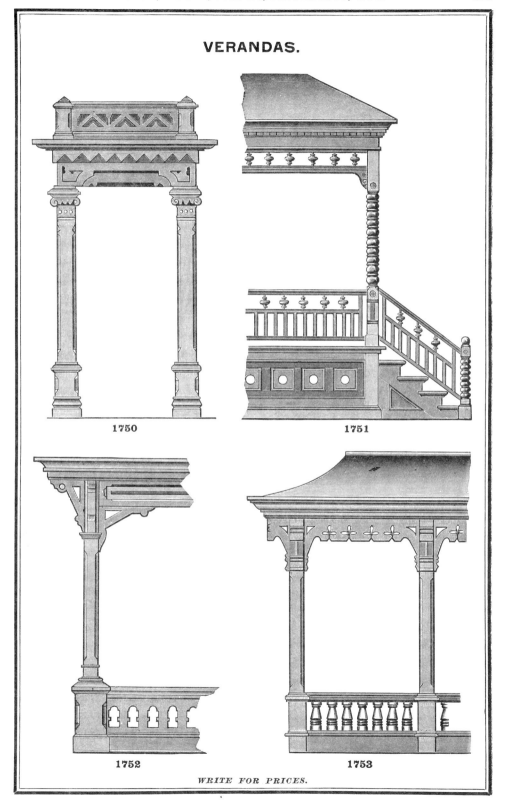

1750

1751

1752

1753

VERANDAS.

1754   1755

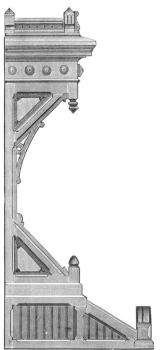

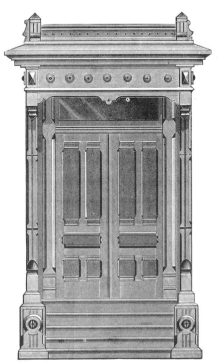

1756
WRITE FOR PRICES.

VERANDAS.

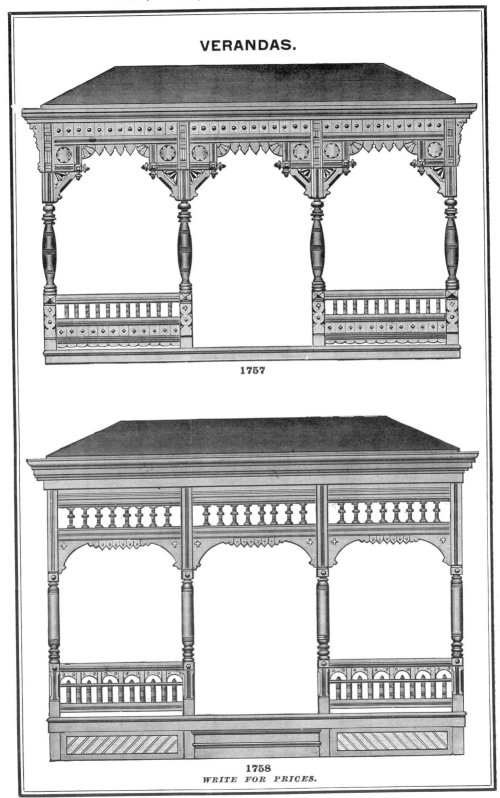

1757

1758
WRITE FOR PRICES.

VERANDAS.

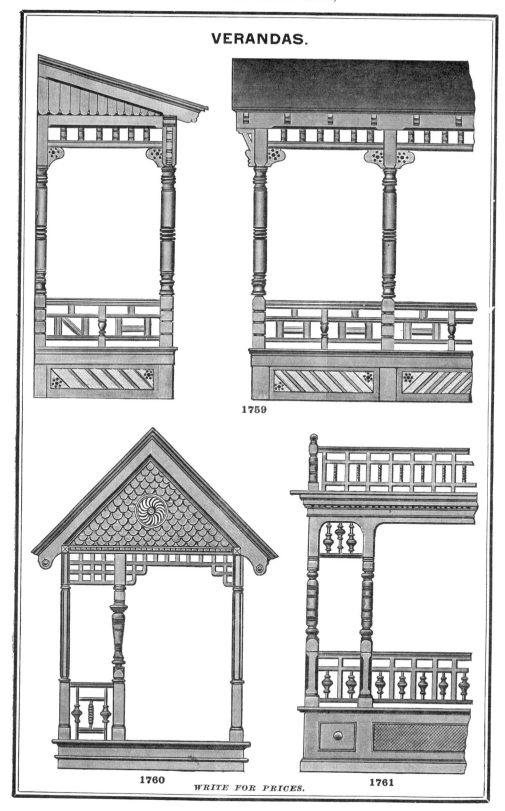

1759

1760 *WRITE FOR PRICES.* 1761

VERANDAS.

1771

1772
WRITE FOR PRICES.

BAY WINDOWS.

1780

1781

1782

1783

WRITE FOR PRICES.

BAY WINDOWS.

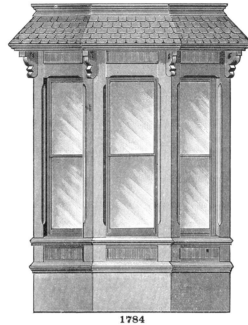

1784

1785

WRITE FOR PRICES.

BRACKETS.

BRACKETS.

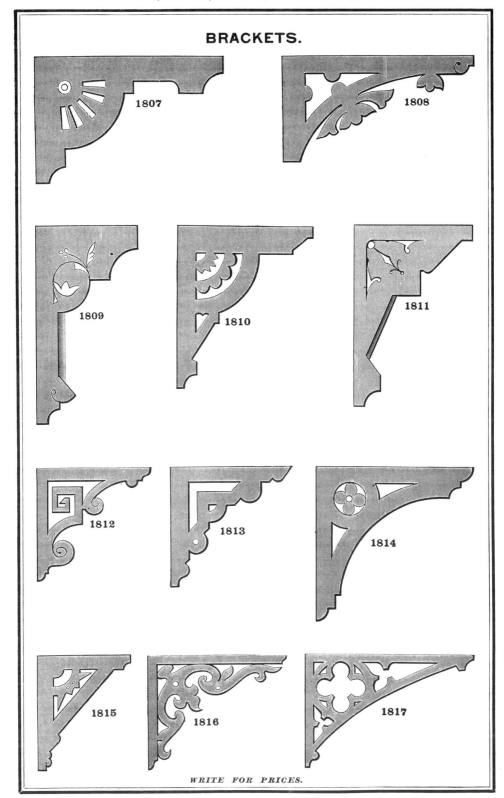

BRACKETS.

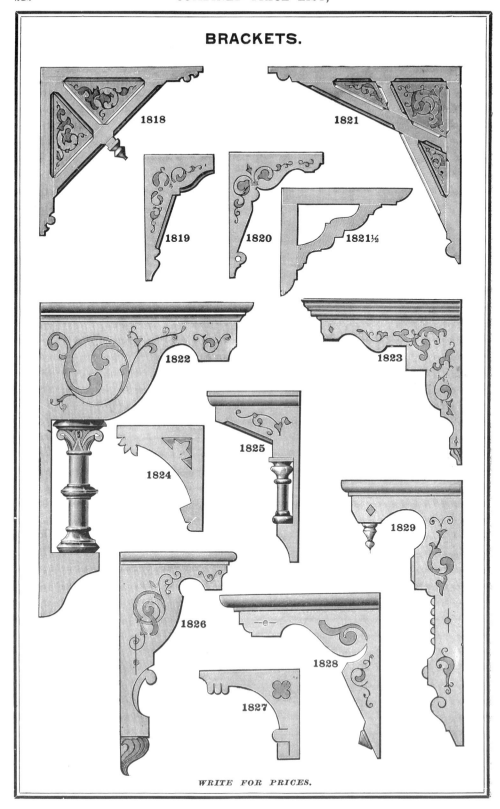

BRACKETS.

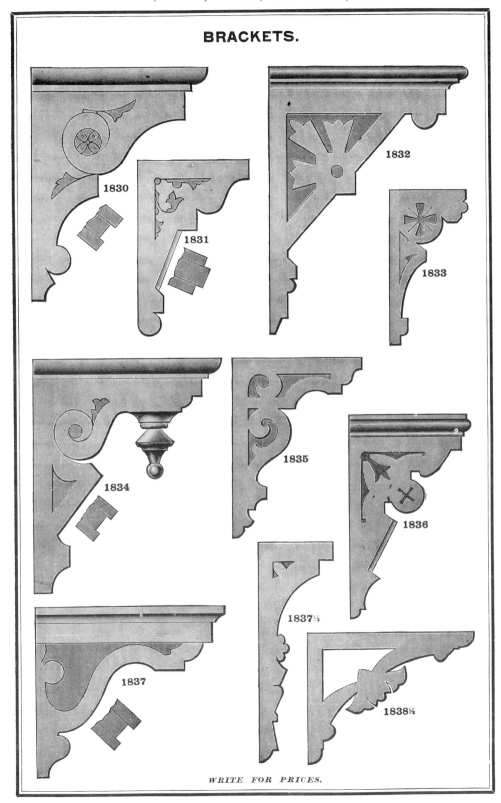

1830

1831

1832

1833

1834

1835

1836

1837

1837½

1838½

BRACKETS.

1839

1840

1841

1842

1843

1845

1845½

1846

1847

WRITE FOR PRICES.

WINDOW HOODS AND BRACKETS.

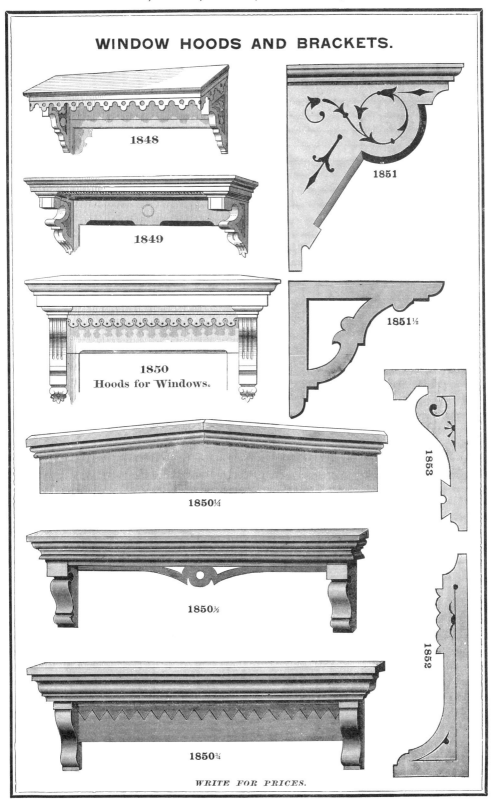

1848

1849

1851

1851½

1850
Hoods for Windows.

1853

1850¼

1850½

1852

1850¾

WRITE FOR PRICES.

BRACKETS.

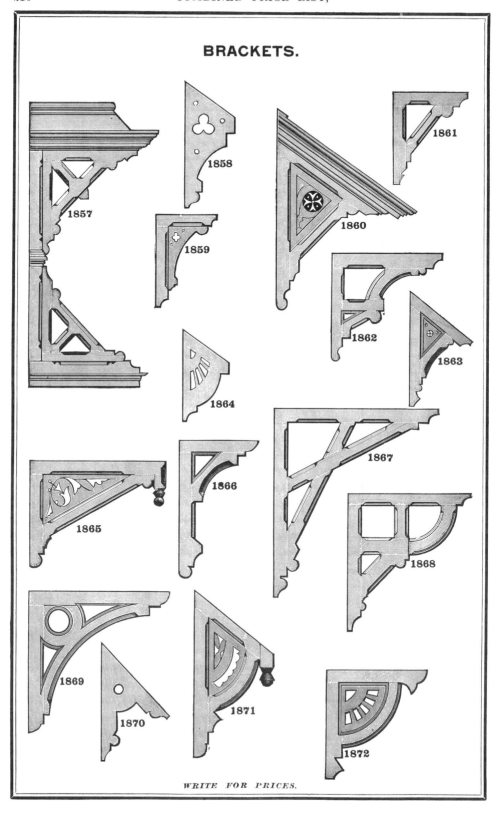

BRACKETS.

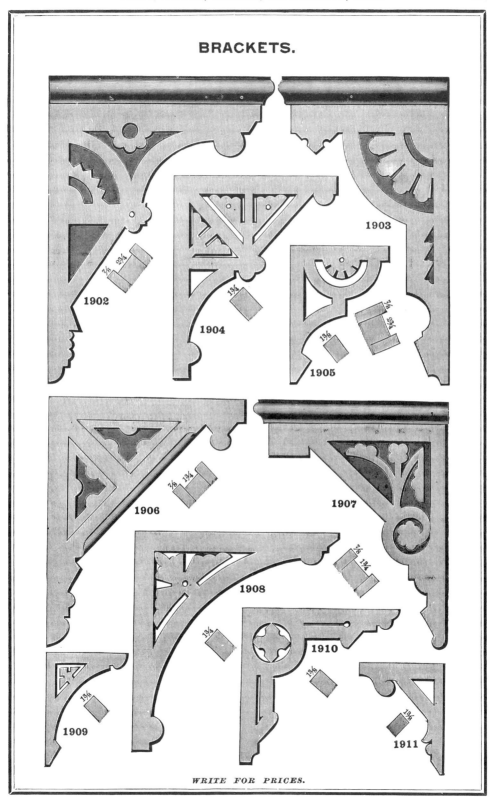

BRACKETS.

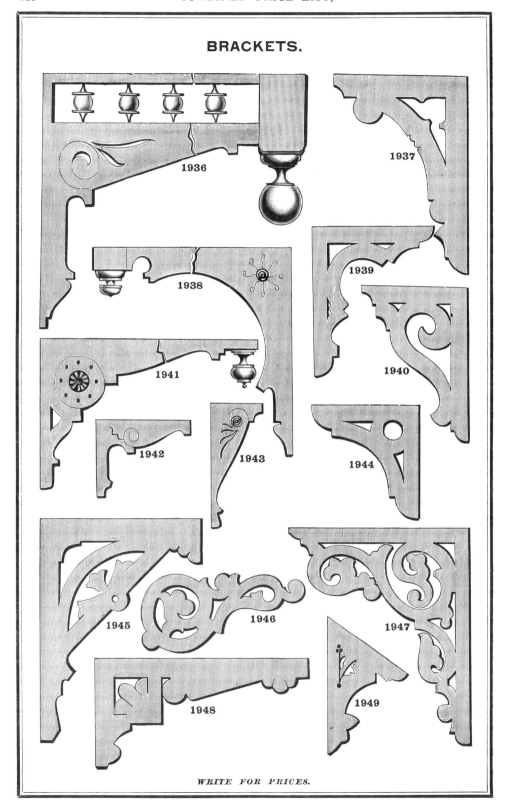

CORNICE DRAPERY, VERGE BOARDS, ETC.

WRITE FOR PRICES.

GABLE FINISH.

2014

2015

2016

2017

2018

2019

2020

2021

2022

2023

GABLE FINISH AND WOOD ROSETTES.

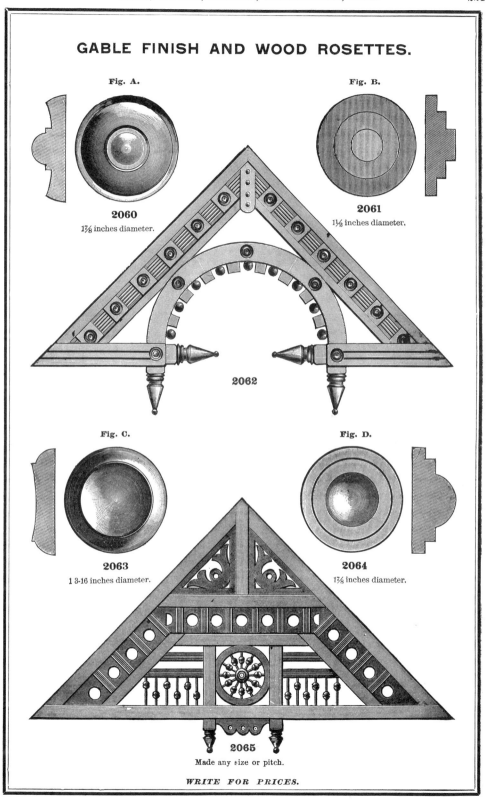

Fig. A.

2060

1⅞ inches diameter.

Fig. B.

2061

1½ inches diameter.

2062

Fig. C.

2063

1 3-16 inches diameter.

Fig. D.

2064

1⅞ inches diameter.

2065

Made any size or pitch.

WRITE FOR PRICES.

GABLE FINISH AND WOOD ROSETTES.

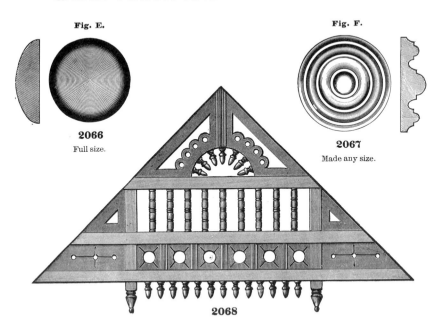

Fig. E.

2066

Full size.

Fig. F.

2067

Made any size.

2068

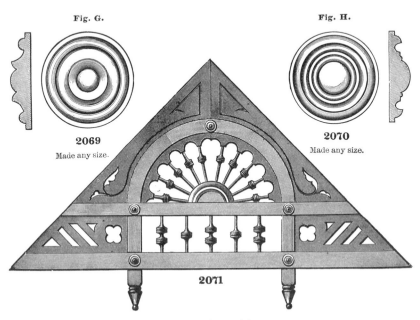

Fig. G.

2069

Made any size.

Fig. H.

2070

Made any size.

2071

Made any size or pitch.

WRITE FOR PRICES.

GABLE FINISH AND WOOD ROSETTES.

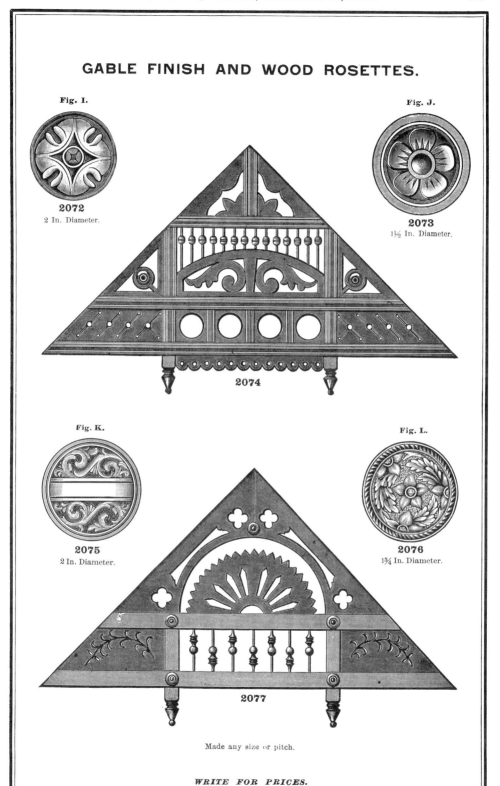

Fig. I.

2072

2 In. Diameter.

Fig. J.

2073

1½ In. Diameter.

2074

Fig. K.

2075

2 In. Diameter.

Fig. L.

2076

1¾ In. Diameter.

2077

Made any size or pitch.

WRITE FOR PRICES.

MANTELS.

2100

From 18 to 30 inches long.

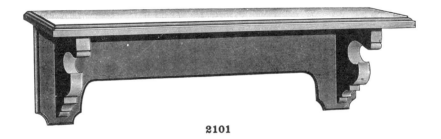

2101

2102

WRITE FOR PRICES.

MANTELS.

2103

From 30 to 48 inches long.

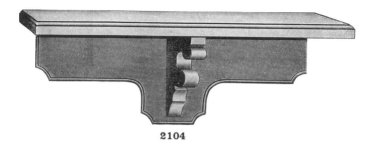

2104

2105

WRITE FOR PRICES.

MANTELS.

2106

2107

MANTELS.

2108

2109

WRITE FOR PRICES.

MANTEL.

2110

MANTEL.

2111

MANTEL.

2112

MANTEL.

2113

MANTEL.

2114

MANTEL.

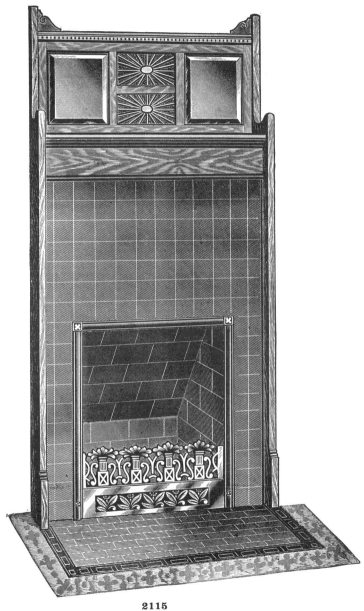

2115

MANTEL.

2116

WRITE FOR PRICES.

MANTEL.

2117

MANTEL.

2118

MANTEL.

2119

Length of Shelf..	5 feet.				
Width of Opening	2 "	11½ inches.			
Width of Opening may be varied up to.....................................	3 "	6 "			
Height of Opening...	2 "	11¾ "			
Profile...	4 "				
Height of Mantel from floor to highest point	6 "	5 "			
Size of Mirror	40 x 18 "				

If length of Shelf is increased, the size and cost of Mirror will be increased proportionately.

WRITE FOR PRICES.

MANTEL.

2120

Length of Shelf.. 5 feet.
Width of Opening .... 2 " 11½ inches.
Width of Opening may be varied up to................................ 3 " 6 "
Height of Opening.. 2 " 11¾ "
Profile.. 7 "
Height of Mantel from floor to highest point .... 6 "
Size of Mirror .... 40 x 12 "
      If length of Shelf is increased, the size and cost of Mirror will be increased proportionately.

WRITE FOR PRICES.

MANTEL.

2121

Length of Shelf	5	feet.	
Width of Opening	2 "	11½	inches.
Width of Opening may be varied up to	3 "	6	"
Height of Opening	2 "	11¾	"
Profile		8	"
Height of Mantel from floor to highest point	6 "	8	"
Size of Mirror	28 x 20		"

If length of Shelf is increased, the size and cost of Mirror will be increased proportionately.

WRITE FOR PRICES.

MANTEL.

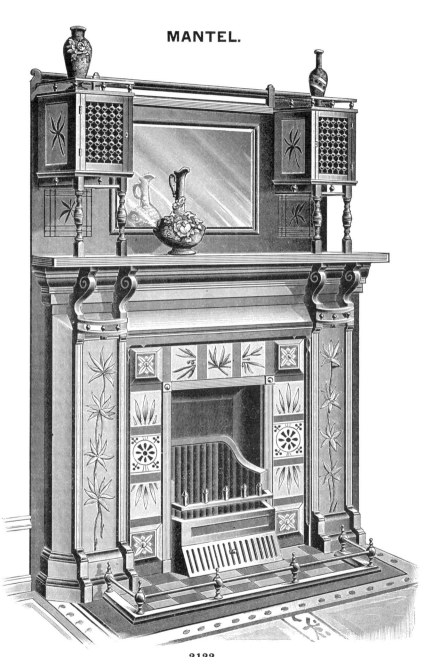

2122

Length of Shelf	5 feet.	
Width of Opening	2 '' 11½ inches.	
Width of Opening can not be increased without increasing length of Shelf.		
Height of Opening	2 '' 11¾	''
Profile	7	''
Height of Mantel from floor to highest point	6 ' 5	''
Size of Mirror	28 x 20	''

WRITE FOR PRICES.

MANTEL.

2123

Length of Shelf	5 feet.	
Width of Opening	2 "	11½ inches.
Height of Opening	2 "	11¼ "
By moving back Side Linings, width of Opening may be varied up to	3 "	6 "

WRITE FOR PRICES.

MANTEL.

2124

Length of Shelf... 5 feet.
Width of Opening .... 2 " 11½ inches
Height of Opening... 2 " 11¾ "

WRITE FOR PRICES.

MANTEL.

2125

Length of Shelf	5 feet.	
Width of Opening	2 "	11½ inches.
Height of Opening	2 "	11¾ "

MANTEL.

2126

Length of Shelf.. 5 feet.
Width of Opening.. 2 " 11½ inches.
Height of Opening... 2 " 11¼ "

WRITE FOR PRICES.

MANTEL.

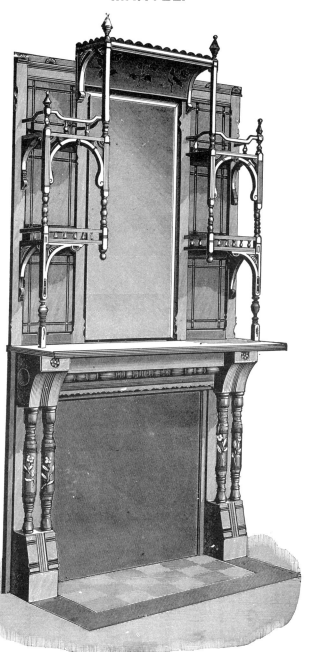

2127

Length of Shelf		5 feet.
Width of Opening	2 "	11½ inches.
Height of Opening	2 "	11¾ "
By moving back Side Linings, width of Opening may be varied up to	3 "	6 "

WRITE FOR PRICES.

MANTEL.

2128

Any width to	5 feet 6 inches.
Height	7 " 8 "
Profile	5¾ "
Mirror	16 x 42 "
Tile Opening	3 feet 6 inches wide x 3 feet 3 inches high.

WRITE FOR PRICES.

OFFICE AND BANK COUNTERS.

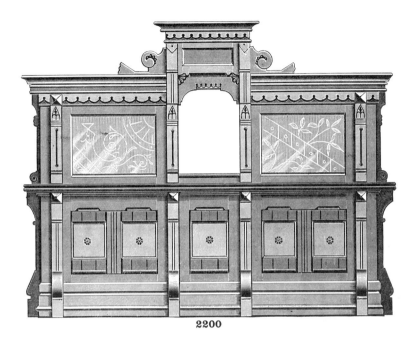

2200

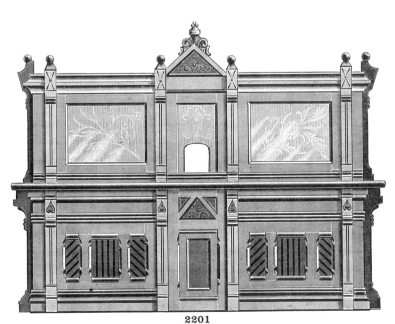

2201

WRITE FOR PRICES.

PULPITS.

2225

2226

2227

2228

2232

2233

WRITE FOR PRICES.

PEW ENDS.

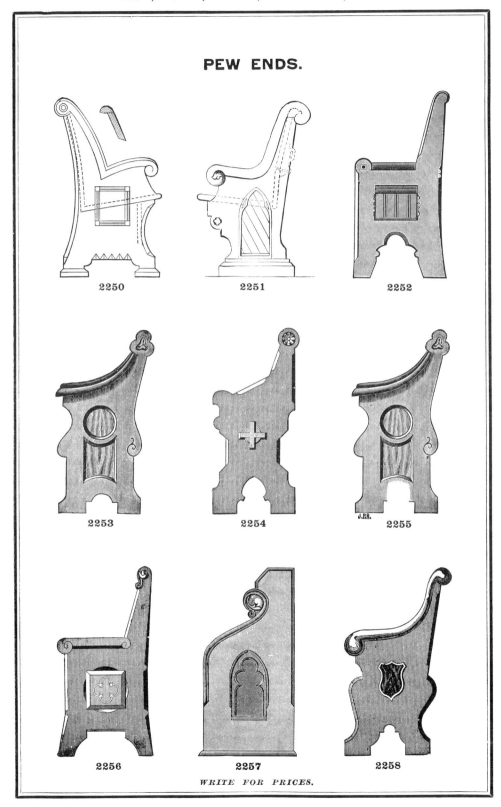

2250

2251

2252

2253

2254

2255

2256

2257

2258

WRITE FOR PRICES.

DIMENSION SHINGLES.

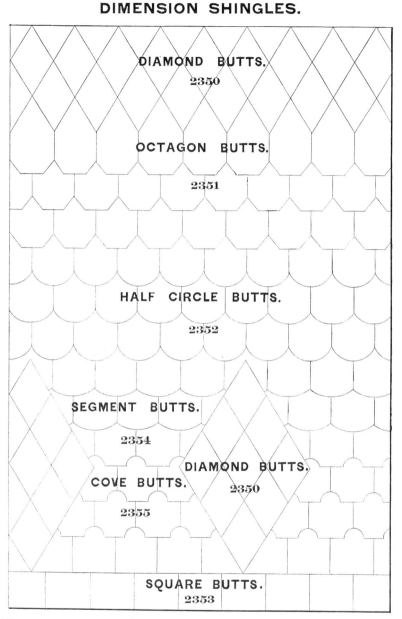

We are prepared to furnish Ornamental Shingles, cut to any shape desired, and can offer inducements in prices. Write for quotations.

SHINGLES REQUIRED IN A ROOF.

To the square foot it takes 9 if exposed 4 inches, 8 if exposed $4\frac{1}{2}$ inches, and 7 1-5 if exposed 5 inches to the weather.

Find the number of Shingles required to cover a roof 38 feet long and the rafters on each side 14 feet. Shingles exposed $4\frac{1}{2}$ inches:

Ans. $28 \times 38 = 1064$ (sq. ft.) $\times 8 = 8512$ Shingles.

PICKETS.

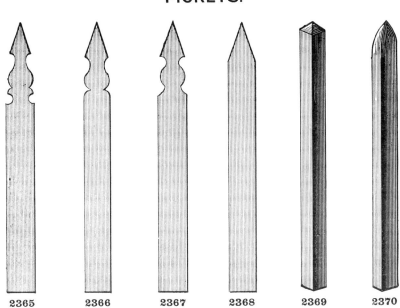

| 2365 | 2366 | 2367 | 2368 | 2369 | 2370 |

PRICE OF PICKETS.

No. 2365 1st Quality	....Net price per 1,000 Pickets,	$——
" 2366 "	.... " " "	——
" 2367 "	.... " " "	——
" 2368 "	.... " " "	——
" 2369 "	.... " " "	——
" 2370 "	.... " " "	——

CONVENIENT FACTS FOR BUILDERS.

Bricks Required for Walls of Various Thickness.

Number for each square foot of face of wall.		Number for each square foot of face of wall.	
Thickness of Wall.	No. Bricks.	Thickness of Wall.	No. Bricks.
4 inches.	7 1-2	24 inches.	45
8 "	15	28 "	52 1-2
12 "	22 1-2	32 "	60
16 "	30	36 "	67 1-2
20 "	37 1-2	42 "	75

Cubic Yard—600 bricks in wall.

Perch (22 cubic feet)—500 bricks in wall.

To pave 1 square yard on flat requires 41 bricks.

To pave 1 square yard on edge requires 68 bricks.

One-fifth more siding and flooring is needed than the number of square feet of surface to be covered, because of the lap in the siding and matching in the flooring.

One thousand lath will cover 70 yards of surface, and 11 pounds of lath nails will nail them on. Eight bushels of good lime, 16 bushels of sand, and 1 bushel of hair will make good enough mortar to plaster 100 square yards.

A cord of stone, 3 bushels of lime, and a cubic yard of sand will lay 100 cubic feet of wall.

Five courses of brick will lay 1 foot in height on a chimney. Six bricks in a course will make a a flue 4 inches wide and 12 inches long, and 16 bricks in a course will make a flue 8 inches wide and 16 inches long.

LUMBER MEASUREMENT.

READY RECKONER.

A table showing the number of feet, board measure, contained in each piece of scantling, joist or timber of the sizes given.

Size in Inches.	LENGTH IN FEET.														
	10	12	14	16	18	20	22	24	26	28	30	32	34	36	40
	NUMBER OF FEET, BOARD MEASURE, IN EACH PIECE.														
2 x 4	6⅔	8	9⅓	10⅔	12	13⅓	14⅔	16	17⅓	18⅔	20	21⅓	22⅔	24	25⅓
2 x 6	10	12	14	16	18	20	22	24	26	28	30	32	34	36	40
2 x 8	13⅓	16	18⅔	21⅓	24	26⅔	29⅓	32	34⅔	37⅓	40	42⅔	45⅓	48	53⅓
2 x 10	16⅔	20	23⅓	26⅔	30	33⅓	36⅔	40	43⅓	46⅔	50	53⅓	56⅔	60	66⅔
2 x 12	20	24	28	32	36	40	44	48	52	56	60	64	68	72	80
3 x 4	10	12	14	16	18	20	22	24	26	28	30	32	34	36	40
3 x 6	15	18	21	24	27	30	34	36	39	42	45	48	51	54	60
3 x 8	20	24	28	32	36	40	44	48	52	56	60	64	68	72	80
3 x 10	25	30	35	40	45	50	55	60	65	70	75	80	85	90	100
3 x 12	30	36	42	48	54	60	66	72	78	84	90	96	102	108	120
4 x 4	13⅓	16	18⅔	21⅓	24	26⅔	29⅓	32	34⅔	37⅓	40	42⅔	45⅓	48	53⅓
4 x 6	20	24	28	32	36	40	44	48	52	56	60	64	68	72	80
4 x 8	26⅔	32	37⅓	42⅔	48	53⅓	58⅔	64	69⅓	74⅔	80	85⅓	90⅔	96	106⅔
4 x 10	33⅓	40	46⅔	53⅓	60	66⅔	73⅓	80	86⅔	93⅓	100	106⅔	113⅓	120	133⅓
4 x 12	40	48	56	64	72	80	88	96	104	112	120	128	136	144	160
6 x 6	30	36	42	48	54	60	66	72	78	84	90	96	102	108	120
6 x 8	40	48	56	64	72	80	88	96	104	112	120	128	136	144	160
6 x 10	50	60	70	80	90	100	110	120	130	140	150	160	170	180	200
6 x 12	60	72	84	96	108	120	132	144	156	168	180	192	204	216	240
8 x 8	53⅓	64	74⅔	85⅓	96	106⅔	117⅓	128	138⅔	149⅓	160	170⅔	181⅓	192	213⅓
8 x 10	66⅔	80	93⅓	106⅔	120	133⅓	146⅔	160	173⅓	186⅔	200	213⅓	226⅔	240	266⅔
8 x 12	80	96	112	128	144	160	176	192	208	224	240	256	272	288	320
10 x 10	83⅓	100	116⅔	133⅓	150	166⅔	183⅓	200	216⅔	233⅓	250	266⅔	283⅓	300	333⅓
10 x 12	100	120	140	160	180	200	220	240	260	280	300	320	340	360	400
12 x 12	120	144	168	192	216	240	264	288	312	336	360	384	408	432	480
12 x 14	140	168	196	224	252	280	308	336	364	392	420	448	476	504	560

APPROXIMATE WEIGHTS OF WINDOWS, DOORS, BLINDS, ETC.

BLINDS. Four-Lighted Windows.			TWO-LIGHTED WINDOWS. Check Rail Sash.				EIGHT-LIGHTED WINDOWS. Plain Rail Sash.		
SIZE.	Thickness.	Weight.	SIZE.	Thickness.	Glazed, Single Strength.	Glazed, Double Strength.	SIZE.	Weight Glazed.	Weight Unglazed.
12 × 20	1 1-8	14 lbs.	20 × 24	1 3-8	21 lbs.	23 lbs.	8 × 10	12 lbs.	5 lbs.
12 × 24	"	16 "	20 × 28	"	22 "	25 "	8 × 12	12 "	5 "
12 × 28	"	18 "	20 × 32	"	23 "	26 "	8 × 14	14 "	7 "
12 × 32	"	20 "	20 × 36	"	25 "	28 "	9 × 12	14 "	6 "
12 × 36	"	23 "	20 × 40	"	26 "	30 "	9 × 14	17 "	7 "
12 × 40	"	25 "	24 × 30	"	24 "	26 "	10 × 12	15 "	8 "
12 × 44	"	28 "	24 × 32	"	25 "	28 "	10 × 14	18 "	8 "
Eight-Lighted Windows.			24 × 36	"	27 "	30 "	10 × 16	20 "	9 "
9 × 12	1 1-8	15 lbs.	24 × 40	"	29 "	33 "	12 × 14	19 "	9 "
9 × 16	"	18 "	26 × 30	"	25 "	28 "	12 × 16	22 "	11 "
10 × 14	"	18 "	26 × 32	"	26 "	30 "	12 × 18	25 "	12 "
12 × 14	"	18 "	26 × 34	"	27 "	31 "	Check Rail Sash.		
12 × 16	"	20 "	26 × 36	"	28 "	32 "	9 × 12	17 lbs.	8 lbs.
12 × 20	"	25 "	26 × 40	"	30 "	34 "	9 × 14	18 "	9 "
Twelve-Lighted Windows.			26 × 44	"	32 "	36 "	10 × 12	18 "	9 "
8 × 10	1 1-8	14 lbs.	26 × 48	"	34 "	39 "	10 × 14	19 "	11 "
9 × 12	"	18 "	28 × 32	"	28 "	32 "	10 × 16	22 "	12 "
9 × 16	"	23 "	28 × 36	"	30 "	34 "	12 × 14	23 "	11 "
10 × 14	"	22 "	28 × 40	"	32 "	36 "	12 × 16	24 "	12 "
10 × 18	"	27 "	28 × 44	"	34 "	38 "	12 × 18	27 "	13 "
10 × 20	"	30 "	28 × 48	"	36 "	40 "	12 × 20	32 "	14 "
							14 × 20	35 "	15 "
							14 × 24	40 "	17 "

Weight of a Four-Lighted Window is practically the same as Two-Lighted of same length.

TWELVE-LIGHTED WINDOWS.						O G FOUR-PANEL DOORS.				
Plain Rail Sash.			Check Rail Sash.				Thickness.			
SIZE.	Weight Glazed.	Weight Unglazed	SIZE.	Weight Glazed.	Weight Unglazed	SIZE.	1 inch.	1⅛ in.	1⅜ in.	1¾ in.
8 × 10	14 lbs.	6 lbs.	8 × 12	20 lbs.	8 lbs.	2 0 × 6 0	17 lbs.	22 lbs.		
8 × 12	18 "	8 "	8 × 14	22 "	8 "	2 4 × 6 4	21 "	26 "		
8 × 14	19 "	8 "	9 × 12	22 "	9 "	2 6 × 6 6	23 "	28 "	33 lbs.	40 lbs.
9 × 12	20 "	9 "	9 × 14	24 "	10 "	2 8 × 6 8	24 "	30 "	35 "	44 "
9 × 14	22 "	9 "	9 × 16	27 "	11 "	2 10 × 6 10		33 "	37 "	47 "
9 × 16	26 "	9 "	10 × 12	23 "	11 "	3 0 × 7 0		35 "	40 "	49 "
10 × 12	21 "	9 "	10 × 14	26 "	11 "	3 0 × 7 6			42 "	53 "
10 × 14	23 "	9 "	10 × 16	29 "	12 "					
10 × 16	26 "	10 "	10 × 18	32 "	13 "					
12 × 14	25 "	10 "	10 × 20	34 "	14 "					
12 × 16	28 "	10 "	12 × 20	36 "	14 "					
12 × 18	31 "	10 "	12 × 24	42 "	15 "					

For Moulded Doors add to above 5 pounds for each side moulded.

WEIGHT OF MOULDINGS. —1 x 1 inch, per one hundred lineal feet, fifteen pounds.

ORNAMENTAL GLASS.

2400—Beveled Glass, Showing Center and One End of Transom Light.

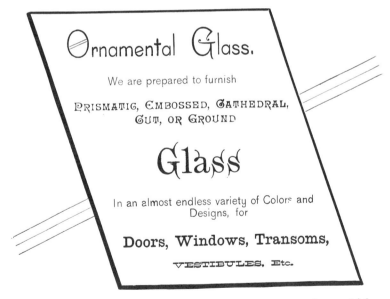

Ornamental Glass.

We are prepared to furnish

Prismatic, Embossed, Cathedral,
Cut, or Ground

Glass

In an almost endless variety of Colors and
Designs, for

Doors, Windows, Transoms,

VESTIBULES, Etc.

We give, on pages following, a number of patterns from which customers can make selections. Cut and Embossed Glass can be adapted to
any shape of Windows, Doors, or Transoms. Prismatic Glass is so moulded
as to produce an external effect of elaborately Cut Glass, and is susceptible
of numerous pleasing combinations, both as to form and colors, and is
especially adapted to Queen Anne work. We solicit correspondence and
estimates.

PATTERNS OF CUT GLASS.

2416
80 cents

2418
80 cents

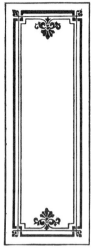

2441
50 cents

2444
$1.15

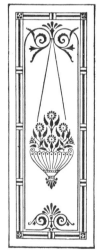

2462
80 cents

2473
65 cents

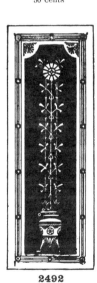

2492
$1.00

2497
$1.00

Order by Numbers.

The dark parts represent Clear Glass and the light parts the Ground Glass

NOTE.—The price under each pattern is the net price per square foot, and includes glazing.   For the number of square feet in different sizes of Doors, see Table of Sizes on page 265

These prices are for Double Strength Glass.

PATTERNS OF CUT GLASS.

2501
80 cents

2505
$1.30

2507
80 cents

2510
85 cents.   Letters Extra

2519
$1.00

2521
$1.00

2527
$1.30

2530
$1.30

Order by Numbers.

The dark parts represent Clear Glass and the light parts the Ground Glass.

To arrive at the cost see foot-note on page 255

2873
$1.00

2874
90 cents

PATTERNS OF CUT GLASS.

2601
80 cents

2609
80 cents

2616
$1.20

2617
$1.00

2618
$1.00

2621
$1.00

2627
$1.00

2628
$1.00

Order by Numbers.
The dark parts represent Clear Glass and the light parts the Ground Glass.
To arrive at the cost see foot-note on page 255

2883
90 cents

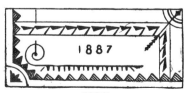

2884
$1.00

PATTERNS OF CUT GLASS.

| **2629** | **2638** | **2641** | **2644** |
| $1.10 | 80 cents | $1.00 | $1.20 |

| **2645** | **2646** | **2647** | **2648** |
| $1.20 | 80 cents | 80 cents | $1.00 |

Order by Numbers.
The dark parts represent Clear Glass and the light parts the Ground Glass.
To arrive at the cost see foot-note on page 255

2893
$1.00

ORNAMENTAL GLASS.

2838—5¾ × 5¾ Inches.

2839—5¾ × 5¾ Inches.
2840—3¾ × 3¾ Inches.

2842—Beveled Glass.

2841—5¼ × 5¼ Inches.

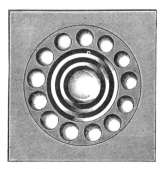

2843—5¾ × 5¾ Inches.
2844—3¾ × 3¾ Inches.

Prices on application.

PATTERNS OF EMBOSSED GLASS.

2845   2846   2847

2848

Order by Numbers.

Price of any of above patterns 80 cents per square foot.

This price is net, but includes glazing and is to be added to the net price of open work.

PATTERNS OF EMBOSSED GLASS.

2849

2850

2851

2852

Order by Numbers.

Price of any of above patterns, 80 cents per square foot.

This price is net, but includes glazing, and is to be added to the net price of open work.

PATTERNS OF EMBOSSED GLASS.

2853

2854

Letters Extra

2855

Letters Extra.

2856

Order by numbers.

Price of any of above patterns, 80 cents per square foot.

This price is net, but includes glazing, and is to be added to the net price of open work.

PATTERNS OF CUT GLASS.

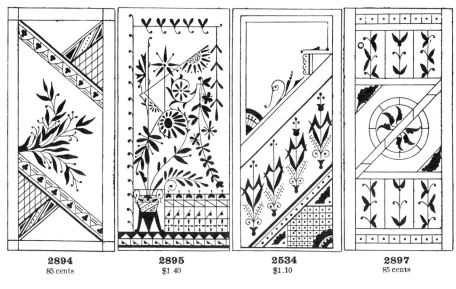

2894
85 cents

2895
$1.40

2534
$1.10

2897
85 cents

2898
$1.25

2899
85 cents

2900
$1.15

2901
$1.20

Order by Numbers.
The dark parts represent Clear Glass and the light parts the Ground Glass.
To arrive at the cost see foot-note on page 255

2902
$1.00

PATTERNS OF CUT GLASS.

2903
90 cents

2904
90 cents

2907
$1.25

2905
90 cents

2906
$1.00

2908
$1.25

Order by Numbers.
The dark parts represent Clear Glass and the light parts the Ground Glass.
To arrive at the cost see foot-note on page 255

2909
$1.25

ENAMELED GLASS AND GLASS MEASURE.

PRICE OF ENAMELED GLASS.

DESCRIPTION.	Single Thick, per Square Foot.	Double Thick, per Square Foot.
Clear per Square Foot.	25 cents.	30 cents.
Obscure " "	30 "	35 "

We keep a variety of choice patterns in Enameled Glass, and customers can rely on neat and tasty designs when selections are left to us.

SIZES OF GLASS IN DOORS.

SIZES OF DOORS.				TWO-LIGHT SASH DOORS.		ONE-LIGHT SASH DOORS.		GARFIELD and JENNY LIND DOORS.	
				Width.	Length.	Width.	Length.	Width.	Length.
Ft.	In.	Ft.	In.	Inches.	Inches.	Inches.	Inches.	Inches.	Inches.
2	6	× 6	6	9 1-2	38	20 3-4	38	21	36
2	8	× 6	8	10 1-2	40	22 3-4	40	23	38
2	10	× 6	10	11 1-2	42	24 3-4	42	25	40
3	0	× 7	0	12 1-2	44	26 3-4	44	27	42

SIZES OF DOORS.				CONGRESS DOORS.		LINCOLN DOORS.		BISMARCK DOORS.	
				Width.	Length.	Width.	Length.	Width.	Length.
Ft.	In.	Ft.	In.	Inches.	Inches.	Inches.	Inches.	Inches.	Inches.
2	6	× 6	6	21	38	17	32	21	22
2	8	× 6	8	23	40	19	34	23	24
2	10	× 6	10	25	42	21	36	25	26
3	0	× 7	0	27	44	23	38	27	28

SIZES OF DOORS.				GRANT DOORS.		OSHKOSH DOORS.		INDIANA DOORS.	
				Width.	Length.	Width.	Length.	Width.	Length.
Ft.	In.	Ft.	In.	Inches.	Inches.	Inches.	Inches.	Inches.	Inches.
2	6	× 6	6	21	36	21	32	21	38
2	8	× 6	8	23	38	23	34	23	40
2	10	× 6	10	25	40	25	36	25	42
3	0	× 7	0	27	42	27	38	27	44

Any addition to the length of above sizes of Doors adds the same difference to the length of Glass. For example: a Door 3-0 x 7-6 requires a Glass 6 inches longer than a 3-7, etc.

SQUARE FEET OF GLASS IN DOORS.

To obtain the number of square feet of Glass in above Doors, take the sizes of Glass as given above, and refer to the table on following page. Odd and fractional parts of inches are charged at the price of the next highest even inches. For example: a light 22½ x 41½ will be figured at 24 x 42.

WEIGHTS OF DIFFERENT ARTICLES.

Lime (quick), per cubic foot	50 Lbs.	Granite, per cubic foot..................	165 Lbs.
" " " barrel...................	220 "	Marble, " " "	169 "
Cement, Hydraulic, per barrel............	300 "	Oil, Linseed (usage), per gallon.........	7½ "
Brick, common, per M...	4,500 "	Coal, Anthracite, per cubic foot.........	54 "
" 8 x 4¼ x 2½, per M..	6,185 "	" Bituminous, " " "	50 "
Sand (dry), per cubic foot.	95 "	(24¾ cubic feet of Stone = 1 Perch.)	

GLASS MEASUREMENT.

A Table Giving the Number of Square Feet in Glass of Given Dimensions.

LENGTH	WIDTH OF GLASS														
	6	7	8	9	10	12	14	16	18	20	22	24	26	28	30
20	$0\frac{5}{6}$	1	$1\frac{1}{12}$	$1\frac{1}{4}$	$1\frac{5}{12}$	$1\frac{2}{3}$	$1\frac{11}{12}$	$2\frac{1}{4}$	$2\frac{1}{2}$	$2\frac{3}{4}$	....	....	....	....	....
22	$0\frac{11}{12}$	$1\frac{1}{12}$	$1\frac{1}{4}$	$1\frac{5}{12}$	$1\frac{1}{2}$	$1\frac{5}{6}$	$2\frac{1}{8}$	$2\frac{5}{12}$	$2\frac{3}{4}$	$3\frac{1}{12}$	$3\frac{1}{3}$	....	....	....	....
24	1	$1\frac{1}{6}$	$1\frac{1}{3}$	$1\frac{1}{2}$	$1\frac{2}{3}$	2	$2\frac{1}{3}$	$2\frac{2}{3}$	3	$3\frac{1}{3}$	$3\frac{2}{3}$	4	....	....	....
26	$1\frac{1}{12}$	$1\frac{1}{4}$	$1\frac{5}{12}$	$1\frac{2}{3}$	$1\frac{5}{6}$	$2\frac{1}{8}$	$2\frac{1}{2}$	$2\frac{11}{12}$	$3\frac{1}{4}$	$3\frac{7}{12}$	4	$4\frac{1}{3}$	$4\frac{2}{3}$	....	....
28	$1\frac{1}{6}$	$1\frac{1}{3}$	$1\frac{7}{12}$	$1\frac{3}{4}$	$1\frac{11}{12}$	$2\frac{1}{3}$	$2\frac{3}{4}$	$3\frac{1}{12}$	$3\frac{1}{2}$	$3\frac{11}{12}$	$4\frac{1}{4}$	$4\frac{2}{3}$	$5\frac{1}{12}$	$5\frac{5}{12}$	....
30	$1\frac{1}{4}$	$1\frac{1}{2}$	$1\frac{2}{3}$	$1\frac{11}{12}$	$2\frac{1}{12}$	$2\frac{1}{2}$	$2\frac{11}{12}$	$3\frac{1}{3}$	$3\frac{3}{4}$	$4\frac{1}{6}$	$4\frac{7}{12}$	5	$5\frac{5}{12}$	$5\frac{5}{6}$	$6\frac{1}{4}$
32	$1\frac{1}{3}$	$1\frac{7}{12}$	$1\frac{3}{4}$	2	$2\frac{1}{4}$	$2\frac{2}{3}$	$3\frac{1}{12}$	$3\frac{7}{12}$	4	$4\frac{5}{12}$	$4\frac{11}{12}$	$5\frac{1}{3}$	$5\frac{3}{4}$	$6\frac{1}{4}$	$6\frac{2}{3}$
34	$1\frac{5}{12}$	$1\frac{2}{3}$	$1\frac{11}{12}$	$2\frac{1}{8}$	$2\frac{1}{3}$	$2\frac{5}{6}$	$3\frac{1}{3}$	$3\frac{3}{4}$	$4\frac{1}{4}$	$4\frac{3}{4}$	$5\frac{1}{6}$	$5\frac{2}{3}$	$6\frac{1}{6}$	$6\frac{7}{12}$	$7\frac{1}{12}$
36	$1\frac{1}{2}$	$1\frac{3}{4}$	2	$2\frac{1}{4}$	$2\frac{1}{2}$	3	$3\frac{1}{2}$	4	$4\frac{1}{2}$	5	$5\frac{1}{2}$	6	$6\frac{1}{2}$	7	$7\frac{1}{2}$
38	$1\frac{7}{12}$	$1\frac{5}{6}$	$2\frac{1}{12}$	$2\frac{5}{12}$	$2\frac{2}{3}$	$3\frac{1}{6}$	$3\frac{2}{3}$	$4\frac{1}{4}$	$4\frac{3}{4}$	$5\frac{1}{4}$	$5\frac{5}{6}$	$6\frac{1}{3}$	$6\frac{5}{8}$	$7\frac{5}{12}$	$7\frac{11}{12}$
40	$1\frac{2}{3}$	$1\frac{11}{12}$	$2\frac{1}{4}$	$2\frac{1}{2}$	$2\frac{3}{4}$	$3\frac{1}{3}$	$3\frac{11}{12}$	$4\frac{5}{12}$	5	$5\frac{7}{12}$	$6\frac{1}{12}$	$6\frac{2}{3}$	$7\frac{1}{4}$	$7\frac{3}{4}$	$8\frac{1}{3}$
42	$1\frac{3}{4}$	$2\frac{1}{12}$	$2\frac{1}{3}$	$2\frac{2}{3}$	$2\frac{11}{12}$	$3\frac{1}{2}$	$4\frac{1}{12}$	$4\frac{2}{3}$	$5\frac{1}{4}$	$5\frac{5}{6}$	$6\frac{5}{12}$	7	$7\frac{7}{12}$	$8\frac{1}{8}$	$8\frac{3}{4}$
44	$1\frac{5}{6}$	$2\frac{1}{6}$	$2\frac{5}{12}$	$2\frac{3}{4}$	$3\frac{1}{12}$	$3\frac{2}{3}$	$4\frac{1}{4}$	$4\frac{11}{12}$	$5\frac{1}{2}$	$6\frac{1}{12}$	$6\frac{3}{4}$	$7\frac{1}{3}$	$7\frac{11}{12}$	$8\frac{7}{12}$	$9\frac{1}{6}$
46	$1\frac{11}{12}$	$2\frac{1}{4}$	$2\frac{7}{12}$	$2\frac{11}{12}$	$3\frac{1}{6}$	$3\frac{5}{6}$	$4\frac{1}{2}$	$5\frac{1}{12}$	$5\frac{3}{4}$	$6\frac{5}{12}$	7	$7\frac{2}{3}$	$8\frac{1}{3}$	$8\frac{11}{12}$	$9\frac{7}{12}$
48	2	$2\frac{1}{3}$	$2\frac{2}{3}$	3	$3\frac{1}{3}$	4	$4\frac{2}{3}$	$5\frac{1}{3}$	6	$6\frac{2}{3}$	$7\frac{1}{3}$	8	$8\frac{2}{3}$	$9\frac{1}{3}$	10
50	$2\frac{1}{12}$	$2\frac{5}{12}$	$2\frac{3}{4}$	$3\frac{1}{8}$	$3\frac{1}{2}$	$4\frac{1}{6}$	$4\frac{5}{6}$	$5\frac{7}{12}$	$6\frac{1}{4}$	$6\frac{11}{12}$	$7\frac{2}{3}$	$8\frac{1}{3}$	9	$9\frac{3}{4}$	$10\frac{5}{12}$
52	$2\frac{1}{6}$	$2\frac{1}{2}$	$2\frac{11}{12}$	$3\frac{1}{4}$	$3\frac{7}{12}$	$4\frac{1}{3}$	$5\frac{1}{12}$	$5\frac{3}{4}$	$6\frac{1}{2}$	$7\frac{1}{4}$	$7\frac{11}{12}$	$8\frac{2}{3}$	$9\frac{5}{12}$	$10\frac{1}{12}$	$10\frac{5}{6}$
54	$2\frac{1}{4}$	$2\frac{2}{3}$	3	$3\frac{5}{12}$	$3\frac{3}{4}$	$4\frac{1}{2}$	$5\frac{1}{4}$	6	$6\frac{3}{4}$	$7\frac{1}{2}$	$8\frac{1}{4}$	9	$9\frac{3}{4}$	$10\frac{1}{2}$	$11\frac{1}{4}$
56	$2\frac{1}{3}$	$2\frac{3}{4}$	$3\frac{1}{12}$	$3\frac{1}{2}$	$3\frac{11}{12}$	$4\frac{2}{3}$	$5\frac{5}{12}$	$6\frac{1}{4}$	7	$7\frac{3}{4}$	$8\frac{7}{12}$	$9\frac{1}{3}$	$10\frac{1}{12}$	$10\frac{11}{12}$	$11\frac{2}{3}$
58	$2\frac{5}{12}$	$2\frac{5}{6}$	$3\frac{1}{4}$	$3\frac{2}{3}$	4	$4\frac{5}{6}$	$5\frac{2}{3}$	$6\frac{5}{12}$	$7\frac{1}{4}$	$8\frac{1}{12}$	$8\frac{5}{6}$	$9\frac{2}{3}$	$10\frac{1}{2}$	$11\frac{1}{4}$	$12\frac{1}{12}$
60	$2\frac{1}{2}$	$2\frac{11}{12}$	$3\frac{1}{3}$	$3\frac{3}{4}$	$4\frac{1}{6}$	5	$5\frac{5}{6}$	$6\frac{2}{3}$	$7\frac{1}{2}$	$8\frac{1}{3}$	$9\frac{1}{6}$	10	$10\frac{5}{6}$	$11\frac{2}{3}$	$12\frac{1}{2}$
62	$2\frac{7}{12}$	3	$3\frac{5}{12}$	$3\frac{11}{12}$	$4\frac{1}{3}$	$5\frac{1}{6}$	6	$6\frac{11}{12}$	$7\frac{3}{4}$	$8\frac{7}{12}$	$9\frac{1}{2}$	$10\frac{1}{3}$	$11\frac{1}{6}$	$12\frac{1}{12}$	$12\frac{11}{12}$
64	$2\frac{2}{3}$	$3\frac{1}{12}$	$3\frac{7}{12}$	4	$4\frac{5}{12}$	$5\frac{1}{3}$	$6\frac{1}{4}$	$7\frac{1}{12}$	8	$8\frac{11}{12}$	$9\frac{3}{4}$	$10\frac{2}{3}$	$11\frac{7}{12}$	$12\frac{5}{12}$	$13\frac{1}{3}$
66	$2\frac{3}{4}$	$3\frac{1}{4}$	$3\frac{2}{3}$	$4\frac{1}{6}$	$4\frac{7}{12}$	$5\frac{1}{2}$	$6\frac{5}{12}$	$7\frac{1}{3}$	$8\frac{1}{4}$	$9\frac{1}{6}$	$10\frac{1}{12}$	11	$11\frac{11}{12}$	$12\frac{5}{6}$	$13\frac{3}{4}$
68	$2\frac{5}{6}$	$3\frac{1}{3}$	$3\frac{3}{4}$	$4\frac{1}{4}$	$4\frac{3}{4}$	$5\frac{2}{3}$	$6\frac{7}{12}$	$7\frac{7}{12}$	$8\frac{1}{2}$	$9\frac{5}{12}$	$10\frac{5}{12}$	$11\frac{1}{3}$	$12\frac{1}{4}$	$13\frac{1}{4}$	$14\frac{1}{6}$
70	$2\frac{11}{12}$	$3\frac{5}{12}$	$3\frac{11}{12}$	$4\frac{5}{12}$	$4\frac{5}{6}$	$5\frac{5}{6}$	$6\frac{5}{6}$	$7\frac{3}{4}$	$8\frac{3}{4}$	$9\frac{3}{4}$	$10\frac{2}{3}$	$11\frac{2}{3}$	$12\frac{2}{3}$	$13\frac{7}{12}$	$14\frac{7}{12}$
72	3	$3\frac{1}{2}$	4	$4\frac{1}{2}$	5	6	7	8	9	10	11	12	13	14	15

Window Glass Price Current, March 6, 1890.

PRICE LIST OF AMERICAN WINDOW GLASS.

Price per Box of Fifty Square Feet.

United Inches.	SIZES.	Single Strength.				Double Strength.			
		AA	A	B	C	AA	A	B	C
		$ cts.	$ cts.	$ cts.	$ cts.	$ cts.	$ cts.	$ cts.	$ cts.
25	6 × 8 to 10 × 15	12.50	10.75	10 00	9.50	17.00	15.00	14.00	13.50
40	11 × 14 to 16 × 24	14.50	12 75	12.00	11.00	21.00	18.50	17.00	
50	18 × 22 to 20 × 30	19.00	16 50	15.00	14.25	26 50	23.50	21.00	
54	15 × 36 to 24 × 30	20.50	17 50	15 50		29.00	25.50	22.00	
60	26 × 28 to 24 × 36	22.00	19.50	17.00		31.50	27.50	24.00	
70	26 × 36 to 26 × 44	23.50	20.50	17.50		33.00	29.50	25.00	
80	26 × 46 to 30 × 50	26.00	23 00	19.50		36.00	32.00	27.00	
84	30 × 52 to 30 × 54	27.00	24.00	20.50		38.00	33.50	28.50	
90	30 × 56 to 34 × 56	29.00	25.50	22.00		40.00	35.00	31.00	
94	34 × 58 to 34 × 60	30.00	27.00	25.00		43.00	39.00	34.00	
100	36 × 60 to 40 × 60	34.00	31.00	27.00		47.00	43.00	38.00	

Sizes above—$10.00 per box extra for every five inches.

An additional 10 per cent. will be charged for all Glass more than 40 inches wide.

All sizes above 52 inches in length, and not making more than 81 united inches, will be charged in the 84 united inches bracket. All fractional inches counted as full inches.

No. of Lights per Box of Fifty Feet.

6× 8	150	12×17	35	15×18	27	18×38	11	22×56	6	28×42	6	34×54	4
6½× 8½	130	18	34	20	24	40	10	60	5	44	6	56	4
7 × 9	115	20	30	22	22	42	10	24×24	12	46	6	60	4
8 × 10	90	22	27	24	20	44	9	26	12	50	5	66	3
8½× 10½	81	24	25	26	19	46	9	28	11	56	5	36×40	5
8 × 11	82	26	23	28	17	50	8	30	10	60	4	42	5
8 × 12	75	28	22	30	16	52	8	32	10	66	4	44	5
9 × 11	73	30	20	32	15	56	7	34	9	30×34	7	46	4
12	67	32	19	34	14	60	7	36	9	36	7	48	4
13	62	34	18	36	13	20×22	16	38	8	38	7	50	4
14	57	36	17	38	13	24	15	40	8	40	6	52	4
15	53	13×14	40	40	12	26	14	42	7	42	6	54	4
16	50	15	37	16×16	28	28	13	46	7	44	6	56	4
18	45	16	35	18	25	30	12	48	6	46	5	60	3
10 × 12	60	18	31	20	23	32	11	50	6	48	5	64	3
13	55	20	28	22	21	34	11	54	6	50	5	66	3
14	52	22	25	24	19	36	10	56	5	52	5	70	3
15	48	24	23	26	17	38	10	60	5	54	4	38×42	5
16	45	26	21	28	16	40	9	66	5	56	4	44	4
17	43	28	20	30	15	42	9	26×28	10	60	4	52	4
18	40	30	19	32	14	44	8	30	9	64	4	56	3
20	36	32	17	34	13	46	8	32	9	66	4	62	3
22	33	14×15	34	36	13	48	8	34	8	70	3	66	3
24	30	16	32	38	12	50	7	36	8	32×34	7	40×44	4
26	28	17	31	40	11	54	7	38	7	36	6	50	4
28	26	18	29	42	11	58	6	40	7	38	6	54	3
30	24	20	26	44	10	64	6	42	7	40	6	60	3
11 × 12	55	22	24	46	10	22×24	14	44	6	42	6	66	3
13	51	24	22	48	9	26	13	48	6	44	5	72	3
14	47	26	20	52	9	28	12	50	6	46	5	42×42	4
15	44	28	19	54	8	30	11	52	5	48	5	48	4
16	41	30	17	60	8	32	10	54	5	50	5	52	3
17	39	32	16	18×20	20	34	10	56	5	56	4	62	3
18	37	34	15	22	18	36	9	58	5	60	4	68	3
20	33	36	14	24	17	38	9	60	5	66	3	44×46	4
22	30	38	14	26	16	40	8	28×30	9	34×36	6	50	3
24	27	40	13	28	14	42	8	32	8	40	6	56	3
12 × 13	46	42	12	30	14	44	7	34	8	44	5	46×54	3
14	43	44	12	32	13	48	7	36	7	46	5	64	3
15	40	46	11	34	12	50	7	38	7	48	5		
16	38	15×16	30	36	11	52	6	40	7	50	4		

PRICE LIST OF AMERICAN GLASS.

PRICE PER SINGLE LIGHT.

SIZES.	SINGLE.			DOUBLE.		
	Aa	A	B	Aa	A	B
6 × 8	$ .09	$ .08	$ .07			
7 × 9	.11	.10	.09			
8 × 10	.14	.12	.12	$ .19	$ .17	$ .16
12	.17	.15	.14	.23	.20	.19
13	.19	.16	.15	.25	.22	.21
14	.20	.17	.16	.27	.24	.22
15	.21	.18	.17	.29	.25	.24
16	.23	.20	.18	.31	.27	.25
18	.29	.28	.24	.42	.37	.34
20	.33	.29	.27	.47	.42	.38
9 × 11	.18	.15	.14	.24	.21	.20
12	.19	.17	.15	.26	.23	.21
13	.21	.18	.17	.28	.25	.23
14	.22	.19	.18	.30	.27	.25
15	.24	.21	.19	.33	.29	.27
16	.25	.22	.20	.34	.30	.28
18	.33	.29	.27	.47	.42	.38
20	.37	.32	.30	.53	.47	.43
22	.41	.36	.34	.59	.52	.48
10 × 12	.21	.18	.17	.29	.25	.24
13	.23	.20	.19	.31	.28	.26
14	.25	.21	.20	.33	.29	.27
15	.27	.23	.21	.36	.32	.30
16	.33	.29	.27	.47	.42	.38
17	.34	.30	.28	.50	.44	.40
18	.37	.32	.30	.53	.47	.43
19	.39	.34	.32			
20	.41	.36	.34	.59	.52	.48
22	.44	.39	.37	.64	.57	.52
24	.49	.43	.40	.70	.62	.57
26	.52	.46	.43	.75	.67	.61
28	.56	.50	.47	.81	.72	.66
30	.61	.54	.50	.88	.78	.71
32	.83	.72	.66	1.16	1.03	.92
34	.91	.79	.72	1.27	1.12	1.00
36	.95	.83	.75	1.33	1.18	1.05
38	1.00	.87	.79	1.40	1.24	1.11
40	1.06	.92	.84	1.48	1.31	1.17
42	1.21	1.03	.92	1.71	1.50	1.30
44	1.29	1.10	.97	1.82	1.60	1.38
11 × 12	.23	.20	.19	.31	.28	.26
13	.25	.22	.20			
14	.31	.28	.26	.45	.40	.37
15	.33	.29	.28	.48	.43	.39
16	.36	.32	.30	.52	.46	.42
17	.38	.33	.31			
18	.40	.35	.33	.57	.50	.46
19	.43	.38	.36	.62	.55	.50
20	.44	.39	.37	.64	.57	.52
22	.49	.43	.40	.70	.62	.57
24	.54	.48	.45	.78	.69	.63
26	.58	.51	.48	.84	.74	.68
28	.64	.56	.53	.92	.81	.74
30	.87	.75	.69	1.21	1.07	.96
32	.95	.83	.75	1.33	1.18	1.05
34	1.00	.87	.79	1.40	1.24	1.11
36	1.06	.92	.84	1.48	1.31	1.17
38				1.56	1.39	1.24
40				1.82	1.60	1.38
42				1.82	1.60	1.38
44				2.10	1.84	1.60
12 × 12	.25	.22	.20	.34	.30	.28
13	.32	.28	.27	.46	.41	.37
14	.34	.30	.28	.49	.44	.40
15	.37	.32	.30	.53	.47	.43
16	.39	.34	.32	.56	.49	.45
17	.42	.37	.35	.60	.53	.49
18	.43	.38	.36	.62	.55	.50
20	.49	.43	.40	.70	.62	.57
22	.54	.48	.45	.78	.69	.63
24	.58	.51	.48	.84	.74	.68
26	.64	.56	.53	.92	.81	.74

PRICE PER SINGLE LIGHT.

SIZES.	SINGLE.			DOUBLE.		
	Aa	A	B	Aa	A	B
12 × 28	$ .66	$ .58	$ .55	$ .96	$ .85	$ .78
30	.95	.83	.75	1.33	1.18	1.05
32	1.00	.87	.79	1.40	1.24	1.11
34	1.06	.92	.84	1.48	1.31	1.17
36	1.12	.98	.89	1.56	1.39	1.24
38	1.19	1.04	.94	1.66	1.47	1.32
40	1.37	1.17	1.04	1.94	1.70	1.47
42	1.47	1.25	1.11	2.08	1.83	1.58
44	1.58	1.40	1.22	2.25	1.97	1.72
46	1.70	1.50	1.31	2.43	2.12	1.85
48	1.70	1.50	1.31	2.43	2.12	1.85
50	1.96	1.71	1.46	2.75	2.46	2.09
13 × 14	.37	.32	.30	.53	.47	.43
15	.40	.35	.33	.57	.50	.46
16	.42	.37	.35	.60	.53	.49
18	.47	.42	.39	.68	.60	.55
20	.52	.46	.43	.75	.67	.61
22	.58	.51	.48	.84	.74	.68
24	.64	.56	.53	.92	.81	.74
26	.70	.61	.58	1.00	.89	.81
28	.95	.83	.75	1.33	1.18	1.05
30	1.00	.87	.79	1.40	1.24	1.11
32	1.12	.98	.89	1.56	1.39	1.24
34	1.19	1.04	.94	1.66	1.47	1.32
36	1.27	1.10	1.00	1.77	1.57	1.40
38	1.37	1.17	1.04	1.94	1.70	1.47
40	1.47	1.25	1.11	2.08	1.83	1.58
42				2.43	2.12	1.85
44				2.43	2.12	1.85
46				2.63	2.30	2.00
48				2.75	2.46	2.09
14 × 14	.40	.35	.33	.57	.50	.46
16	.46	.40	.38	.66	.58	.54
17	.47	.42	.39	.68	.60	.55
18	.50	.44	.42	.73	.64	.59
20	.56	.50	.47	.81	.72	.66
22	.61	.54	.50	.88	.78	.71
24	.66	.58	.55	.96	.85	.78
26	.73	.64	.60	1.05	.93	.85
28	1.00	.87	.79	1.40	1.24	1.11
30	1.12	.98	.89	1.56	1.39	1.24
32	1.19	1.04	.94	1.66	1.47	1.32
34	1.27	1.10	1.00	1.77	1.57	1.40
36	1.36	1.18	1.08	1.90	1.68	1.50
38	1.47	1.25	1.11	2.08	1.83	1.58
40	1.58	1.35	1.20	2.24	1.97	1.70
42	1.84	1.63	1.42	2.63	2.30	2.00
44	1.84	1.63	1.42	2.63	2.30	2.00
46	2.00	1.78	1.55	2.87	2.50	2.19
48	2.14	1.87	1.60	3.00	2.69	2.28
50	2.35	2.05	1.75	3.30	2.95	2.50
52	2.35	2.05	1.75	3.30	2.95	2.50
54				3.80	3.35	2.85
56				4.23	3.73	3.17
58				4.23	3.73	3.17
15 × 15	.46	.40	.38	.66	.58	.54
16	.49	.43	.40	.70	.62	.57
18	.54	.48	.45	.78	.69	.63
20	.61	.54	.50	.88	.78	.71
22	.66	.58	.55	.96	.85	.78
24	.73	.64	.60	1.05	.93	.85
26	1.00	.87	.79	1.40	1.24	1.11
28	1.12	.98	.89	1.56	1.39	1.24
30	1.19	1.04	.94	1.66	1.47	1.32
32	1.27	1.10	1.00	1.77	1.57	1.40
34	1.36	1.18	1.08	1.90	1.68	1.50
36	1.58	1.35	1.20	2.24	1.97	1.70
38	1.58	1.35	1.20	2.24	1.97	1.70
40	1.84	1.63	1.42	2.63	2.30	2.00
42	2.00	1.78	1.55	2.87	2.50	2.19
44	2.00	1.78	1.55	2.87	2.50	2.19
46	2.35	2.05	1.75	3.30	2.95	2.50

PRICE LIST OF AMERICAN GLASS.

PRICE PER SINGLE LIGHT.						PRICE PER SINGLE LIGHT.					
SIZES.	SINGLE.			DOUBLE.							
	AA	A	B	AA	A	B					
15 × 48	2.35	2.05	1.75	3.30	2.95	2.50					
50	2.35	2.05	1.75	3.30	2.95	2.50					
16 × 16	.52	.46	.43	.75	.67	.61					
18	.58	.51	.48	.84	.74	.68					
20	.64	.56	.53	.92	.81	.74					
22	.70	.61	.58	1.00	.89	.81					
24	.77	.68	.64	1.11	.98	.90					
26	1.12	.98	.89	1.56	1.39	1.24					
28	1.19	1.04	.94	1.66	1.47	1.32					
30	1.27	1.10	1.00	1.77	1.57	1.40					
32	1.36	1.18	1.08	1.90	1 68	1 50					
34	1.47	1.27	1.16	2 04	1.81	1.62					
36	1.58	1.35	1 20	2.24	1.97	1.70					
38	1.71	1.46	1.30	2.42	2.13	1.84					
40	2 00	1.78	1.55	2.87	2.50	2.19					
42	2.00	1.78	1.55	2.87	2.50	2.19					
44	2.20	1.95	1.70	3.15	2.75	2.40					
46	2.35	2.05	1.75	3.30	2.95	2.50					
48	2.62	2.28	1.95	3.67	3.28	2.78					
50	2.62	2.28	1.95	3.67	3.28	2.78					
18 × 18	.66	.58	.55	.96	.85	.78					
20	.73	.64	.60	1.05	.93	.85					
22	1.06	.92	.84	1.48	1.31	1.17					
24	1.12	.98	.89	1.56	1.39	1.24					
26	1.19	1.04	.94	1.66	1.47	1.32					
28	1.36	1.18	1.08	1.90	1.68	1.50					
30	1.36	1.18	1.08	1.90	1.68	1.50					
32	1.47	1.27	1.16	2.04	1.81	1.62					
34	1.71	1.46	1.30	2.42	2.13	1.84					
36	1.87	1.60	1.41	2.64	2.32	2 00					
38	2.00	1.78	1.55	2.87	2.50	2.19					
40	2.20	1.95	1.70	3.15	2.75	2.40					
42	2.20	1.95	1.70	3.15	2.75	2.40					
44	2.62	2.28	1.95	3.67	3.28	2.78					
46	2.62	2.28	1 95	3.67	3.28	2.78					
48	2.94	2.57	2.19	4.13	3.69	3.13					
50	2.94	2.57	2.19	4.13	3.69	3.13					
52	2.94	2.57	2.19	4.13	3.69	3.13					
54				5.43	4.79	4.08					
20 × 20	1.06	.92	.84	1.48	1.31	1.17					
22	1.19	1.04	.94	1.66	1.47	1.32					
24	1.27	1.10	1.00	1.77	1.57	1.40					
26	1.36	1.18	1.08	1.90	1.68	1.50					
28	1.47	1.27	1 16	2.04	1 81	1.62					
30	1.59	1.38	1.25	2.21	1.96	1.75					
32	1.87	1.60	1.41	2.64	2.32	2.00					
34	1.87	1.60	1.41	2 64	2.32	2.00					
36	2.20	1.95	1.70	3.15	2.75	2.40					
38	2.20	1 95	1.70	3.15	2.75	2.40					
40	2.45	2.17	1.89	3.50	3.06	2.67					
42	2.62	2.28	1.95	3.67	3.28	2.78					
44	2.94	2.57	2.19	4.13	3.69	3.13					
46	2.94	2.57	2.19	4.13	3.69	3.13					
48	2.94	2.57	2.19	4.13	3.69	3.13					
50	3.36	2.93	2.50	4.72	4.22	3.58					
52	3.72	3.29	2.79	5.15	4.58	3.86					
54				5.43	4.79	4.08					
56				6.34	5.59	4.75					
22 × 22	1.27	1.10	1.00	1.77	1.57	1.40					
24	1.36	1.18	1.08	1.90	1.68	1.50					
26	1.47	1.27	1.16	2.04	1.81	1.62					
28	1.59	1.38	1.25	2.21	1.96	1.75					
30	1.87	1.60	1.41	2.64	2.32	2.00					
32	2.05	1.75	1.55	2.90	2.55	2.20					
34	2.20	1.95	1.70	3.15	2.75	2.40					
36	2.45	2.17	1.89	3.50	3.06	2.67					
38	2.45	2.17	1.89	3 50	3.06	2.67					
40	2.94	2.57	2.19	4.13	3.69	3.13					
42	2.94	2.57	2.19	4.13	3.69	3.13					
44	3.36	2.93	2.50	4.72	4.22	3.58					
46	3.36	2.93	2.50	4.72	4.22	3 58					
48	3.36	2.93	2.50	4.72	4.22	3.58					

SIZES.	SINGLE.			DOUBLE.		
	AA	A	B	AA	A	B
22 × 50	3.72	3.29	2.79	5.15	4.58	3.86
52	4.34	3.84	3.25	6.00	5.34	4.50
54	....	....	....	6.34	5.59	4.75
56	....	....	....	6.34	5.59	4.75
58	....	....	....	6.34	5.59	4.75
60	....	....	....	7.60	6.70	5.70
24 × 24	1.59	1.38	1.25	2.21	1.96	1.75
26	1.59	1.38	1.25	2.21	1.96	1.75
28	1.87	1.60	1 41	2.64	2.32	2.00
30	2.05	1.75	1.55	2.90	2.55	2.20
32	2.20	1.95	1.70	3.15	2.75	2.40
34	2.45	2.17	1.89	3.50	3.06	2.67
36	2.45	2.17	1.89	3.50	3.06	2.67
38	2.94	2.57	2.19	4.13	3.69	3.13
40	2.94	2.57	2.19	4.13	3 69	3.13
42	3.36	2.93	2.50	4.72	4.22	3.58
44	3.36	2.93	2.50	4.72	4.22	3.58
46	3.36	2.93	2.50	4.72	4.22	3.58
48	4.34	3.84	3.25	6.00	5.34	4.50
50	4.34	3.84	3.25	6.00	5.34	4.50
52	4.34	3.84	3.25	6.00	5.34	4.50
54	....	....	....	6.34	5.59	4.75
56	....	....	....	7.60	6.70	5.70
58	....	....	....	7.60	6.70	5.70
26 × 26	1.87	1.60	1.41	2 64	2.32	2.00
28	2.20	1.95	1.70	3 15	2.75	2.40
30	2.45	2.17	1 89	3.50	3.06	2.67
32	2 45	2.17	1.89	3.50	3.06	2.67
34	2.75	2.44	2.13	3.94	3.44	3.00
36	2.94	2.57	2.19	4 13	3.69	3.13
38	3.36	2.93	2.50	4.72	4.22	3.58
40	3.36	2.93	2.50	4.72	4.22	3.58
42	3.36	2.93	2.50	4.72	4.22	3.58
44	3.92	3.42	2.92	5.50	4.92	4.17
46	4.34	3.84	3.25	6.00	5.34	4.50
48	4.34	3.84	3.25	6 00	5.34	4.50
50	....	....	....	6 00	5.34	4.50
52	....	....	....	.20	6.40	5.40
54	....	....	....	7.60	6.70	5.70
56	....	....	....	7.60	6.70	5.70
58	....	....	....	7.60	6.70	5.70
60	....	....	....	8 00	7.00	6 20
62	....	....	....	10.00	8.75	7.75
28 × 28	....	....	....	3.50	3.06	2.67
30	2.45	2.17	1 89	3.50	3.06	2.67
32	2.75	2.44	2.13	3.94	3.44	3.00
34	2.94	2.57	2.19	4.13	3.69	3.13
36	3.36	2.93	2.50	4.72	4.22	3.58
38	3.36	2.93	2.50	4.72	4.22	3.58
40	3.36	2.93	2.50	4.72	4.22	3.58
42	3.92	3.42	2 92	5.50	4.92	4.17
44	4.34	3.84	3.25	6.00	5.34	4.50
46	4.34	3.84	3.25	6.00	5 34	4 50
48	5.20	4.60	3.90	7.20	6.40	5.40
50	5.20	4.60	3.90	7.20	6.40	5.40
52	....	....	....	7.20	6 40	5.40
54	....	....	....	7.60	6.70	5.70
56	....	....	....	7.60	6.70	5.70
58	....	....	....	10.00	8.75	7.75
60	....	....	....	10.00	8.75	7.75
62	....	....	....	10.00	8.75	7.75
30 × 30	2.75	2.44	2.13	3.94	3.44	3.00
32	2.94	2.57	2.19	4.13	3.69	3.13
34	3.36	2.93	2.50	4.72	4.22	3.58
36	3 36	2.93	2.50	4.72	4.22	3.58
38	3.36	2.93	2 50	4.72	4.22	3.58
40	3.92	3.42	2.92	5.50	4.92	4.17
42	4.34	3.84	3.25	6.00	5.34	4.50
44	4.34	3.84	3.25	6.00	5.34	4.50
46	5.20	4 60	3.90	7.20	6 40	5.40
48	5.20	4.60	3.90	7.20	6.40	5.40
50	5.20	4.60	3.90	7.20	6.40	5.40

PRICE LIST OF AMERICAN GLASS.

PRICE PER SINGLE LIGHT.

SIZES.	DOUBLE. AA	A	B
30 × 52	7.60	6.70	5.70
54	9.50	8.38	7.13
56	10.00	8.75	7.75
58	10.00	8.75	7.75
60	10 00	8.75	7.75
62	10.75	9.75	8.50
64	10.75	9.75	8.50
66	11.75	10.75	9.50
68	11.75	10.75	9.50
70	15.67	14.34	12.67
72	19.00	17.67	16.00
74	19.00	17.67	16.00
76	22.34	21.00	19.34
78	22.34	21.00	19.34
80	22.34	21.00	19.34
82	25.67	24.34	22.67
84	25 67	24.34	22.67
86	29.00	27.67	26.00
88	29.00	27.67	26.00
32 × 32	4.72	4.22	3.58
34	4.72	4.22	3.58
36	5.50	4.92	4.17
38	5.50	4.92	4.17
40	6.00	5.34	4.50
42	6.00	5 34	4.50
44	7.20	6.40	5.40
46	7.20	6.40	5.40
48	7.20	6.40	5 40
50	7.60	6.70	5.70
52	9.50	8.38	7.13
54	10.00	8.75	7.75
56	10.00	8.75	7.75
58	10.00	8.75	7.75
60	10.75	9.75	8.50
62	10.75	9.75	8.50
64	11.75	10.75	9 50
66	15.67	14.34	12 67
68	15.67	14.34	12.67
70	19.00	17.67	16.00
72	19.00	17.67	16.00
74	.....	.....	.....
76	.....	.....	.....
34 × 34	5.50	4 92	4.17
36	5.50	4.92	4.17
38	6.00	5.34	4.50
40	6.00	5.34	4.50
42	7.20	6.40	5.40
44	7.20	6.40	5.40
46	7 20	6.40	5.40
48	7.60	6.70	5.70
50	9.50	8.38	7.13
52	10.00	8.75	7.75
54	10.00	8.75	7.75
56	10.00	8.75	7.75
58	10.75	9.75	8.50
60	10.75	9 75	8 50
62	15.67	14.34	12 67
64	15.67	14.34	12.67
66	15.67	14.34	12.67
68	19.00	17.67	16.00
70	19.00	17.67	16.00
72	22.34	21.00	19.34
74	.....	.....	.....
76	.....	.....	.....
36 × 36	6.00	5.34	4.50
38	7.20	6.40	5.40
40	7.20	6 40	5.40
42	7.20	6 40	5.40

PRICE PER SINGLE LIGHT.

SIZES.	DOUBLE. AA	A	B
36 × 44	7.20	6.40	5.40
46	9.50	8.38	7.13
48	9.50	8.38	7.13
50	10.00	8.75	7.75
52	10.00	8.75	7.75
54	10.00	8.75	7.75
56	10.75	9.75	8.50
58	14.34	13.00	11.34
60	15.67	14.34	12 67
62	15.67	14.34	12.67
64	15.67	14.34	12.67
66	19.00	17.67	16.00
68	19.00	17.67	16.00
70	22.34	21.00	17.00
72	22.34	21.00	17.00
74			
38 × 38	7.20	6 40	5.40
40	7.20	6.40	5.40
42	7 20	6.40	5.40
44	9.50	8 38	7.13
46	9 50	8.38	7.13
48	10.00	8.75	7.75
50	10.00	8.75	7.75
52	10.00	8.75	7.75
54	10.75	9.75	8.50
56	14.34	13.00	11.34
58	15.67	14.34	12.67
60	15.67	14.34	12.67
62	15.67	14.34	12.67
64	19.00	17.67	16.00
66	19.00	17.67	16.00
68	22.34	21.00	19.34
70	22.34	21.00	19.34
72	25.67	24.34	22.67
74	25.67	24.34	22.67
76	29.00	27.67	26.00
78	29.00	27.67	26.00
40 × 40	7.20	6.40	5.40
42	9.50	8.38	7.13
44	9.50	8.38	7.13
46	10.00	8 75	7.75
48	10.00	8.75	7.75
50	10.00	8.75	7.75
52	14.34	13.00	11.34
54	14.34	13.00	11.34
56	15.67	14.34	12 67
58	15 87	14.34	12.67
60	15.67	14.34	12.67
62	19.00	17.67	16.00
64	19.00	17.67	16.00
66	22.34	21.00	19.34
68	22.34	21.00	19.34
70	22.34	21.00	19.34
72	25.67	24.34	22.67
74	25.67	24.34	22.67
76	29.00	27.67	26 00
78	29.00	27.67	26.00
42 × 42	10.45	9.22	7.84
44	11.00	9.63	8.53
46	11.00	9.63	8.53
48	11.00	9.63	8.53
50	15.77	14.30	12.47
52	15.77	14.30	12.47
54	17.24	15.77	13.94
56	17.24	15.77	13.94
58	17.24	15.77	13.94
60	20 90	19.44	17 60
62	20.90	19.44	17 60

PRICE PER SINGLE LIGHT.

SIZES.	DOUBLE. AA	A	B
42 × 64	24.57	23.10	21.27
66	24.57	23.10	21.27
68	24.57	23.10	21.27
70	28 24	26.77	24.94
72	28.24	26.77	24.94
74	31.90	30.44	28.60
76	31.90	30.44	28.60
78	31.90	30.44	28.60
44 × 44	11.00	9 63	8.53
46	11.00	9.63	8.53
48	15.77	14.30	12.47
50	15.77	14.30	12.47
52	17.24	15.77	13.94
54	17.24	15.77	13.94
56	17.24	15.77	13.94
58	20.90	19.44	17.60
60	20.90	19.44	17.60
62	24.57	23.10	21.27
64	24.57	23.10	21.27
66	24.57	23.10	21.27
68	28.24	26.77	24.94
70	28.24	26.77	24.94
72	31.90	30.44	28.60
74	31.90	30.44	28.60
76	31.90	30.44	28.60
78	35.57	34.10	32.27
46 × 46	15.77	14.30	12.47
48	15.77	14 30	12.47
50	17.24	15.77	13.94
52	17.24	15.77	13.94
54	17.24	15.77	13.94
56	20.90	19.44	17.60
58	20.90	19.44	17.60
60	24.57	23.10	21.27
62	24.57	23.10	21.27
64	24.57	23.10	21.27
66	28.24	26.77	24.94
68	28.24	26.77	24.94
70	31.90	30.44	28.60
72	31.90	30.44	28.60
74	31.90	30.44	28.60
48 × 48	17.24	15.77	13.94
50	17.24	15 77	13.94
52	17.24	15 77	13.94
54	20.90	19.44	17.60
56	20.90	19.44	17.60
58	24.57	23.10	21.27
60	24.57	23 10	21.27
62	24.57	23 10	21.27
64	28.24	26.77	24.94
66	28.24	26.77	24.94
68	31.90	30.44	28.60
70	31.90	30.44	28 60
72	31.90	30.44	28.60
74	35.57	34 10	32.27
50 × 50	17.24	15.77	13.94
52	20.90	19.44	17.60
54	20.90	19.44	17.60
56	24.57	23.10	21.27
58	24.57	23.10	21.27
60	24 57	23.10	21.27
62	28.24	26.77	24.94
64	28.24	26.77	24.94
66	31.90	30.44	28 60
68	31.90	30.44	28.60
70	31.90	30.44	28.60
72	35.57	34 10	32.27
74	35.57	34.10	32.27

PRICE LIST PER LIGHT

OF

POLISHED PLATE GLASS.

TARIFF OF FEBRUARY 19, 1892.

Length.	WIDTH.					Length.	WIDTH.				
	6	7	8	9	10		6	7	8	9	10
24	.60	.70	.80	.90	1.00	44	1.10	1.30	1.45	1.65	2.40
26	.65	.75	.85	1.00	1.10	46	1.15	1.35	1.55	1.75	2.50
28	.70	.80	.95	1.05	1.15	48	1.20	1.40	1.60	1.80	2.60
30	.75	.85	1.00	1.15	1.25	50	1.25	1.45	1.65	2.45	2.70
32	.80	.90	1.05	1.20	1.35	52	1.30	1.50	1.75	2.55	2.80
34	.85	1.00	1.15	1 30	1.40	54	1.35	1.60	1.80	2.65	2.95
36	.90	1.05	1.20	1.35	1.50	56	1.40	1.65	2.45	2.75	3.05
38	.95	1.10	1.25	1.45	1.60	58	1.45	1.70	2.50	2.85	3.15
40	1.00	1.15	1.35	1.50	1.65	60	1.50	1.75	2.60	2.95	3.25
42	1.05	1.25	1.40	1.60	1.75						

PLATE GLASS LIST—Continued.

Price per Light.

Length.	12	14	16	18	20	22	24	26	28	30	32	34	36	Length.
12	.60													12
14	.70	.80												14
16	.80	.95	1.05											16
18	.90	1.05	1.20	1.35										18
20	1.00	1.15	1.35	1.50	1.65									20
22	1.10	1.30	1.45	1.65	2.40	2.60								22
24	1.20	1.40	1.60	1.80	2.60	2.85	3.10							24
26	1.30	1.50	1.75	2.25	2.80	3.10	3.40	3.65						26
28	1.40	1.65	2.45	2.75	3.05	3.35	3.65	7.00	7.50					28
30	1.50	1.75	2.60	2.95	3.25	3.60	3.90	7.50	8.05	8.65				30
32	1.60	2.45	2.75	3.10	3.45	3.80	7.35	8.00	8.60	9.20	9.80			32
34	1.70	2.60	2.95	3.30	3.70	7.15	7.80	8.50	9.15	9.80	10.45	11.10		34
36	1.80	2.75	3.10	3.50	3.90	7.60	8.80	8.95	9.65	10.35	11.05	11.75	12.40	36
38	2.45	2.90	3.30	3.70	7.30	8.00	8.75	9.45	10.20	10.95	11.65	12.40	13.10	38
40	2.60	3.05	3.45	3.90	7.65	8.45	9.20	9.95	10.75	11.50	12.25	13.05	13.80	40
42	2.75	3.20	3.65	7.25	8.05	8.85	9.65	10.45	11.25	12.10	12.90	13.70	22.35	42
44	2.85	3 35	3.80	7.60	8.45	9.30	10.10	10.95	11.80	12.65	13.50	22.15	23.45	44
46	3.00	3.50	7.05	7.95	8.80	9.70	10.60	11.45	12.35	13.25	21.80	23.15	24.50	46
48	3.10	3.65	7.35	8.30	9.20	10.10	11.05	11.95	12.90	13.80	22.70	24 15	25.55	48
50	3.25	3.80	7.65	8.65	9.60	10.55	11.50	12.45	13.40	22.20	23.65	25.15	26.65	50
52	3.40	7 00	7.95	8.95	9.95	10.95	11.95	12.95	21.55	23.10	24.60	26.15	27.70	52
54	3.50	7.25	8.30	9.30	10.35	11.40	12.40	13.45	22.35	23.95	25.55	27.15	28.75	54
56	3.65	7.50	8.60	9.65	10.75	11.80	12.90	21.55	23.20	24.85	26.50	28.15	29.80	56
58	3.75	7.80	8.90	10.00	11.10	12.25	13.35	22.30	24.	25.75	27.45	29.15	30.90	58
60	3.90	8.05	9.20	10.35	11.50	12.65	13.80	23.10	24.85	26.65	28.40	30.20	31.95	60
62	7.15	8.30	9.50	10.70	11.90	13.10	22.	23.85	25.70	27.50	29.35	31.20	33.	62
64	7.35	8.60	9.80	11.05	12.25	13.50	22.70	24.60	26.50	28.40	30.30	32.20	34.10	64
66	7.60	8.85	10.10	11.40	12.65	21.50	23.45	25.40	27.35	29.30	31.25	33.20	35.15	66
68	7.80	9.10	10.45	11.75	13.05	22.15	24.15	26.15	28.15	30.20	32.20	34.20	36.20	68
70	8.05	9.40	10.75	12.10	13.40	22.80	24.85	26.90	29.	31.05	33.15	35.20	37.30	70
72	8.30	9.65	11.05	12.40	13.80	23.45	25.55	27.70	29.80	31.95	34.10	36.20	38.35	72
74	8.50	9.95	11.35	12.75	21.90	24.10	26.25	28.45	30.65	32.85	35.05	37.20	39.40	74
76	8.75	10.20	11.65	13.10	22.50	24.75	27.	29.25	31.50	33.75	36.	38.20	40.45	76
78	8.95	10.45	11.95	13.45	23.10	25.40	27.70	30.	32.30	34.60	36.90	39.25	41.55	78
80	9.20	10.75	12.25	13.80	23.65	26.05	28.40	30.75	33.15	35.50	37.85	40.25	42.60	80
82	9.45	11.00	12.60	21.85	24.25	26.70	28.60	31.55	33.95	36.40	38.80	41.25	43.65	82
84	9.65	11.25	12.90	22.35	24.85	27.35	29.80	32.30	34.80	37.30	39.75	42.25	44.75	84
86	9.90	11.55	13.20	22.90	25.45	28.	30.55	33.10	35.60	38.15	40.70	43.25	45.80	86
88	10.10	11.80	13.50	23.45	26.05	28.65	31.25	33.85	36.45	39.05	41.65	44.25	46.85	88
90	10.35	12.10	13.80	23.95	26.65	29.30	31.95	34.60	37.30	39.95	42.60	45.25	47.95	90
92	10.60	12.35	21.80	24.50	27.20	29.95	32.65	35.40	38.10	40.85	43.55	46.25	49.	92
94	10.80	12.60	22.25	25.05	27.80	30.60	33.35	36.15	38.95	41.70	44.50	47.30	50.05	94
96	11.05	12.90	22.70	25.55	28.40	31.25	34.10	36.90	39.75	42.60	45.45	48.30	51.10	96
98	11.25	13.15	23.20	26.10	29.	31.90	34.80	37.70	40.60	43.50	46.40	49.30	52.20	98
100	11.50	13.40	23.65	26.65	29.60	32.55	35.50	38.45	41.40	44.40	47.35	50.30	53.25	100
102	11.75	13.70	24.15	27.15	30.20	33.20	36.20	39.25	42.25	45.25	48.30	51.30	54.30	102
104	11.95	21.55	24.60	27.70	30.75	33.85	36.90	40.	43.10	46.15	49.25	52.30	55.40	104
106	12.20	21.95	25.10	28.20	31.35	34.50	37.65	40.75	43.90	47.05	50.20	53.30	56.45	106
108	12.40	22.35	25.55	28.75	31.95	35.15	38.35	41.55	44.75	47.95	51.10	54.30	57.50	108
110	12.65	22.80	26.05	29.30	32.55	35.80	39.05	42.30	45.55	48.80	52.05	55.30	58.60	110
112	12.90	23.20	26.50	29.80	33.15	36.45	39.75	43.10	46.40	49.70	53.	56.35	59.65	112
114	13.10	23.60	27.	30.35	33.70	37.10	40.45	43.85	47.20	50.60	53.95	57.35	60.70	114
116	13.35	24.	27.45	30.90	34.30	37.75	41.20	44.60	48.05	51.50	54.90	58.35	61.75	116
118	13.55	24.45	27.95	31.40	34.90	38.40	41.90	45.40	48.85	52.35	55.85	59.35	62.85	118
120	13.80	24.85	28.40	31.95	35.50	39.05	42.60	46.15	49.70	53.25	56.80	60.35	63.90	120
122	21.65	25.25	28.90	32.50	36.10	39.70	43.30	46.90	50.55	54.15	57.75	61.35	64.95	122
124	22.	25.70	29.35	33.	36.70	40.35	44.	47.70	51.35	55.05	58.70	62.35	66.05	124
126	22.35	26.10	29.80	33.55	37.30	41.	44.75	48.45	52.20	55.90	59.65	63.35	67.10	126
128	22.70	26.50	30.30	34.10	37.85	41.65	45.45	49.25	53.	56.80	60.60	64.40	68.15	128
130	23.10	26.90	30.75	34.60	38.45	42.30	46.15	50.	53.85	57.70	61.55	65.40	69.25	130
132	23.45	27.35	31.25	35.15	39.05	42.95	46.85	50 75	54.65	58.60	62.50	66.40	70.30	132
134	23.80	27.75	31.70	35.70	39.65	43.60	47.55	51.55	55.50	59.45	63.45	67.40	71.35	134
136	24.15	28.15	32.20	36.20	40.25	44.25	48.30	52.30	56.35	60.35	64.40	68.40	72.40	136

PLATE GLASS LIST—Continued.

Price per Light.

Length.	38	40	42	44	46	48	50	52	54	56	58	Length.
38	21.35	.....	.....	.....	.....	.....	.....	.....	.....	.....	.....	38
40	22.50	23.65	.....	.....	.....	.....	.....	.....	.....	.....	.....	40
42	23.60	24.85	26.10	.....	.....	.....	.....	.....	.....	.....	.....	42
44	24.75	26.05	27.35	28.65	.....	.....	.....	.....	.....	.....	.....	44
46	25.85	27.20	28.60	29.95	31.30	.....	.....	.....	.....	.....	.....	46
48	27.	28.40	29.80	31.25	32.65	34.10	.....	.....	.....	.....	.....	48
50	28.10	29.60	31.05	32.55	34.	35.50	37.	.....	.....	.....	.....	50
52	29.25	30.75	32.30	33.85	35.40	36.90	38.	40.	.....	.....	.....	52
54	30.35	31.95	33.55	35.15	36.75	38.35	40.	42.	43.	.....	.....	54
56	31.50	33.15	34.80	36.45	38.10	39.75	41.	43.	45.	46.	.....	56
58	32.60	34.30	36.05	37.75	39.45	41.20	43.	45.	46.	48.	50.	58
60	33.75	35.50	37.30	39.05	40.85	42.60	44.	46.	48.	50.	51.	60
62	34.85	36.70	38.50	40.35	42.20	44.	46.	48.	50.	51.	53.	62
64	36.	37.85	39.75	41.65	43.55	45.45	47.	49.	51.	53.	55.	64
66	37.10	39.05	41.	42.95	44.90	46.85	49.	51.	53.	55.	57.	66
68	38.20	40.25	42.25	44.25	46.25	48.30	50.	52.	54.	56.	58.	68
70	39.35	41.40	43.50	45.55	47.65	49.70	52.	54.	56.	58.	60.	70
72	40.45	42.60	44.75	46.85	49.	51.10	53.	55.	58.	60.	62.	72
74	41.60	43.80	45.95	48.15	50.35	52.55	55.	57.	59.	61.	63.	74
76	42.70	44.95	47.20	49.45	51.70	53.95	56.	58.	61.	63.	65.	76
78	43.85	46.15	48.45	50.75	53.05	55.40	58.	60.	62.	65.	67.	78
80	44.95	47.35	49.70	52.05	54.45	56.80	59.	62.	64.	66.	69.	80
82	46.10	48.50	50.95	53.35	55.80	58.20	61.	63.	66.	68.	70.	82
84	47.20	49.70	52.20	54.65	57.15	59.65	62.	65.	67.	70.	72.	84
86	48.35	50.90	53.45	55.95	58.50	61.05	64.	66.	69.	71.	74.	86
88	49.45	52.05	54.65	57.30	59.90	62.50	65.	68.	70.	73.	76.	88
90	50.60	53.25	55.90	58.60	61.25	63.90	67.	69.	72.	75.	77.	90
92	51.70	54.45	57.15	59.90	62.60	65.30	68.	71.	73.	76.	79.	92
94	52.85	55.60	58.40	61.20	63.95	66.75	70.	72.	75.	78.	81.	94
96	53.95	56.80	59.65	62.50	65.30	68.15	71.	74.	77.	80.	82.	96
98	55.10	58.	60.90	63.80	66.70	69.60	72.	75.	78.	81.	84.	98
100	56.20	59.15	62.15	65.10	68.05	71.	74.	77.	80.	83.	90.	100
102	57.35	60.35	63.35	66.40	69.40	72.40	75.	78.	81.	84.	92.	102
104	58.45	61.55	64.60	67.70	70.75	73.85	77.	80.	83.	91.	94.	104
106	59.60	62.70	65.85	69.	72.15	75.25	78.	82.	85.	92.	96.	106
108	60.70	63.90	67.10	70.30	73.50	76.70	80.	83.	91.	94.	97.	108
110	61.85	65.10	68.35	71.60	74.85	78.10	81.	85.	92.	96.	99.	110
112	62.95	66.25	69.60	72.90	76.20	79.50	83.	91.	94.	98.	101.	112
114	64.10	67.45	70.80	74.20	77.55	80.95	84.	92.	96.	99.	103.	114
116	65.20	68.65	72.05	75.50	78.95	82.35	90.	94.	97.	101.	105.	116
118	66.35	69.80	73.30	76.80	80.30	83.80	92.	95.	99.	103.	106.	118
120	67.45	71.	74.55	78.10	81.65	85.20	93.	97.	101.	105.	108.	120
122	68.60	72.20	75.80	79.40	83.	91.	95.	99.	102.	106.	110.	122
124	69.70	73.35	77.05	80.70	84.35	93.	96.	100.	104.	108.	112.	124
126	70.80	74.55	78.30	82.	90.	94.	98.	102.	106.	110.	114.	126
128	71.95	75.75	79.50	83.30	92.	96.	100.	104.	108.	112.	115.	128
130	73.05	76.90	80.75	84.60	93.	97.	101.	105.	109.	113.	117.	130
132	74.20	78.10	82.	90.	94.	99.	103.	107.	111.	115.	119.	132
134	75.30	79.30	83.25	92.	96.	100.	104.	108.	113.	117.	121.	134
136	76.45	80.45	84.50	93.	97.	102.	106.	110.	114.	118.	123.	136
138	77.55	81.65	90.	94.	99.	103.	107.	112.	116.	120.	125.	138
140	78.70	82.85	91.	96.	100.	105.	109.	113.	118.	122.	126.	140
142	79.80	84.	93.	97.	102.	106.	110.	115.	119.	124.	128.	142
144	80.95	85.20	94.	99.	103.	108.	112.	116.	121.	125.	130.	144
146	82.05	91.	95.	100.	104	109.	114.	118.	123.	127.	132.	146
148	83.20	92.	97.	101.	106.	111.	115.	120.	124.	129.	134.	148
150	84.30	93.	98.	103.	107.	112.	117.	121.	126.	131.	135.	150
152	97.	102.	107.	112.	118.	123.	128.	133.	138.	143.	148.	152
154	98.	104.	109.	114.	119.	124.	129.	135.	140.	145.	150.	154
156	100.	105.	110.	115.	121.	126.	131.	136.	142.	147.	152.	156
158	101.	106.	112.	117.	122.	127.	133.	138.	143.	149.	154.	158
160	102.	108.	113.	118.	124.	129.	134.	140.	145.	151.	156.	160
162	103.	109.	114.	120.	125.	131.	136.	142.	147.	152.	158.	162
164	105.	110.	116.	121.	127.	132.	138.	143.	149.	154.	160.	164
166	106.	112.	117.	123.	128.	134.	139.	145.	151.	156.	162.	166
168	107.	113.	119.	124.	130.	136.	141.	147.	152.	158.	164.	168
170	109.	114.	120.	126.	131.	137.	143.	149.	154.	160.	166.	170

PLATE GLASS LIST—Continued.

Price per Light.

Length.	|	WIDTH.										|	Length.
	60	62	64	66	68	70	72	74	76	78	80		
60	53.	....	....	....	....	....	....	....	....	....	....		60
62	55.	57.	....	....	....	....	....	....	....	....	....		62
64	57.	59.	61.	....	....	....	....	....	....	....	....		64
66	59.	61.	62.	64.	....	....	....	....	....	....	....		66
68	60.	62.	64.	66.	68.	....	....	....	....	....	....		68
70	62.	64.	66.	68.	70.	72.	....	....	....	....	....		70
72	64.	66.	68.	70.	72.	75.	77.	....	....	....	....		72
74	66.	68.	70.	72.	74.	77.	79.	81.	....	....	....		74
76	67.	70.	72.	74.	76.	79.	81.	83.	90.	....	....		76
78	69.	72.	74.	76.	78.	81.	83.	90.	92.	95.	....		78
80	71.	73.	76.	78.	80.	83.	85.	92.	95.	97.	100.		80
82	73.	75.	78.	80.	82.	85.	92.	94.	97.	99.	102.		82
84	75.	77.	80.	82.	84.	91.	94.	97.	99.	102.	105.		84
86	76.	79.	81.	84.	91.	94.	96.	99.	102.	104.	107.		86
88	78.	81.	83.	90.	93.	96.	99.	101.	104.	107.	110.		88
90	80.	83.	85.	92.	95.	98.	101.	104.	106.	109.	112.		90
92	82.	84.	92.	94.	97.	100.	103.	106.	109.	112.	114.		92
94	83.	91.	94.	97.	99.	102.	105.	108.	111.	114.	117.		94
96	85.	93.	96.	99.	102.	105.	108.	111.	113.	116.	119.		96
98	91.	95.	98.	101.	104.	107.	110.	113.	116.	119.	122.		98
100	93.	96.	100.	103.	106.	109.	112.	115.	118.	121.	124.		100
102	95.	98.	102.	105.	108.	111.	114.	117.	121.	124.	127.		102
104	97.	100.	104.	107.	110.	113.	116.	120.	123.	126.	129.		104
106	99.	102.	106.	109.	112.	115.	119.	122.	125.	129.	132.		106
108	101.	104.	108.	111.	114.	118.	121.	124.	128.	131.	134.		108
110	103.	106.	110.	113.	116.	120.	123.	127.	130.	133.	137.		110
112	105.	108.	112.	115.	118.	122.	125.	129.	132.	136.	139.		112
114	106.	110.	113.	117.	121.	124.	128.	131.	135.	138.	142.		114
116	108.	112.	115.	119.	123.	126.	130.	134.	137.	141.	144.		116
118	110.	114.	117.	121.	125.	128.	132.	136.	140.	143.	147.		118
120	112.	116.	119.	123.	127.	131.	134.	138.	142.	146.	149.		120
122	114.	118.	121.	125.	129.	133.	137.	140.	144.	148.	152.		122
124	116.	120.	123.	127.	131.	135.	139.	143.	147.	150.	154.		124
126	118.	122.	125.	129.	133.	137.	141.	145.	149.	153.	157.		126
128	119.	123.	127.	131.	135.	139.	143.	147.	151.	155.	159.		128
130	121.	125.	129.	133.	138.	142.	146.	150.	154.	158.	162.		130
132	123.	127.	131.	136.	140.	144.	148.	152.	156.	160.	164.		132
134	125.	129.	133.	138.	142.	146.	150.	154.	158.	163.	167.		134
136	127.	131.	135.	140.	144.	148.	152.	157.	161.	165.	169.		136
138	129.	133.	137.	142.	146.	150.	155.	159.	163.	167.	172.		138
140	131.	135.	139.	144.	148.	152.	157.	161.	166.	170.	174.		140
142	133.	137.	141.	146.	150.	155.	159.	163.	168.	172.	177.		142
144	134.	139.	143.	148.	152.	157.	161.	166.	170.	175.	179.		144
146	136.	141.	145.	150.	154.	159.	164.	168.	173.	177.	196.		146
148	138.	143.	147.	152.	157.	161.	166.	170.	175.	194.	199.		148
150	140.	145.	149.	154.	159.	163.	168.	173.	177.	197.	202.		150
152	153.	158.	163.	169.	174.	179.	184.	189.	194.	199.	204.		152
154	155.	160.	166.	171.	176.	181.	186.	192.	197.	202.	207.		154
156	157.	163.	168.	173.	178.	184.	189.	194.	199.	204.	210.		156
158	159.	165.	170.	175.	181.	186.	191.	196.	202.	207.	212.		158
160	161.	167.	172.	177.	183.	188.	194.	199.	204.	210.	215.		160
162	163.	169.	174.	180.	185.	191.	196.	201.	207.	212.	218.		162
164	165.	171.	176.	182.	187.	193.	198.	204.	209.	215.	220.		164
166	167.	173.	179.	184.	190.	195.	201.	206.	212.	218.	223.		166
168	169.	175.	181.	186.	192.	198.	203.	209.	215.	220.	226.		168
170	171.	177.	183.	189.	194.	200.	206.	211.	217.	223.	229.		170

PLATE GLASS LIST—Continued.

Price per Light.

Length.					WIDTH.							Length
	82	84	86	88	90	92	94	96	98	100	102	
82	105.											82
84	107.	110.										84
86	110.	112.	115.									86
88	112.	115.	118.	120.								88
90	115.	118.	120.	123.	126.							90
92	117.	120.	123.	126.	129.	132.						92
94	120.	123.	126.	129.	132.	135.	137.					94
96	122.	125.	128.	131.	134.	137.	140.	143.				96
98	125.	128.	131.	134.	137.	140.	143.	146.	149.			98
100	128.	131.	134.	137.	140.	143.	146.	149.	152.	155.		100
102	130.	133.	136.	140.	143.	146.	149.	152.	155.	158.	175.	102
104	133.	136.	139.	142.	146.	149.	152.	155.	158.	161.	178.	104
106	135.	139.	142.	145.	148.	152.	155.	158.	161.	164.	182.	106
108	138.	141.	144.	148.	151.	155.	158.	161.	164.	167.	185.	108
110	140.	144.	147.	151.	154.	157.	161.	164.	167.	170.	188.	110
112	143.	146.	150.	153.	157.	160.	164.	167.	170.	174.	192.	112
114	145.	149.	153.	156.	160.	163.	167.	170.	173.	177.	195.	114
116	148.	152.	155.	159.	162.	166.	170.	173.	176.	195.	199.	116
118	151.	154.	158.	162.	165.	169.	173.	176.	194.	198.	202.	118
120	153.	157.	161.	164.	168.	172.	175.	179.	198.	201.	205.	120
122	156.	159.	163.	167.	171.	175.	178.	197.	201.	205.	209.	122
124	158.	162.	166.	170.	174.	177.	196.	200.	204.	208.	212.	124
126	161.	165.	169.	172.	176.	195.	199.	203.	207.	212.	216.	126
128	163.	167.	171.	175.	179.	198.	202.	207.	211.	215.	219.	128
130	166.	170.	174.	178.	197.	201.	205.	210.	214.	218.	223.	130
132	168.	172.	177.	195.	200.	204.	209.	213.	217.	222.	226.	132
134	171.	175.	194.	198.	203.	207.	212.	216.	221.	225.	230.	134
136	173.	178.	197.	201.	206.	210.	215.	219.	224.	228.	233.	136
138	176.	195.	199.	204.	209.	213.	218.	223.	227.	232.	236.	138
140	179.	198.	202.	207.	212.	216.	221.	226.	230.	235.	240.	140
142	196.	200.	205.	210.	215.	220.	224.	229.	234.	238.	301.	142
144	198.	203.	208.	213.	218.	223.	227.	232.	237.	242.	306.	144
146	201.	206.	211.	216.	221.	226.	231.	236.	240.	304.	310.	146
148	204.	209.	214.	219.	224.	229.	234.	239.	242.	308.	314.	148
150	207.	212.	217.	222.	227.	232.	237.	242.	306.	312.	318.	150
152	209.	215.	220.	225.	230.	235.	240.	304.	310.	316.	322.	152
154	212.	217.	223.	228.	233.	238.	302.	308.	314.	320.	327.	154
156	215.	220.	225.	231.	236.	241.	306.	312.	318.	324.	331.	156
158	218.	223.	228.	234.	239.	303.	309.	316.	322.	329.	335.	158
160	220.	226.	231.	237.	242.	307.	313.	320.	326.	333.	339.	160
162	223.	229.	234.	240.	304.	310.	317.	324.	330.	337.	343.	162
164	226.	232.	237.	301.	307.	314.	321.	328.	334.	341.	348.	164
166	229.	234.	240.	304.	311.	318.	325.	332.	338.	345.	352.	166
168	232.	237.	301.	308.	315.	322.	329.	336.	342.	349.	356.	168
170	235.	240.	305.	312.	319.	326.	333.	340.	347.	354.	434.	170
172	293.	301.	308.	315.	322.	329.	336.	344.	351.	358.	440.	172
174	297.	304.	311.	318.	326.	333.	340.	347.	355.	435.	444.	174
176	300.	308.	315.	322.	329.	337.	344.	351.	359.	440.	449.	176
178	304.	311.	318.	326.	333.	341.	348.	355.	436.	445.	454.	178
180	307.	314.	322.	329.	337.	344.	352.	359.	441.	450.	459.	180
182	373.	382.	391.	400.	410.	419.	428.	437.	446.	455.	464.	182
184	377.	386.	396.	405.	414.	423.	432.	442.	451.	460.	587.	184
186	381.	391.	400.	409.	419.	428.	437.	446.	456.	465.	593.	186
188	385.	395.	404.	414.	423.	432.	442.	451.	461.	588.	599.	188
190	390.	399.	409.	418.	428.	437.	447.	456.	466.	594.	606.	190
192	492.	504.	516.	528.	540.	552.	564.	576.	588.	600.	612.	192
194	497.	509.	521.	534.	546.	558.	570.	582.	594.	606.	618.	194
196	502.	515.	527.	539.	551.	564.	576.	588.	600.	613.	625.	196
198	507.	520.	532.	545.	557.	569.	582.	594.	606.	619.	631.	198
200	512.	525.	537.	550.	562.	575.	588.	600.	613.	626.	638.	200
202	517.	530.	542.	555.	567.	580.	594.	606.	619.	632.	644.	202
204	522.	535.	547.	560.	577.	585.	600.	612.	625.	638.	650.	204
206	527.	540.	552.	565.	582.	595.	606.	618.	632.	644.	657.	206
208	532.	545.	557.	575.	587.	600.	610.	624.	638.	650.	663.	208
210	537.	550.	562.	580.	592.	605.	616.	630.	644.	656.	670.	210
212	542.	555.	567.	585.	597.	610.	622.	636.	650.	662.		212
214	547.	560.	577.	590.	602.	615.	628.	642.	656.	668.		214
216	555.	565.	582.	595.	607.	620.	634.	648.	662.	675.		216

PLATE GLASS LIST—Continued.
Price per Light.

Length	104	106	108	110	112	114	116	118	120	122	124	Length
104	182.											104
106	185.	189.										106
108	189.	192.	196.									108
110	192.	196.	199.	203.								110
112	196.	199.	203.	207.	261.							112
114	199.	203.	207.	211.	266.	270.						114
116	203.	206.	210.	214.	270.	275.	280.					116
118	206.	210.	214.	218.	275.	280.	285.	290.				118
120	210.	214.	218.	222.	280.	285.	290.	295.	300.			120
122	213.	217.	221.	225.	284.	289.	294.	300.	305.	372.		122
124	217.	221.	225.	229.	289.	294.	299.	304.	310.	378.	384.	124
126	220.	224.	229.	233.	294.	299.	304.	309.	314.	384.	391.	126
128	224.	228.	232.	236.	298.	304.	309.	314.	319.	390.	397.	128
130	227.	232.	236.	240.	303.	308.	314.	319.	324.	397.	403.	130
132	231.	235.	240.	302.	308.	313.	318.	324.	329.	403.	409.	132
134	234	239.	301.	307.	312.	318.	323.	329.	334.	409.	415.	134
136	238.	300.	306.	311.	317.	322.	328.	334.	339.	415.	422.	136
138	241.	304.	310.	315.	321.	327.	333.	339.	344.	421.	428.	138
140	303.	309.	314.	320.	326.	332.	338.	343.	349.	427.	434.	140
142	307.	313.	319.	325.	331.	337.	343.	349.	354.	433.	440.	142
144	312.	317.	323.	329.	335.	341.	347.	353.	359.	439.	446.	144
146	316.	322.	328.	334.	340.	346.	352.	358.	438.	445.	453.	146
148	320.	326.	332.	339.	345.	351.	357.	437.	444.	451.	459.	148
150	324.	331.	337.	343.	349.	356.	435.	443.	450.	458.	465.	150
152	329.	335.	341.	348.	354.	433.	441.	448.	456.	464.	589.	152
154	333.	340.	346.	352.	359.	439.	447.	454.	462.	587.	597.	154
156	337.	344	350.	357.	437.	445.	452.	460.	468.	595.	604.	156
158	342.	348.	355.	435.	442.	450.	458.	466.	593.	602.	612.	158
160	346.	353.	359.	440.	448.	456.	464.	590.	600.	610.	620.	160
162	351.	357.	437.	446.	453.	462.	587.	597.	608.	618.	628.	162
164	355.	435.	443.	451.	459.	467.	595.	605.	615.	625.	635.	164
166	359.	440.	448.	457.	465.	591.	602.	612.	623.	633.	643.	166
168	437.	445.	454.	462.	588.	599.	609.	619.	630.	640.	651.	168
170	442.	451.	459.	468.	595.	606.	616.	627.	638.	648.	658.	170
172	447.	456.	464.	591.	602.	618.	624.	634.	645.	656.	667.	172
174	452.	461.	587.	598.	609.	620.	631.	642.	653.	663.	675.	174
176	458.	465.	594.	605.	616.	627.	638.	649.	660.	671.		176
178	463.	590.	601.	612.	623.	634.	645.	656.	668.			178
180	468.	596.	608.	619.	630.	641.	653.	664.	675.			180
182	592.	603.	614.	626.	637.	648.	661.	671.				182
184	598.	609.	621.	632.	644.	655.	668.					184
186	605.	616.	628.	639.	651.	663.	675.					186
188	611.	623.	635.	646.	658.	670.						188
190	618.	629.	641.	653.	665.							190
192	624.	636.	648.	660.	672.							192
194	631.	643.	655.	667.								194
196	637.	649.	662.	674.								196
198	644.	656.	668.									198
200	650.	662.	675.									200
202	657.	668.										202
204	663.	675.										204
206	670.											206

To Approximate Weight of Polished Plate Glass, Boxed.

Extend the glass at 3½ lbs. per square foot. Weight of box equals the contents of a plate of greatest width and length of those packed therein, multiplied by 10. Thus:

$$\left. \begin{array}{l} \text{1 plate } 36'' \times 96'' \\ \text{1 } \quad `` \quad 60'' \times 84'' \end{array} \right\} = 59 \text{ ft.} \times 3\tfrac{1}{2} = 206\tfrac{1}{2} \text{ lbs.}$$

$$\text{Size of box } 60'' \times 96'' = 40 \text{ ft.} \times 10 = \underline{400}$$

$$606\tfrac{1}{2} \text{ lbs.}$$

Irregular shaped glass, or glass cut to patterns, will be charged as it squares.

Plates containing over 120 square feet, list price $5 per square foot or fraction.

On orders for one or two plates only, a charge of 6 foot of box-lid will be invariably made to cover cost of boxing.

Odd and fractional parts of inches are charged at the price of the next highest even inches.

REVISED EDITION

OF THE

New Universal

oulding Book

CONTAINING

Latest Styles of Mouldings,

IN GREAT VARIETY,

Giving Full Size of Mouldings and their Exact Measurement in Inches on each Moulding.

FOR PRICES, SEE PAGES 331 and 332.

Mouldings.

....

We keep in stock a large and complete Assortment of Mouldings ready for shipment, and have facilities unsurpassed for furnishing on very short notice any style of Moulding or

Inside Finish

that may be desired, either in Yellow or White Pine or in any of the native woods.

We give careful attention to the quality of our work, and spare no effort to make it equal, if not superior, to the very best in the market.

In ordering, please use the numbers on each Moulding to indicate the pattern and size wanted.

CROWN MOULDINGS.

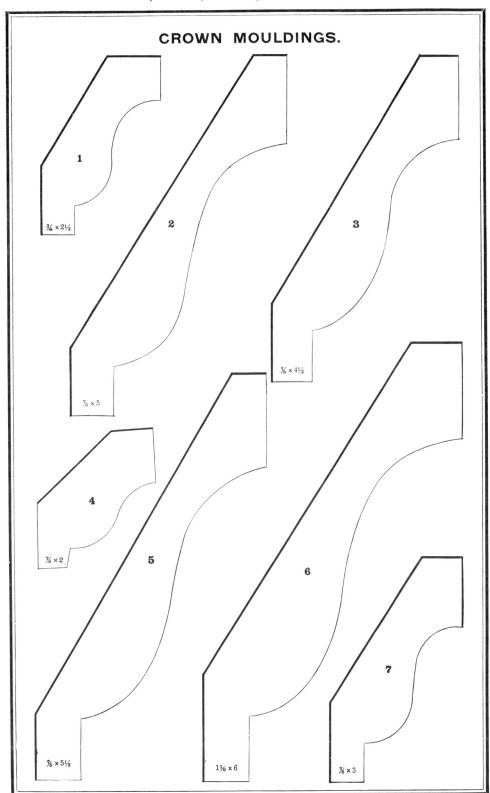

CROWN MOULDINGS.

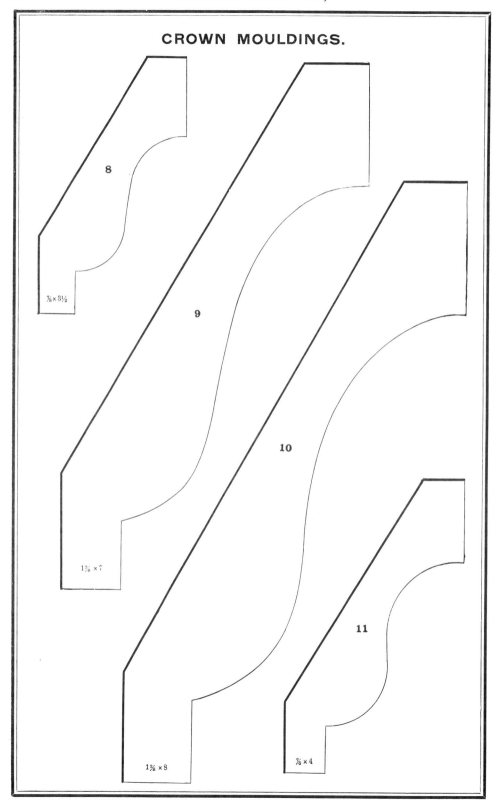

8

⅞ × 3½

9

1⅜ × 7

10

11

1⅜ × 8

⅞ × 4

CROWN MOULDINGS.

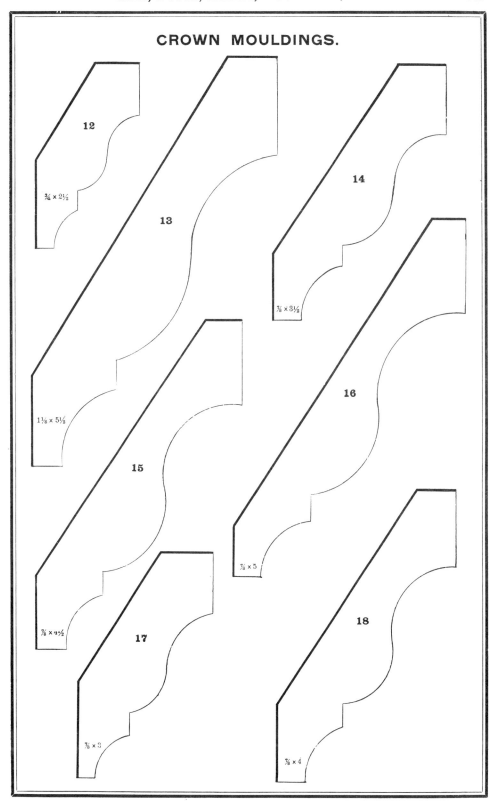

CROWN MOULDINGS.

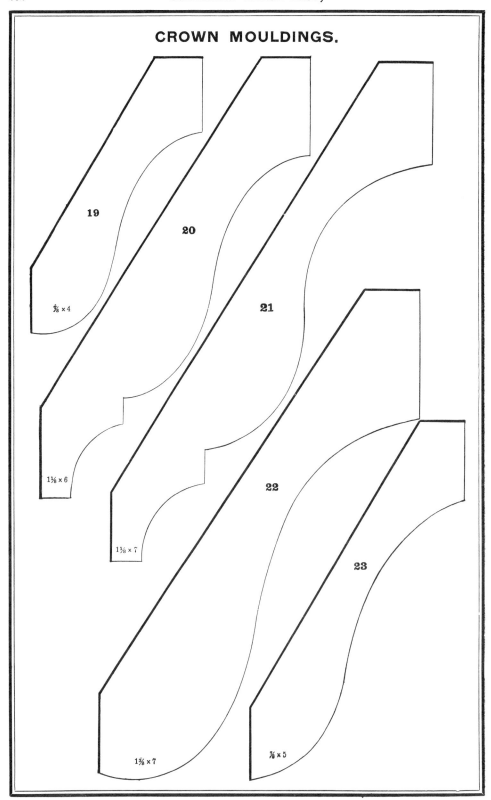

CROWN MOULDINGS.

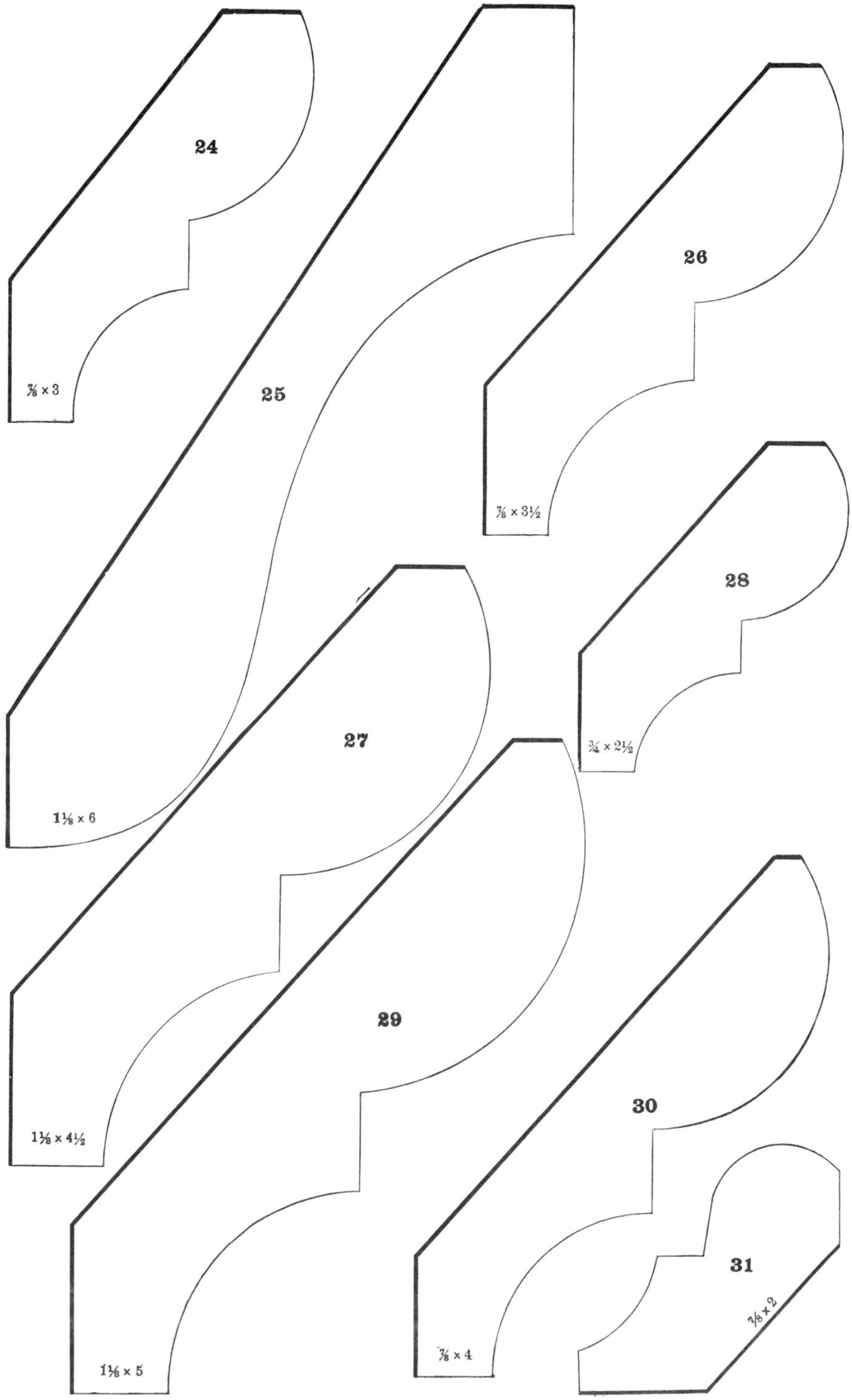
24
⅞ × 3
25
1⅛ × 6
26
⅞ × 3½
27
1⅛ × 4½
28
¾ × 2½
29
1⅛ × 5
30
⅞ × 4
31
⅞ × 2

SPRUNG COVE AND BED MOULDINGS.

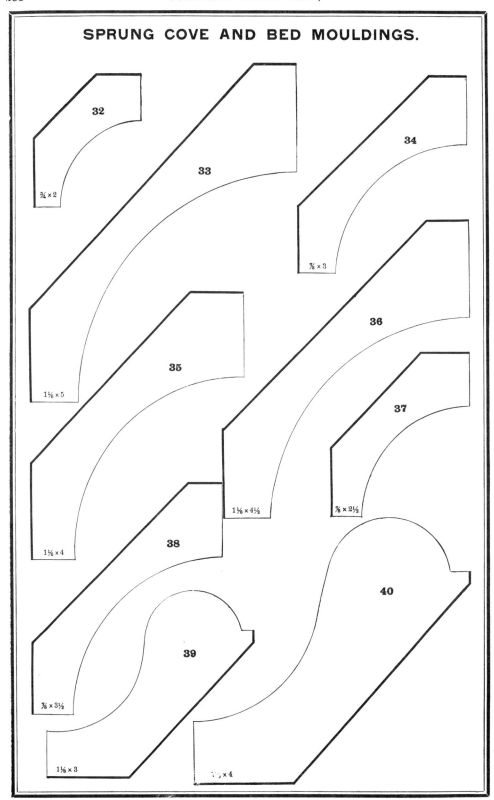

BED MOULDINGS.

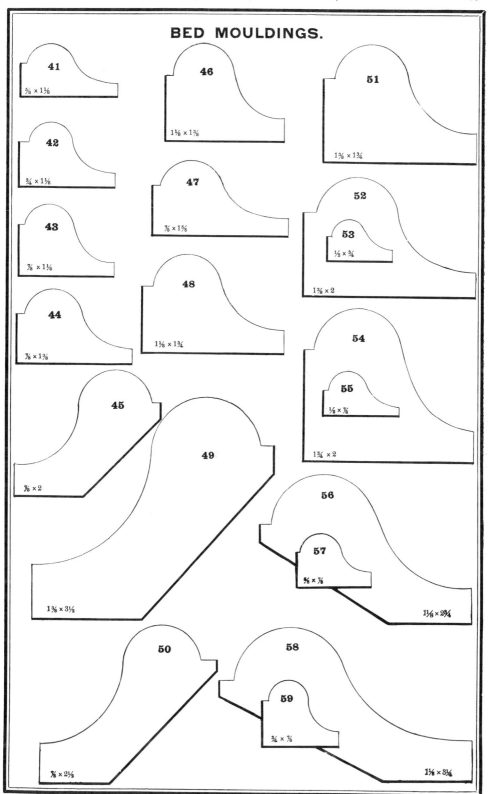

41 ⅝ × 1⅛

42 ¾ × 1⅛

43 ⅞ × 1⅛

44 ⅞ × 1⅜

45 ⅞ × 2

46 1⅛ × 1⅜

47 ⅞ × 1⅝

48 1⅛ × 1¾

49 1⅜ × 3½

50 ⅞ × 2½

51 1⅜ × 1¾

52
53 ½ × ¾
1⅜ × 2

54
55 ½ × ⅞
1¾ × 2

56
57 ⅝ × ⅞
1⅛ × 2¾

58
59 ¾ × ⅞
1¼ × 3¼

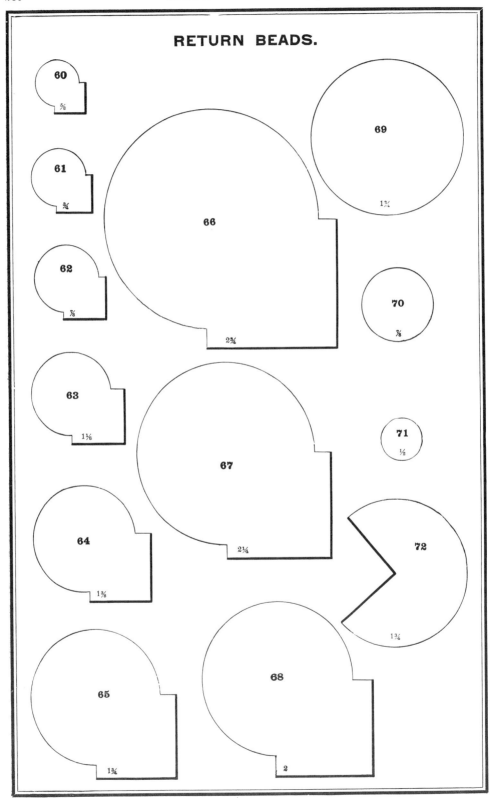

RETURN BEADS.

QUARTER ROUND, HALF ROUND, AND COVE.

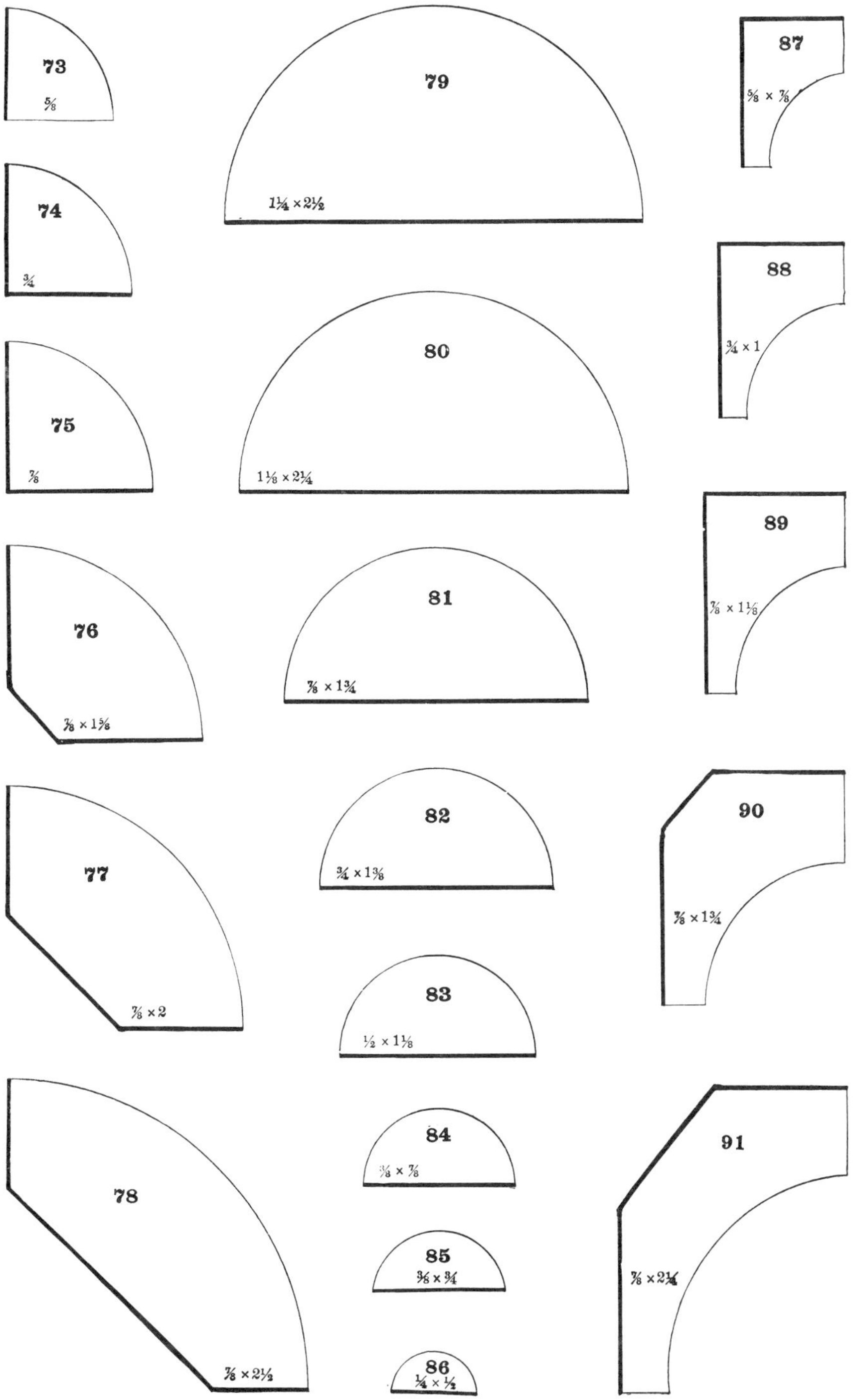
73
⅝
74
¾
75
⅞
76
⅞ × 1⅝
77
⅞ × 2
78
⅞ × 2½
79
1¼ × 2½
80
1⅛ × 2¼
81
⅞ × 1¾
82
¾ × 1⅜
83
½ × 1⅛
84
⅜ × ⅞
85
⅜ × ¾
86
¼ × ½
87
⅝ × ⅞
88
¾ × 1
89
⅞ × 1⅛
90
⅞ × 1¾
91
⅞ × 2¼

O G STOPS.

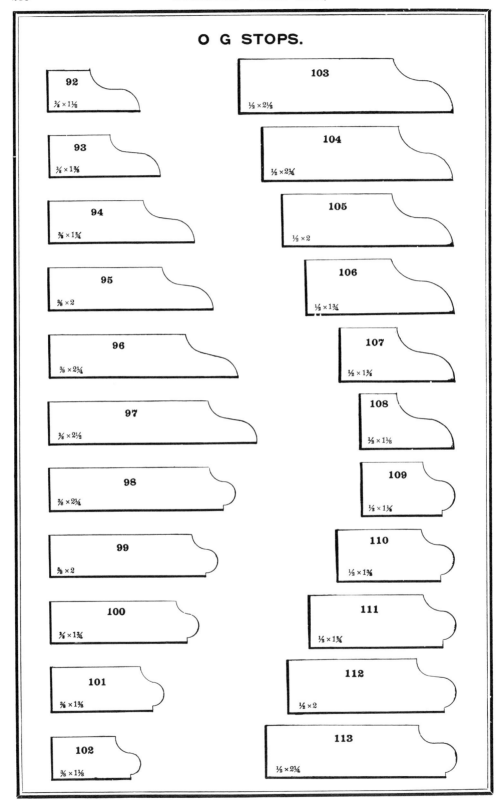

92 — ⅜ × 1⅛

93 — ⅜ × 1⅜

94 — ⅜ × 1¾

95 — ⅜ × 2

96 — ⅜ × 2¼

97 — ⅜ × 2½

98 — ⅜ × 2¼

99 — ⅜ × 2

100 — ⅜ × 1¾

101 — ⅜ × 1⅜

102 — ⅜ × 1⅛

103 — ½ × 2½

104 — ½ × 2¼

105 — ½ × 2

106 — ½ × 1¾

107 — ½ × 1⅜

108 — ½ × 1⅛

109 — ½ × 1¼

110 — ½ × 1⅜

111 — ½ × 1¾

112 — ½ × 2

113 — ½ × 2¼

P G AND BEAD STOPS.

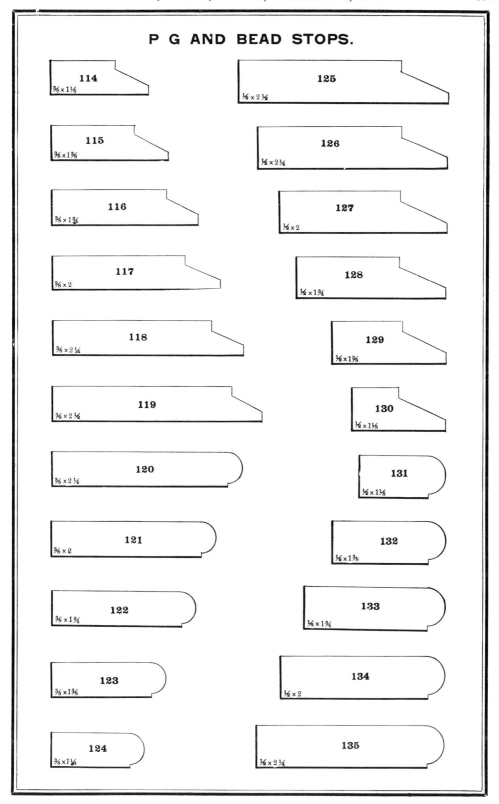

ASTRAGAL MOULDINGS.

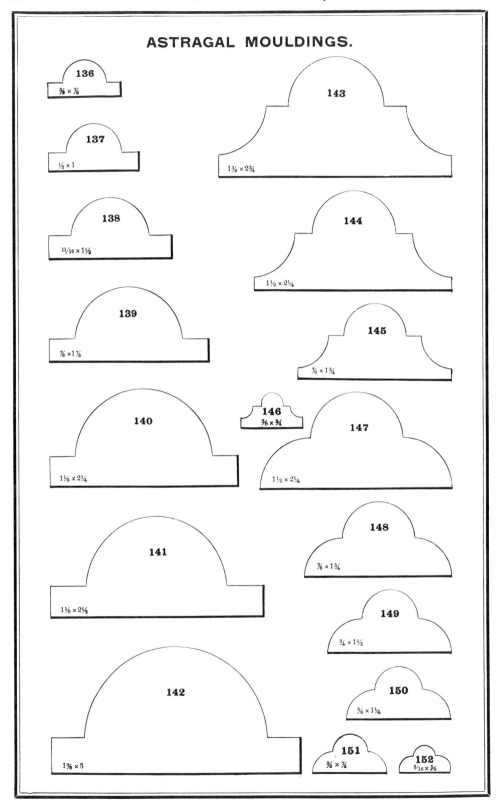

NOSINGS.

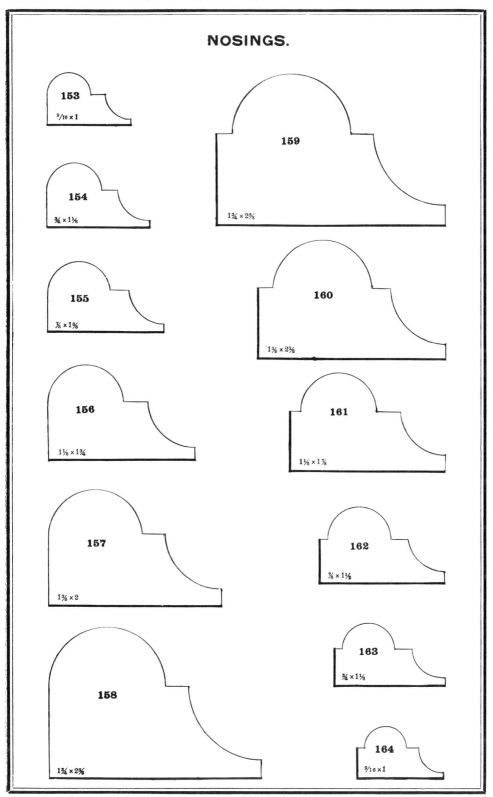

NOSINGS.

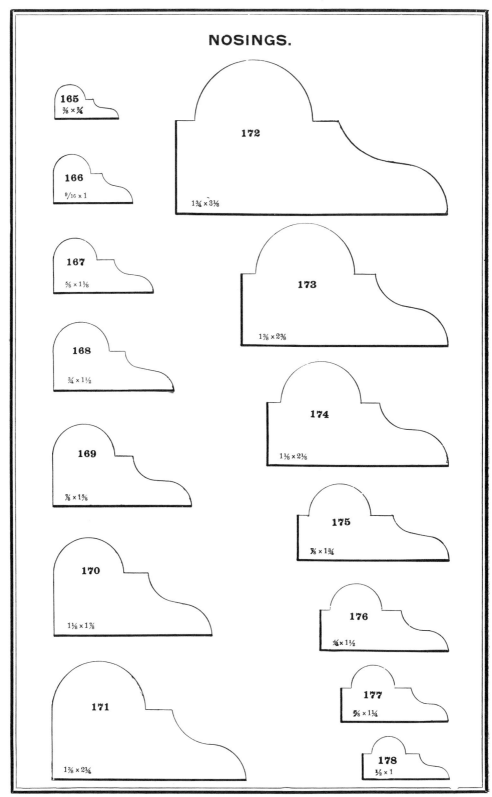

165
⅜ × ¾

166
⁹⁄₁₆ × 1

167
⅝ × 1⅛

168
¾ × 1½

169
⅞ × 1⅝

170
1⅛ × 1⅞

171
1⅜ × 2¼

172
1¾ × 3⅛

173
1⅜ × 2⅜

174
1⅛ × 2⅛

175
⅞ × 1¾

176
¾ × 1½

177
⅝ × 1¼

178
½ × 1

PANEL AND BASE MOULDINGS.

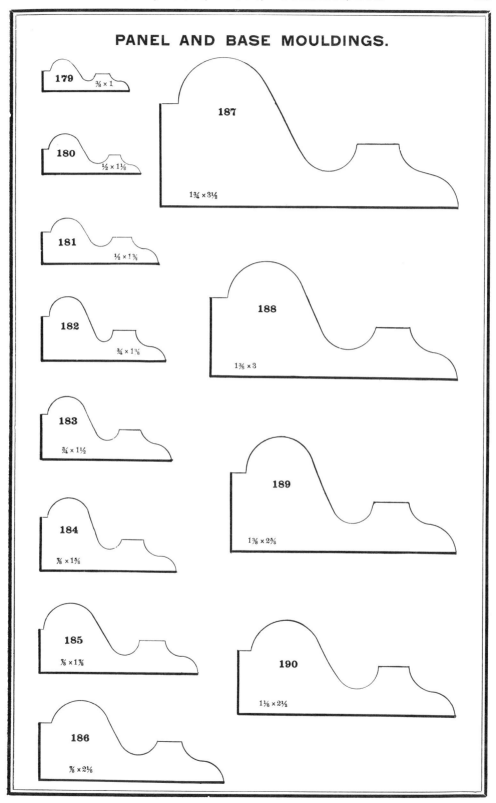

PANEL AND BASE MOULDINGS.

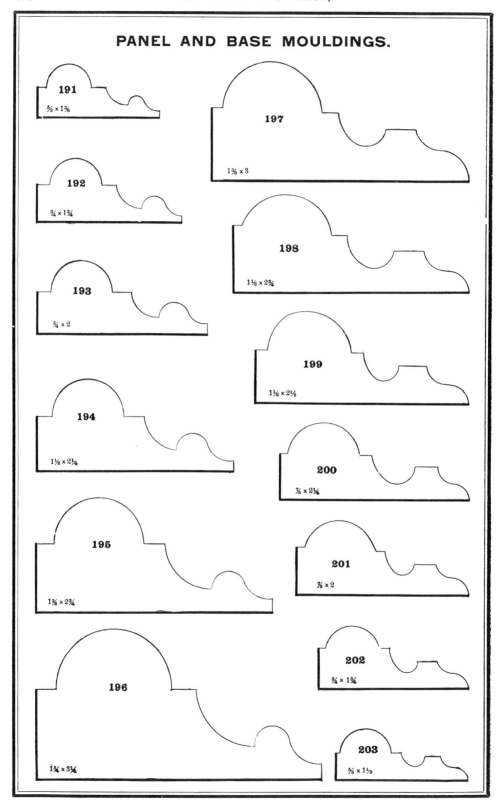

191
⅝ × 1⅜

192
¾ × 1¾

193
¾ × 2

194
1⅛ × 2¼

195
1⅜ × 2¾

196
1¾ × 3¼

197
1⅜ × 3

198
1⅛ × 2¾

199
1⅛ × 2½

200
⅞ × 2¼

201
⅞ × 2

202
¾ × 1¾

203
⅝ × 1½

PANEL AND BASE MOULDINGS.

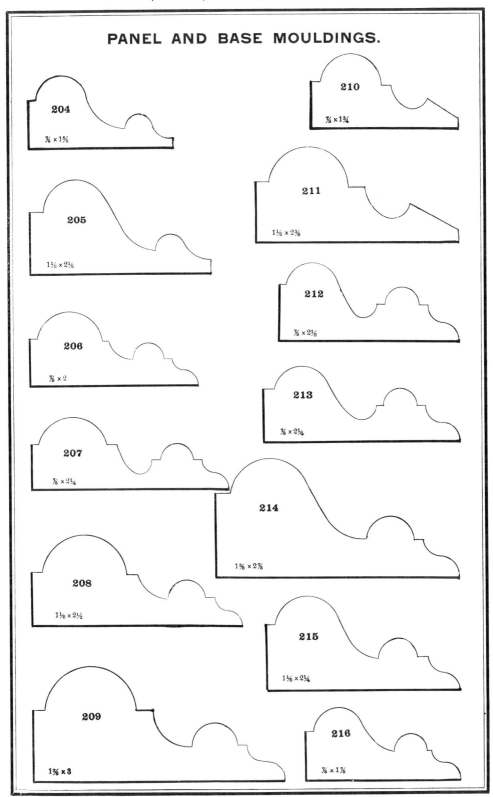

BAND MOULDINGS.

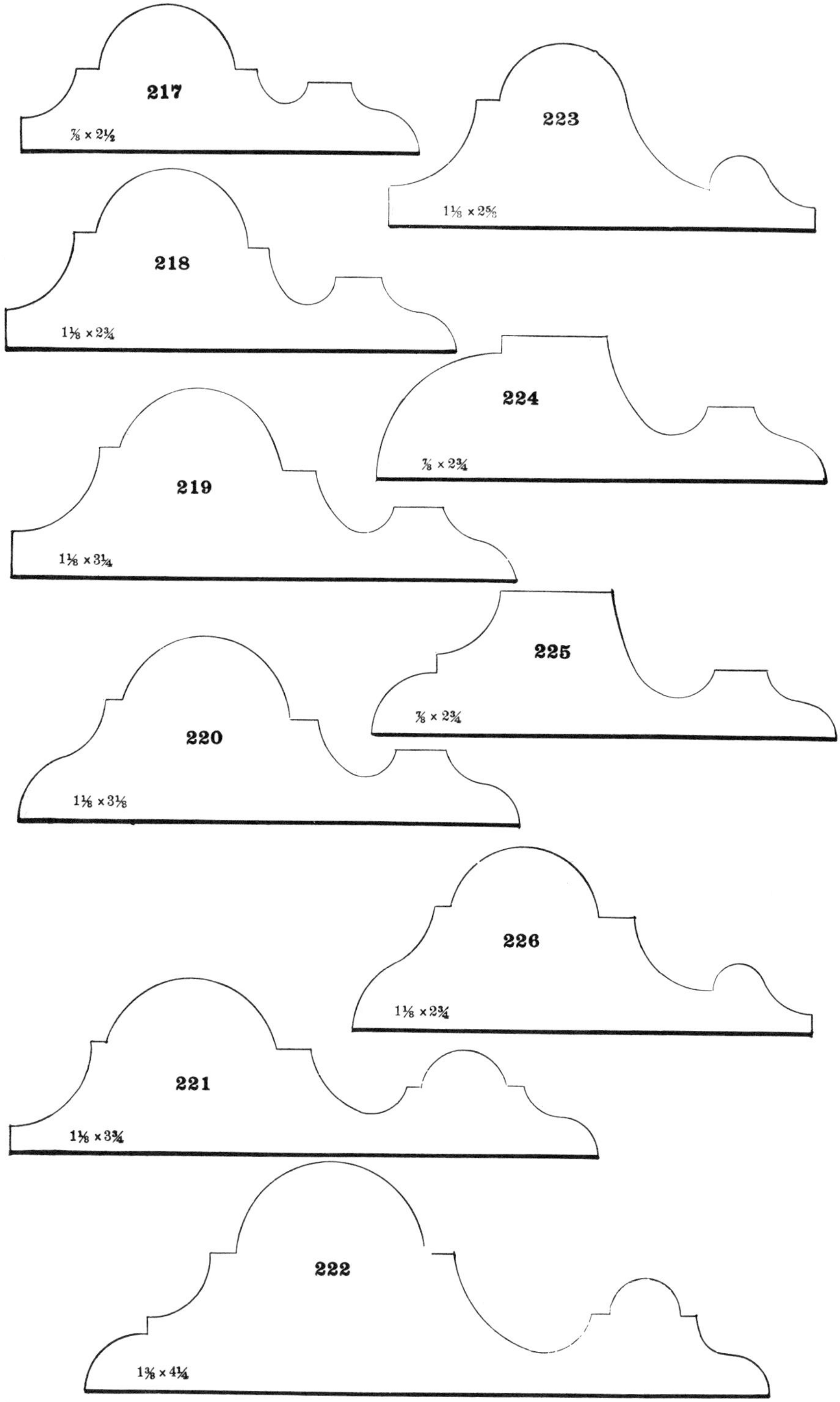
217
⅞ x 2½
223
1⅛ x 2⅝
218
1⅛ x 2¾
224
⅞ x 2¾
219
1⅛ x 3¼
225
⅞ x 2¾
220
1⅛ x 3⅛
226
1⅛ x 2¾
221
1⅛ x 3¾
222
1⅜ x 4¼

BAND MOULDINGS.

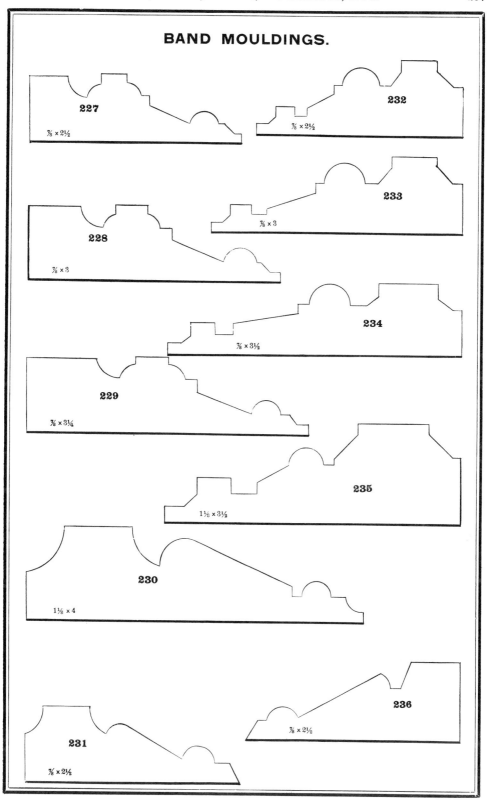

BAND MOULDINGS.

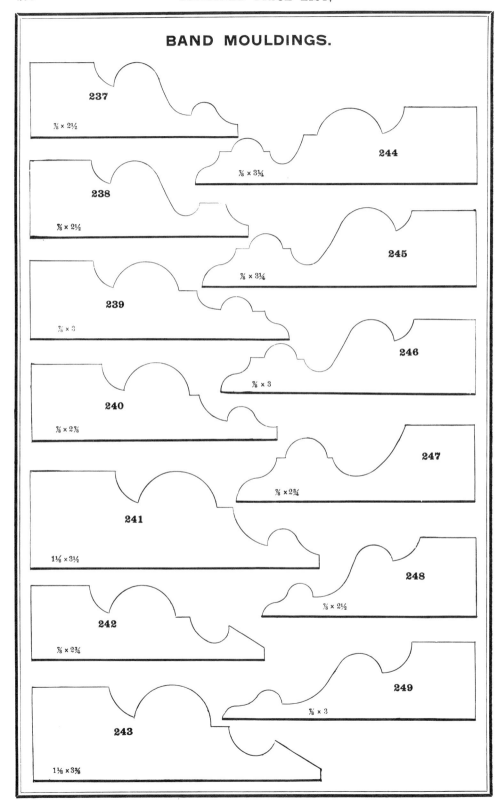

237   ⅞ × 2½

238   ⅞ × 2½

239   ⅞ × 3

240   ⅞ × 2⅞

241   1⅛ × 3½

242   ⅞ × 2¾

243   1⅛ × 3⅜

244   ⅞ × 3¼

245   ⅞ × 3¼

246   ⅞ × 3

247   ⅞ × 2¾

248   ⅞ × 2½

249   ⅞ × 3

BAND MOULDINGS.

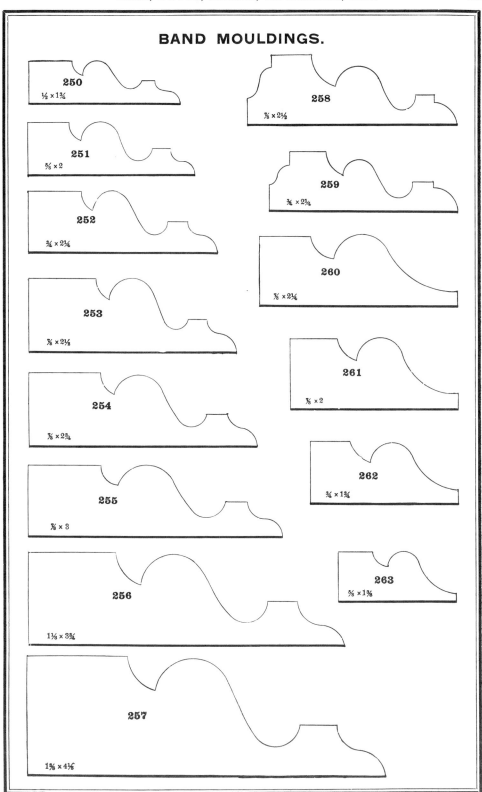

250
½ × 1¾

251
⅝ × 2

252
¾ × 2¼

253
⅞ × 2½

254
⅞ × 2¾

255
⅞ × 3

256
1⅛ × 3¾

257
1⅜ × 4⅛

258
⅞ × 2½

259
¾ × 2¼

260
⅞ × 2¼

261
⅞ × 2

262
¾ × 1¾

263
⅝ × 1⅝

BAND MOULDINGS.

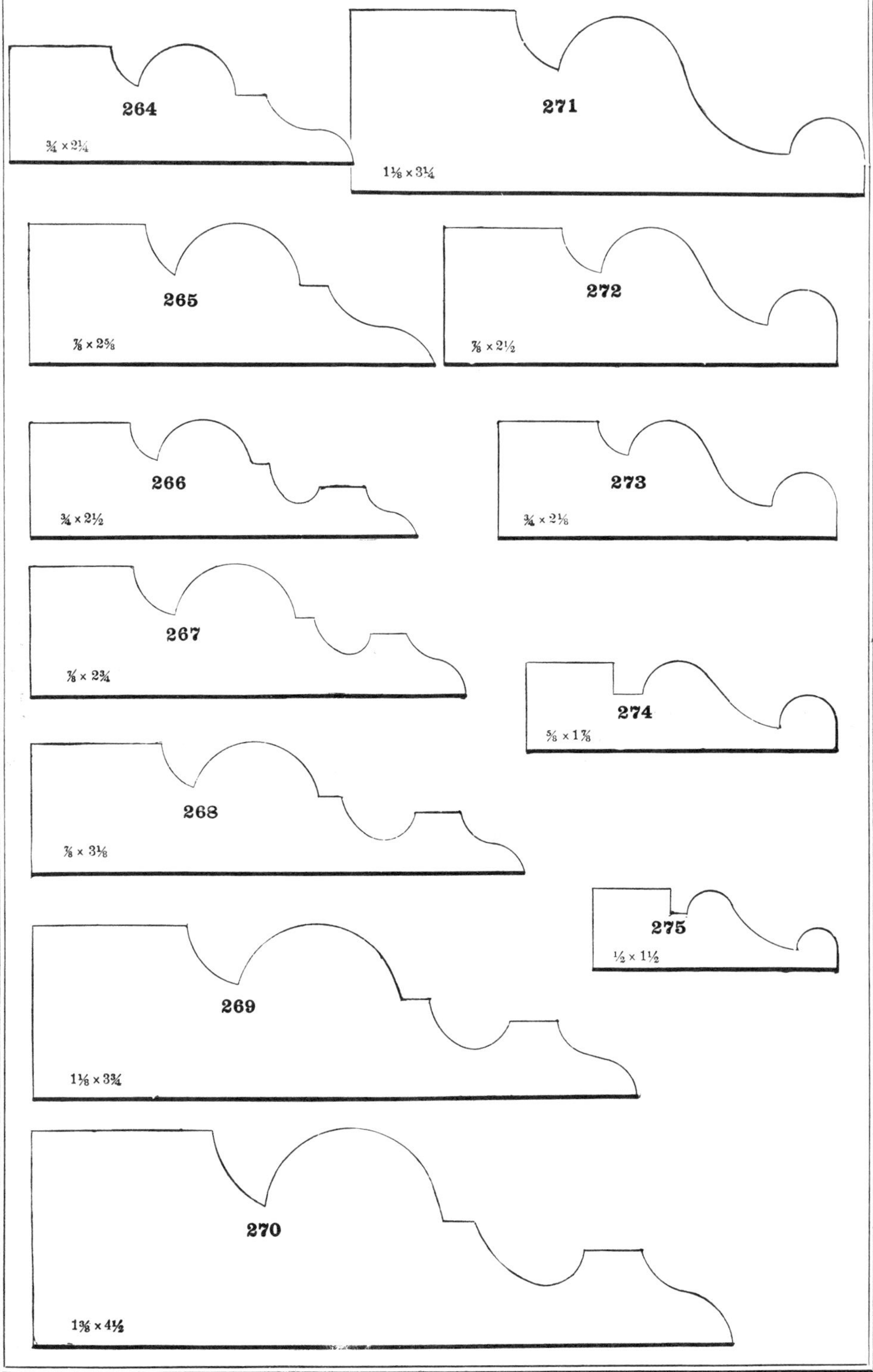
264
¾ × 2¼
271
1⅛ × 3¼
265
⅞ × 2⅝
272
⅞ × 2½
266
¾ × 2½
273
¾ × 2⅛
267
⅞ × 2¾
274
⅝ × 1⅞
268
⅞ × 3⅛
275
½ × 1½
269
1⅛ × 3¾
270
1⅜ × 4½

RABBETED PANEL AND BASE MOULDINGS.

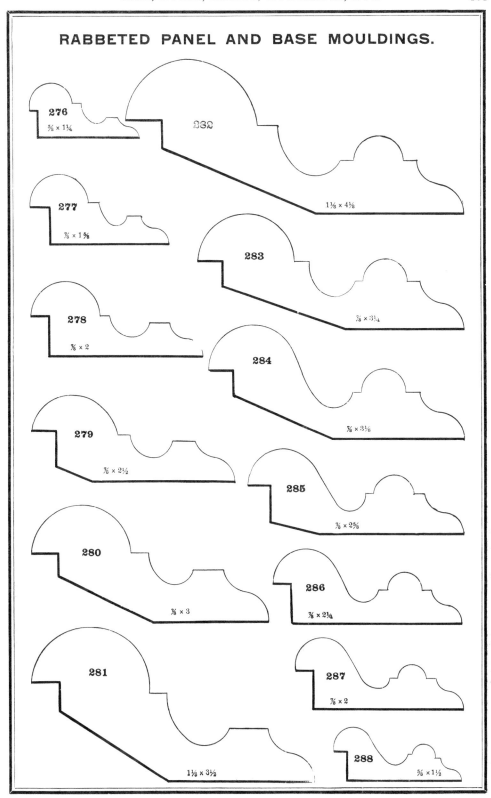

276
⅝ × 1¼

282
1⅛ × 4⅛

277
⅞ × 1⅝

283
⅞ × 3¼

278
⅞ × 2

284
⅞ × 3⅛

279
⅞ × 2½

285
⅞ × 2⅝

280
⅞ × 3

286
⅞ × 2¼

281
1⅛ × 3½

287
⅞ × 2

288
⅝ × 1½

RABBETED PANEL AND BASE MOULDINGS.

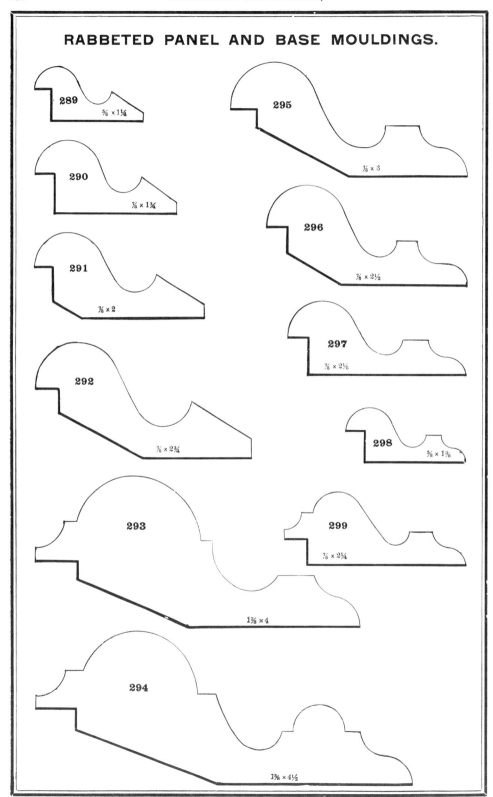

RABBETED PANEL AND BASE MOULDINGS.

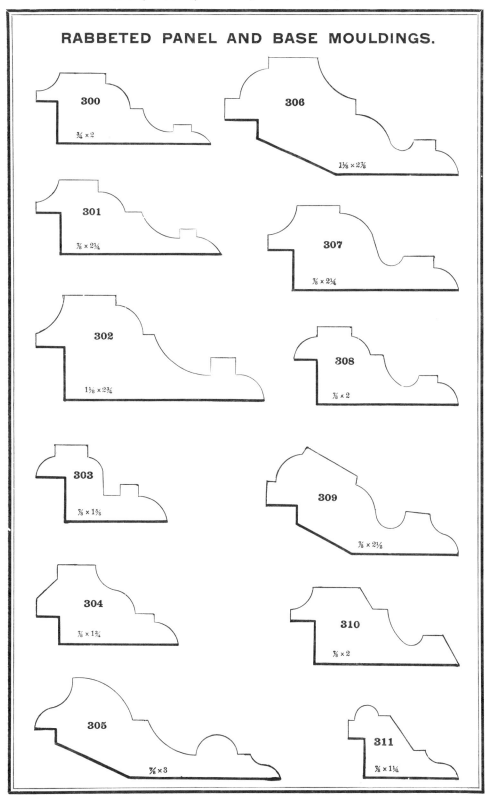

300
¾ × 2

306
1⅛ × 2⅞

301
⅞ × 2¼

307
⅞ × 2¼

302
1⅛ × 2¾

308
⅞ × 2

303
⅞ × 1⅝

309
⅞ × 2½

304
⅞ × 1¾

310
⅞ × 2

305
⅞ × 3

311
⅞ × 1¼

RABBETED PANEL AND BASE MOULDINGS.

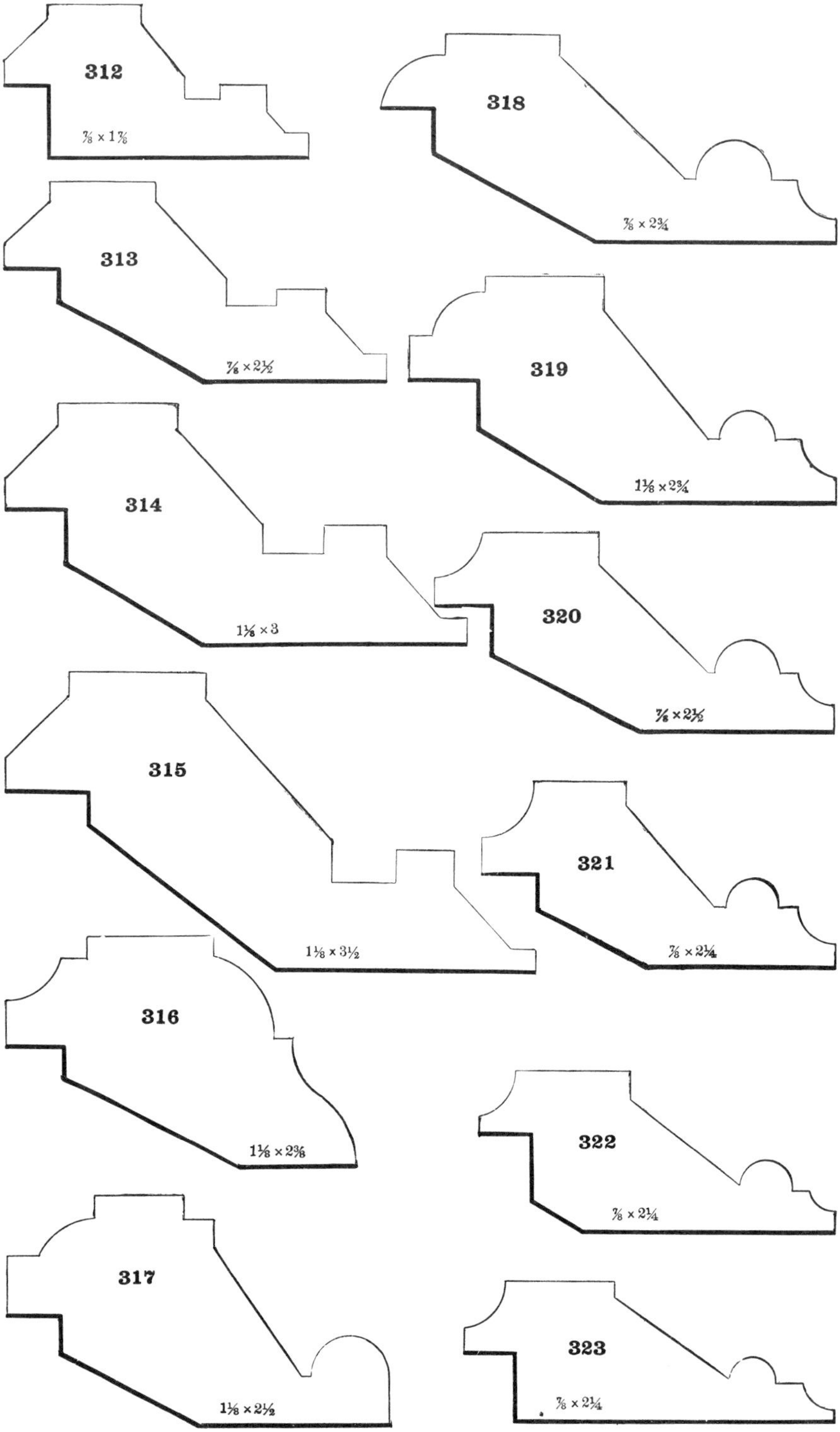
312
⅞ × 1⅞
318
⅞ × 2¾
313
⅞ × 2½
319
1⅛ × 2¾
314
1⅛ × 3
320
⅞ × 2½
315
1⅛ × 3½
321
⅞ × 2¼
316
1⅛ × 2⅜
322
⅞ × 2¼
317
1⅛ × 2½
323
⅞ × 2¼

RABBETED PANEL AND BASE MOULDINGS.

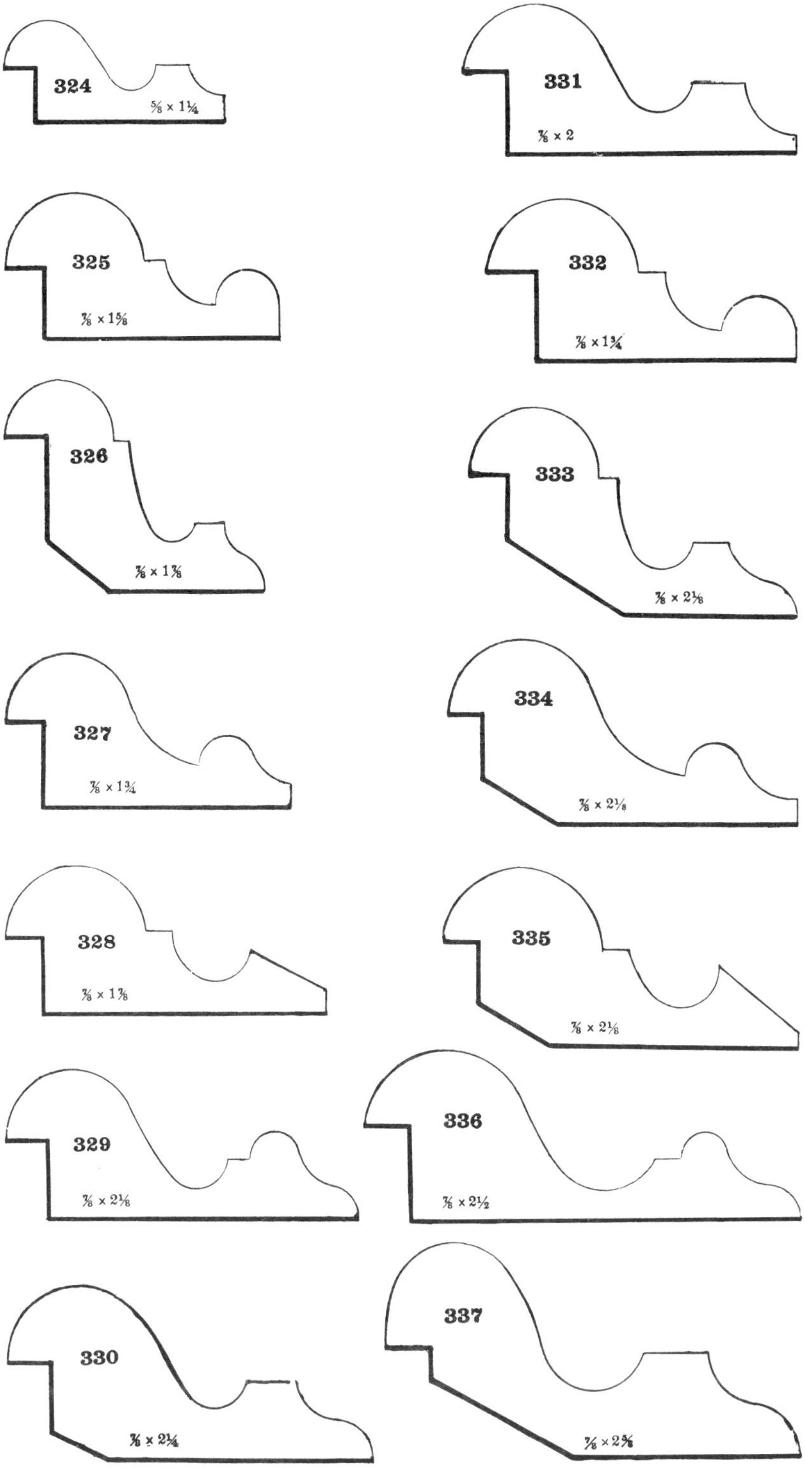
324
⅝ × 1¼
331
⅞ × 2
325
⅞ × 1⅝
332
⅞ × 1¾
326
⅞ × 1⅞
333
⅞ × 2⅛
327
⅞ × 1¾
334
⅞ × 2⅛
328
⅞ × 1⅞
335
⅞ × 2⅛
329
⅞ × 2⅛
336
⅞ × 2½
330
⅞ × 2¼
337
⅞ × 2⅝

ASTRAGAL AND BATTENS.

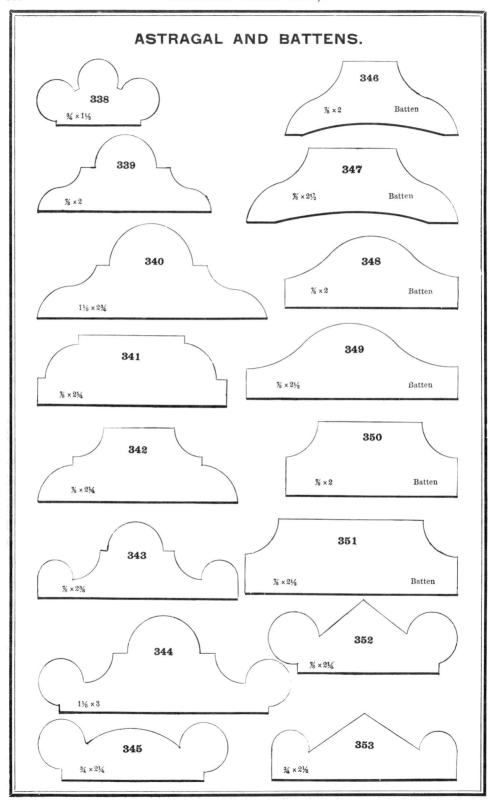

NOSINGS.

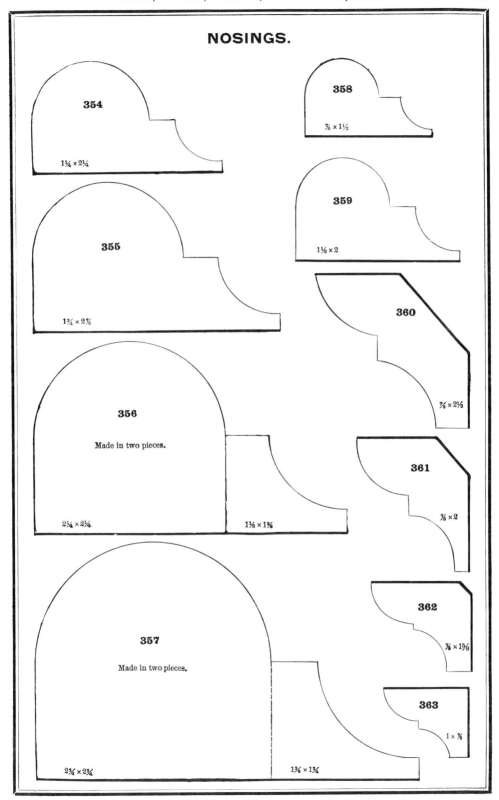

354 — $1\frac{1}{4} \times 2\frac{1}{4}$

355 — $1\frac{3}{4} \times 2\frac{7}{8}$

356 — Made in two pieces. — $2\frac{1}{4} \times 2\frac{1}{4}$ — $1\frac{1}{8} \times 1\frac{3}{4}$

357 — Made in two pieces. — $2\frac{3}{4} \times 2\frac{3}{4}$ — $1\frac{3}{8} \times 1\frac{3}{4}$

358 — $\frac{7}{8} \times 1\frac{1}{2}$

359 — $1\frac{1}{8} \times 2$

360 — $\frac{7}{8} \times 2\frac{1}{2}$

361 — $\frac{7}{8} \times 2$

362 — $\frac{7}{8} \times 1\frac{5}{8}$

363 — $1 \times \frac{7}{8}$

PEW BACK RAIL, WAINSCOTING CAP, AND THRESHOLDS.

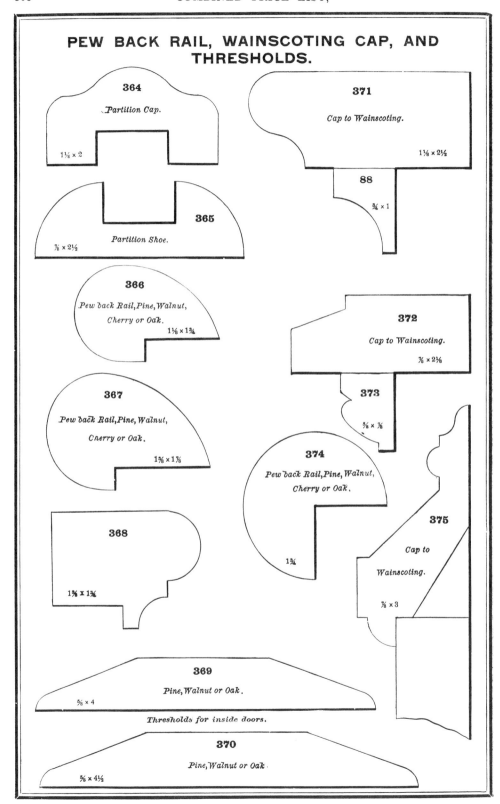

364

Partition Cap.

1⅛ × 2

371

Cap to Wainscoting.

1⅛ × 2½

88

¾ × 1

365

Partition Shoe.

⅞ × 2½

366

Pew back Rail, Pine, Walnut, Cherry or Oak.

1⅛ × 1¾

372

Cap to Wainscoting.

⅞ × 2⅛

373

⅝ × ⅞

367

Pew back Rail, Pine, Walnut, Cherry or Oak.

1⅜ × 1⅞

374

Pew back Rail, Pine, Walnut, Cherry or Oak.

1¾

375

Cap to Wainscoting.

⅞ × 3

368

1⅜ × 1¾

369

Pine, Walnut or Oak.

⅝ × 4

Thresholds for inside doors.

370

Pine, Walnut or Oak.

⅝ × 4½

SUNK PANEL MOULDINGS.

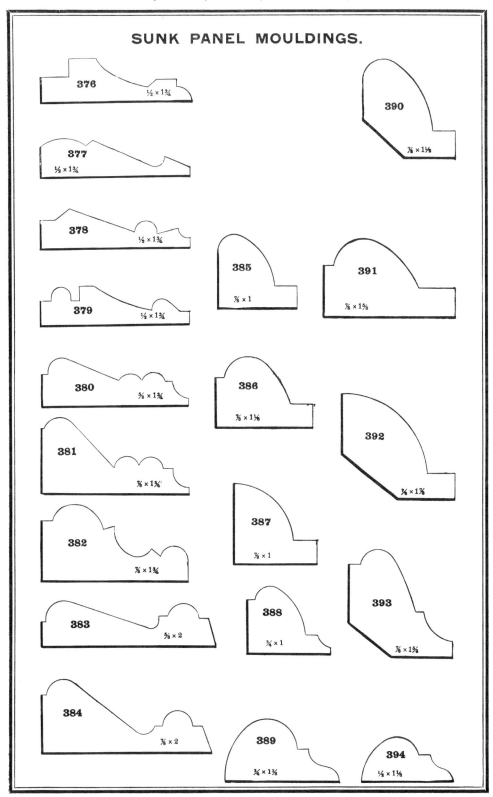

LATTICE, BACK BAND, AND TRANSOM BAR MOULDING.

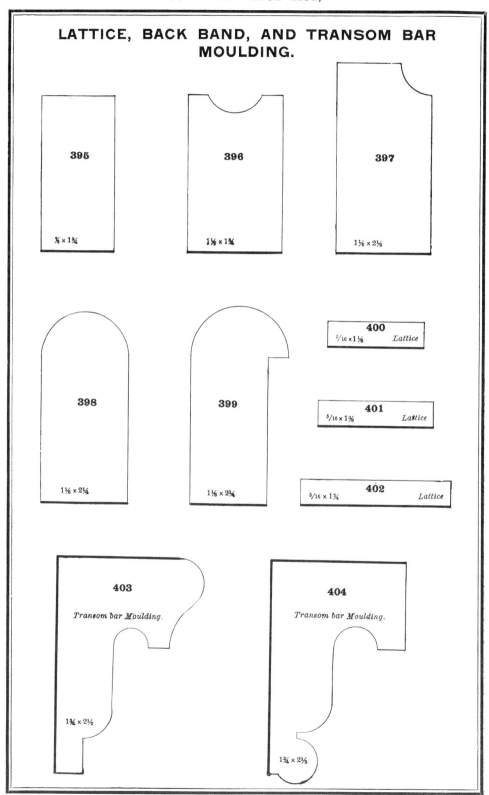

INTERIOR CORNICE.

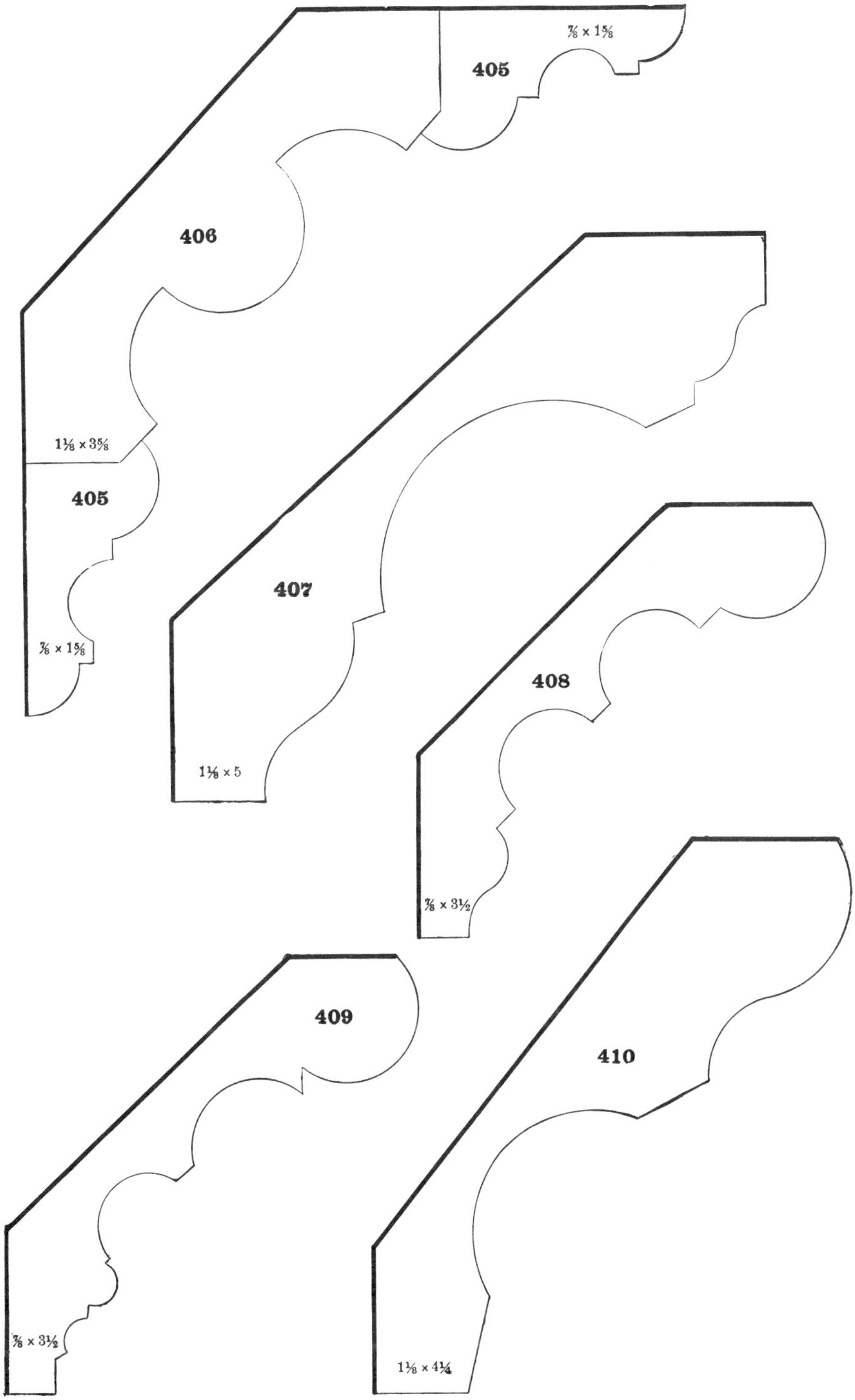
⅞ × 1⅝
405
406
1⅛ × 3⅝
405
⅞ × 1⅝
407
1⅛ × 5
408
⅞ × 3½
409
⅞ × 3½
410
1⅛ × 4¼

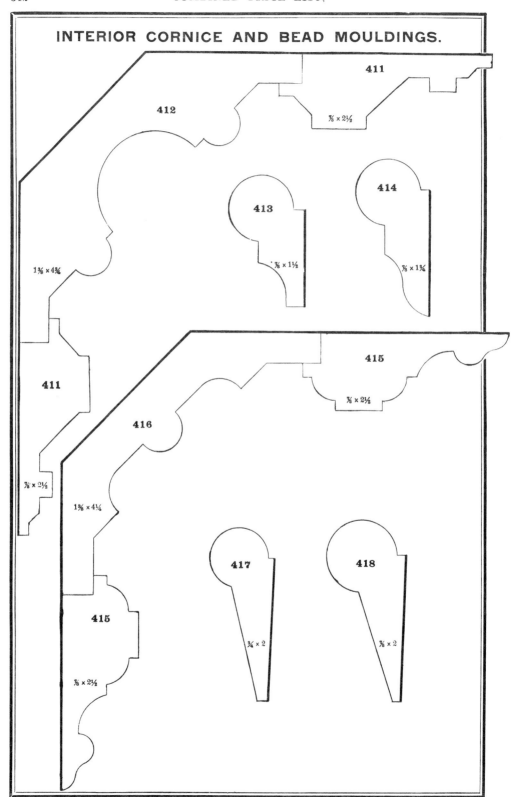

INTERIOR CORNICE AND BEAD MOULDINGS.

SECTION OF WINDOW FRAME.

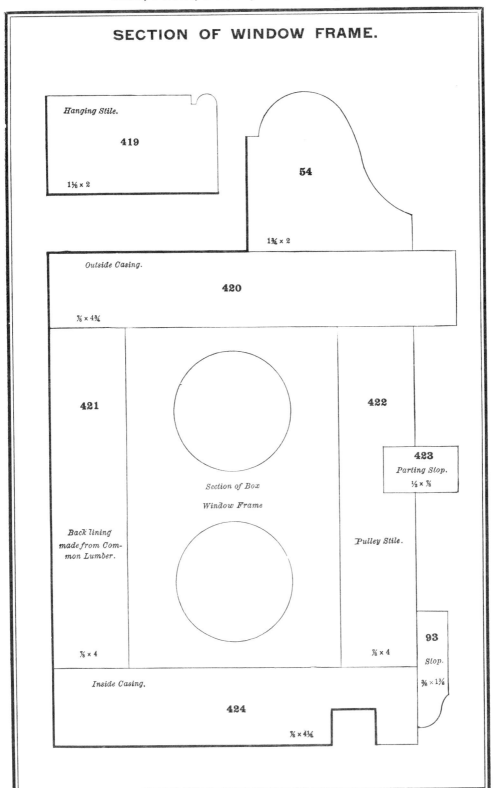

Hanging Stile.

419

1⅛ × 2

54

1¾ × 2

Outside Casing.

420

⅞ × 4¾

421

422

423

Parting Slop.

½ × ⅞

Section of Box

Window Frame

Back lining made from Common Lumber.

Pulley Stile.

⅞ × 4

⅞ × 4

93

Slop.

⅜ × 1⅜

Inside Casing.

424

⅞ × 4¼

SECTION OF WINDOW FRAME.

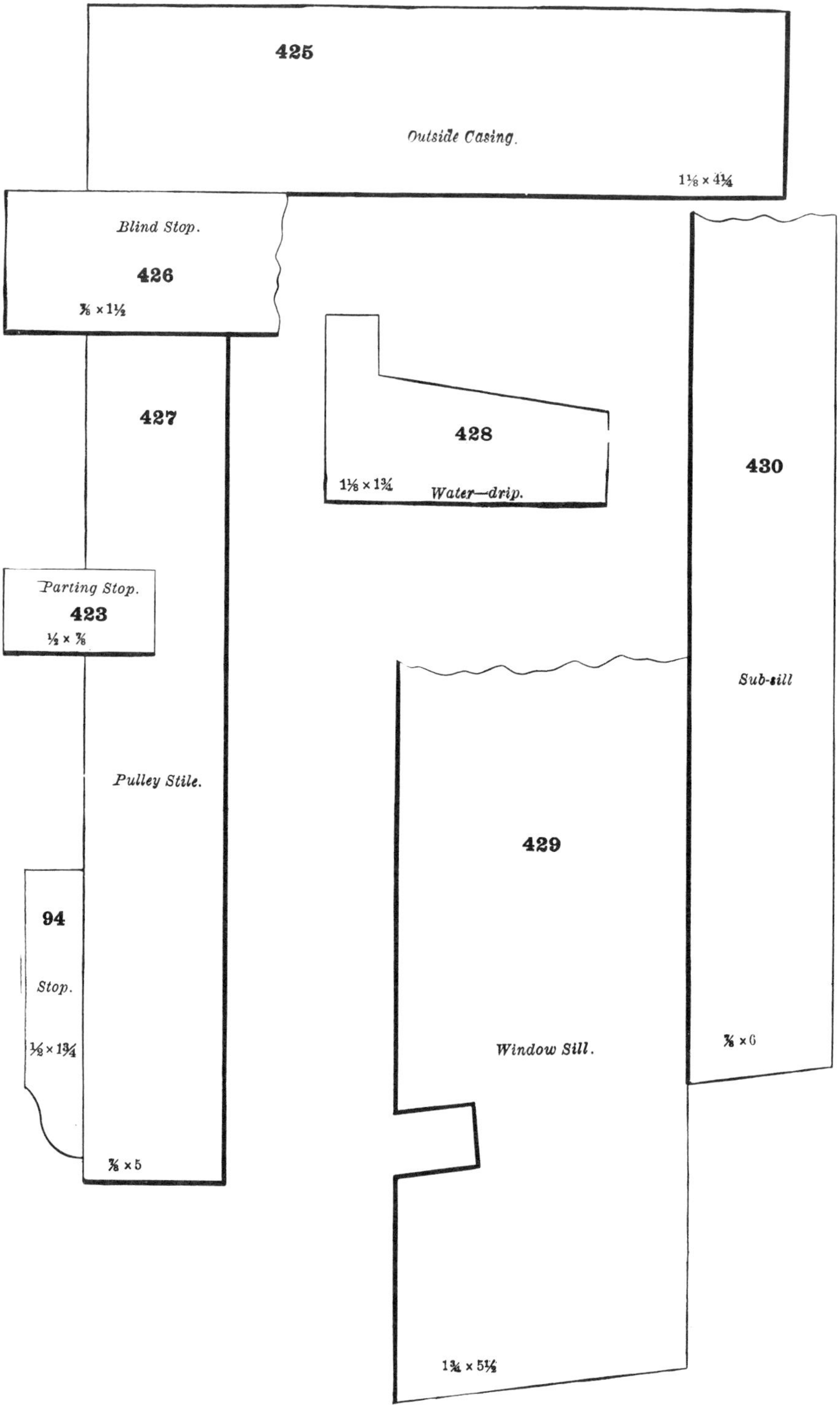
425
Outside Casing.
1⅛ × 4¼
Blind Stop.
426
⅜ × 1½
427
428
1⅛ × 1¾
Water—drip.
430
Parting Stop.
423
½ × ⅞
Sub-sill
Pulley Stile.
429
94
Stop.
½ × 1¾
Window Sill.
⅞ × 6
⅞ × 5
1¾ × 5⅛

WATER TABLE OR DRIP CAP.

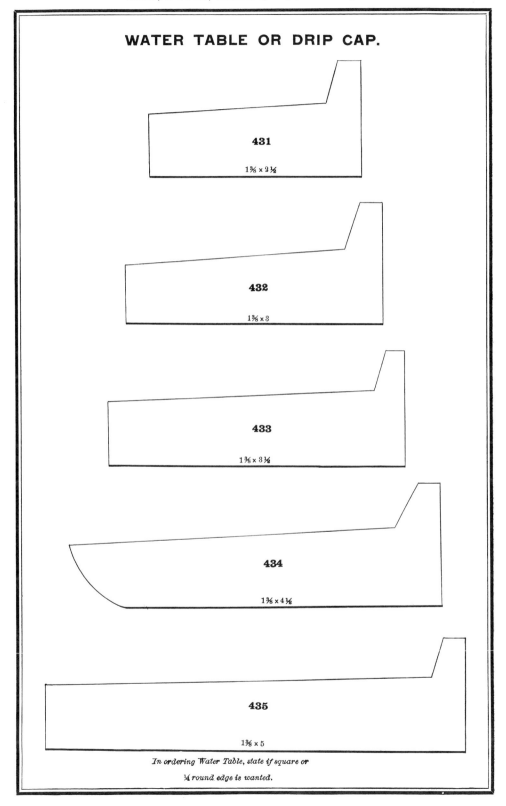

431

1⅜ × 2½

432

1⅜ × 3

433

1⅜ × 3½

434

1⅜ × 4½

435

1⅜ × 5

In ordering Water Table, state if square or
¼ round edge is wanted.

CEILING AND WINDOW STOOLS.

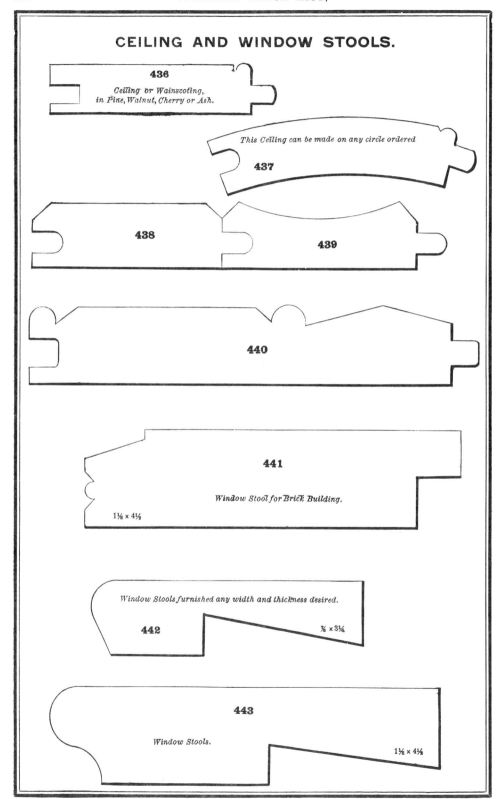

436
*Ceiling or Wainscoting,
in Pine, Walnut, Cherry or Ash.*

This Ceiling can be made on any circle ordered
437

438

439

440

441

Window Stool for Brick Building.

1⅛ × 4½

442

Window Stools furnished any width and thickness desired.

⅞ × 3¼

443

Window Stools.

1⅛ × 4½

INSIDE FINISH.

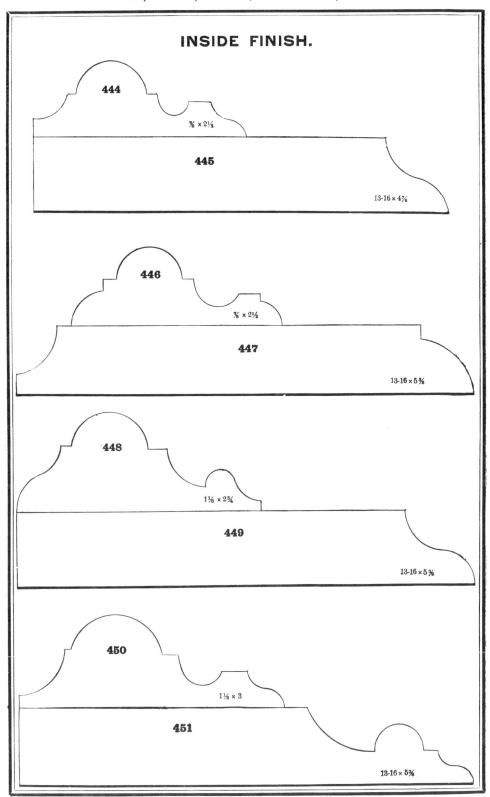

444

⅞ × 2½

445

13-16 × 4⅞

446

⅞ × 2½

447

13-16 × 5⅜

448

1⅛ × 2¾

449

13-16 × 5⅜

450

1⅛ × 3

451

13-16 × 5⅜

INSIDE FINISH.

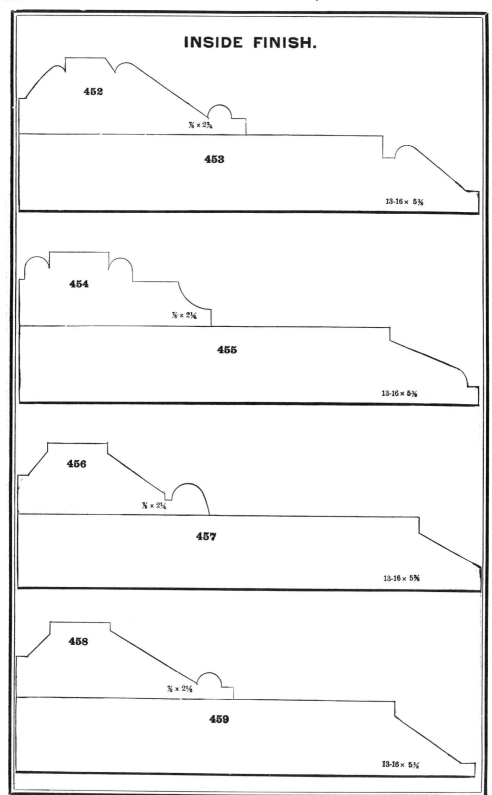

452

453

⅞ × 2¾

13-16 × 5⅜

454

455

⅞ × 2¼

13-16 × 5⅜

456

457

⅞ × 2¼

13-16 × 5⅜

458

459

⅞ × 2½

13-16 × 5⅜

CASINGS.

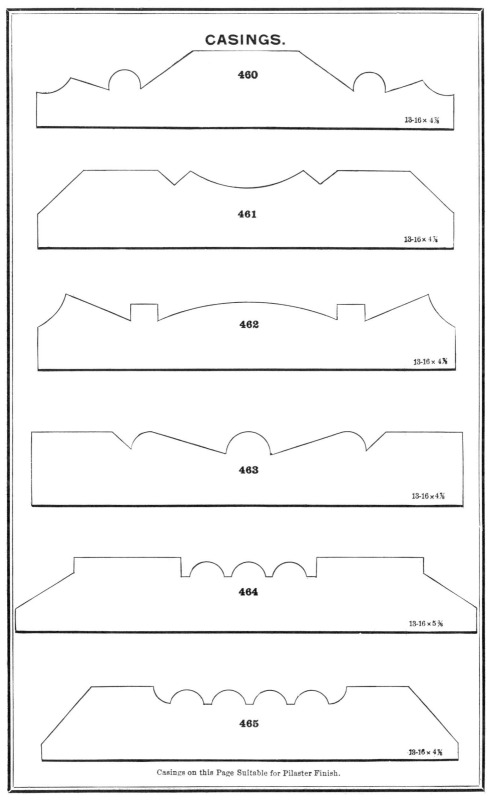

460

13-16 × 4⅞

461

13-16 × 4⅞

462

13-16 × 4⅞

463

13-16 × 4⅞

464

13-16 × 5⅜

465

13-16 × 4⅞

Casings on this Page Suitable for Pilaster Finish.

EASTLAKE AND QUEEN ANNE CASINGS.

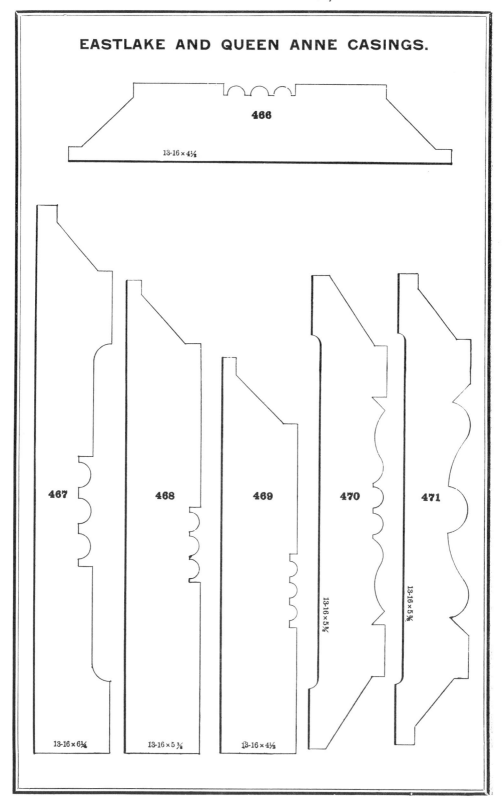

466

13-16 × 4½

467   468   469   470   471

13-16 × 6¼   13-16 × 5⅜   13-16 × 4½   13-16 × 5⅜   13-16 × 5¾

EASTLAKE AND QUEEN ANNE CASINGS.

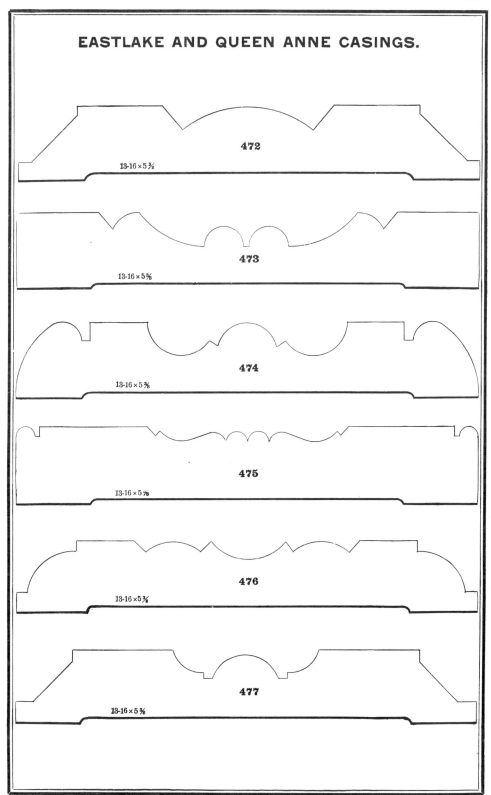

472

13-16 × 5 ⅜

473

13-16 × 5 ⅜

474

13-16 × 5 ⅜

475

13-16 × 5 ⅞

476

13-16 × 5 ⅜

477

13-16 × 5 ⅜

CASINGS.

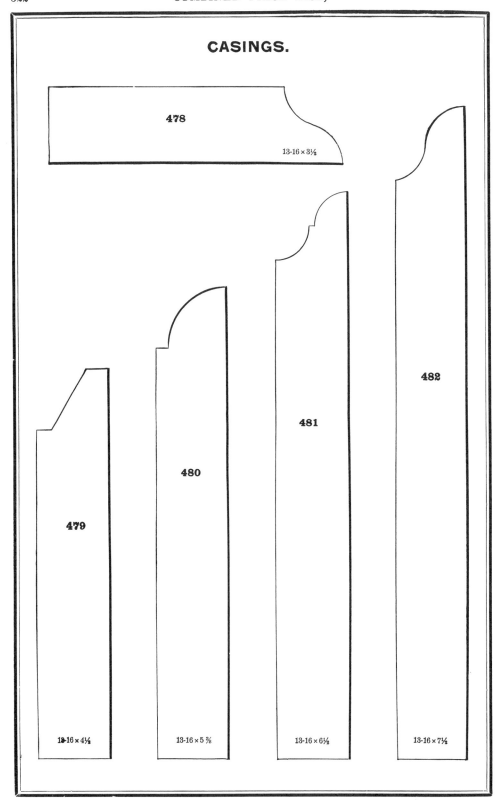

478   13-16 × 3½

482

481

480

479

13-16 × 4½   13-16 × 5⅝   13-16 × 6½   13-16 × 7½

BASE.

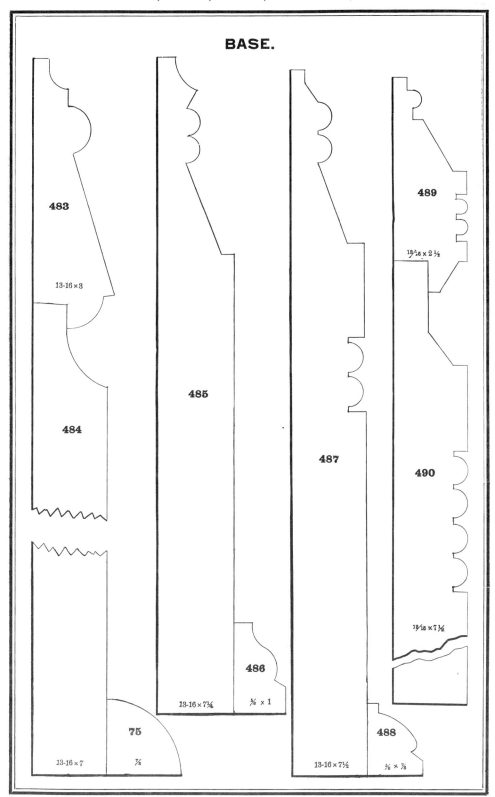

483

13-16 × 3

484

485

487

486

⅝ × 1

75

13-16 × 7½

13-16 × 7

⅞

489

13⁄16 × 2 ½

490

13⁄16 × 7 ⅛

488

⅝ × ⅞

13-16 × 7½

DROP SIDING, FLOORING, AND SHIP LAP.

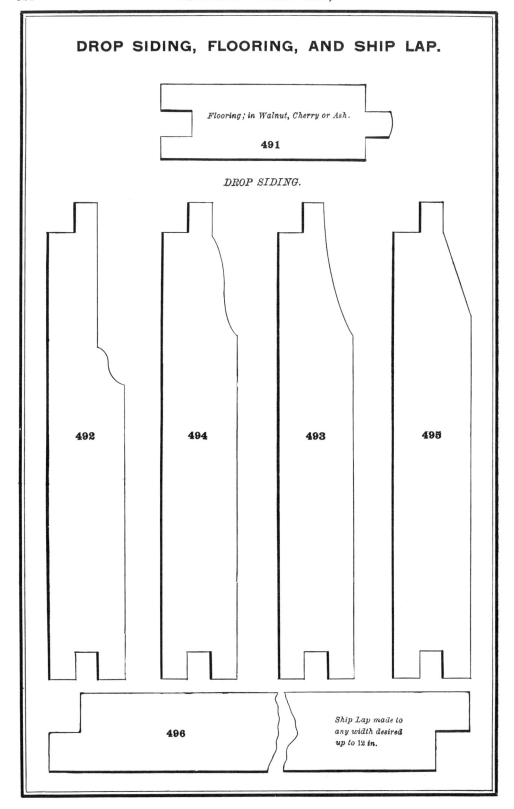

Flooring; in Walnut, Cherry or Ash.

491

DROP SIDING.

492

494

493

495

496

Ship Lap made to any width desired up to 12 in.

CASINGS.

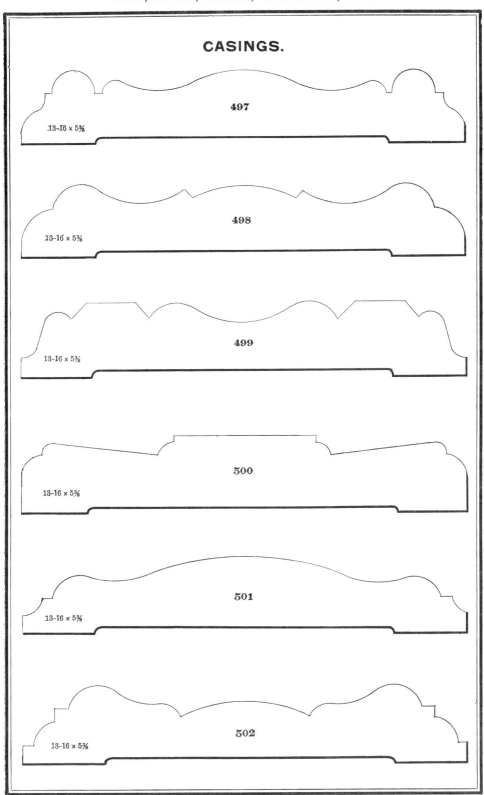

497

13–16 x 5⅝

498

13–16 x 5⅝

499

13–16 x 5⅝

500

13–16 x 5⅝

501

13–16 x 5⅝

502

13–16 x 5⅝

CASINGS.

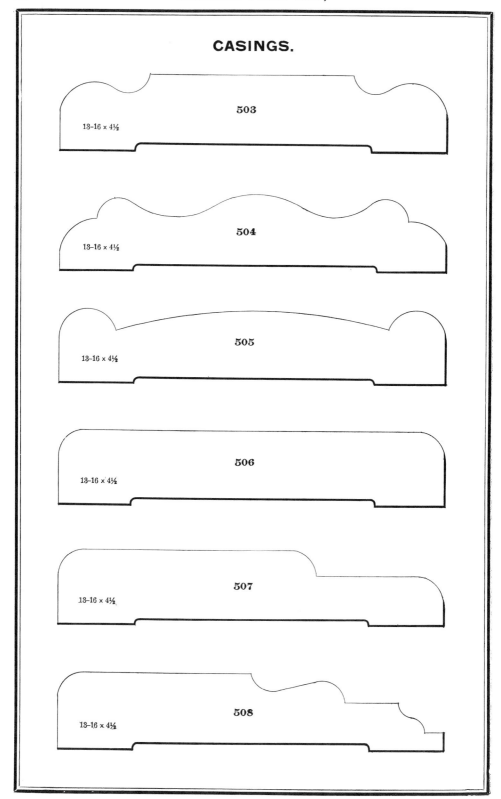

CASINGS.

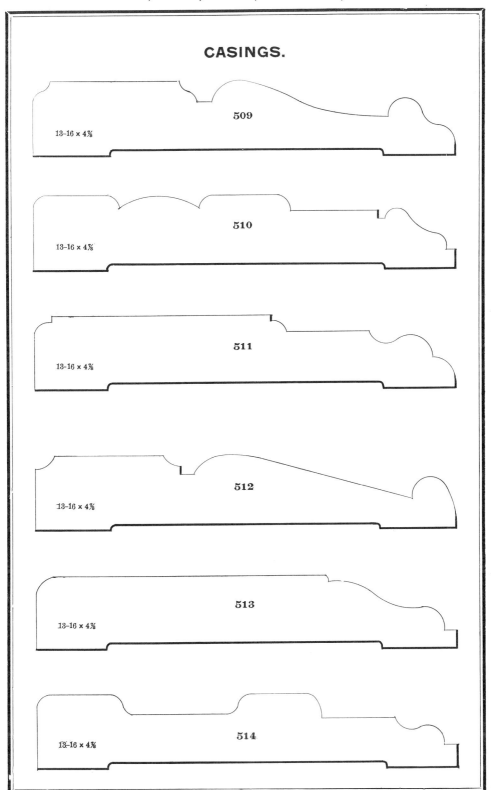

509

13–16 x 4⅝

510

13–16 x 4⅝

511

13–16 x 4⅝

512

13–16 x 4⅝

513

13–16 x 4⅝

514

13–16 x 4⅝

INSIDE FINISH.

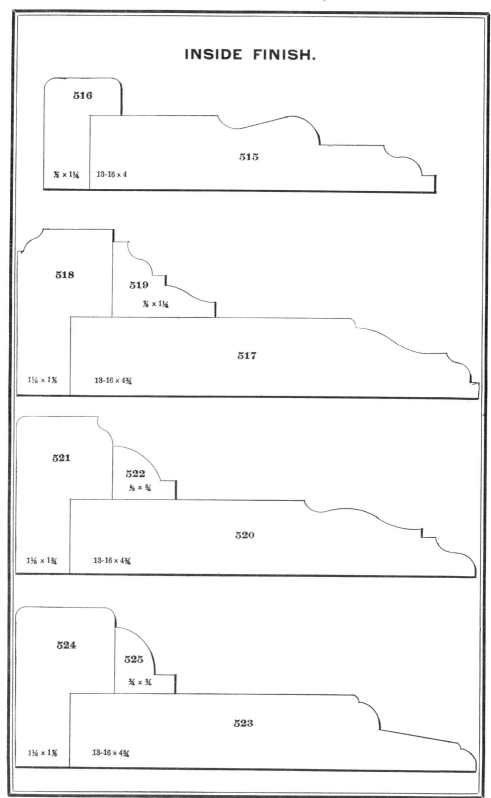

BASE.

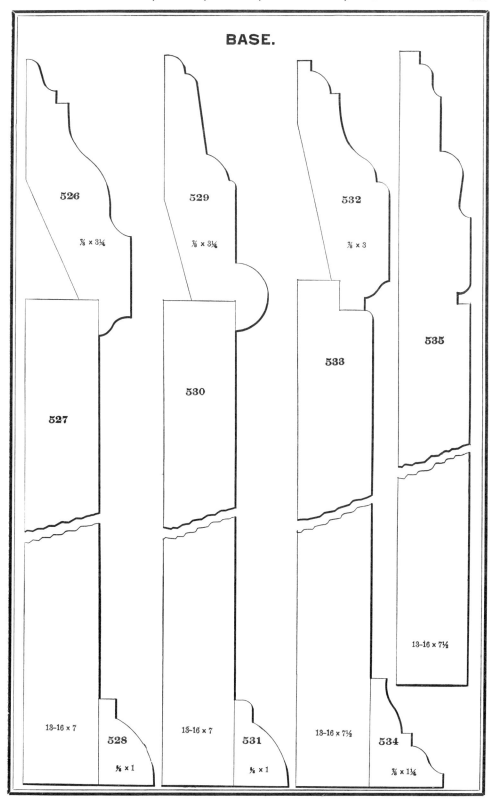

526 ⅞ × 3¼

529 ⅞ × 3¼

532 ⅞ × 3

535

527

530

533

13-16 × 7½

528 ⅝ × 1

531 ⅝ × 1

534 ⅞ × 1¼

13-16 × 7

13-16 × 7

13-16 × 7½

BASE.

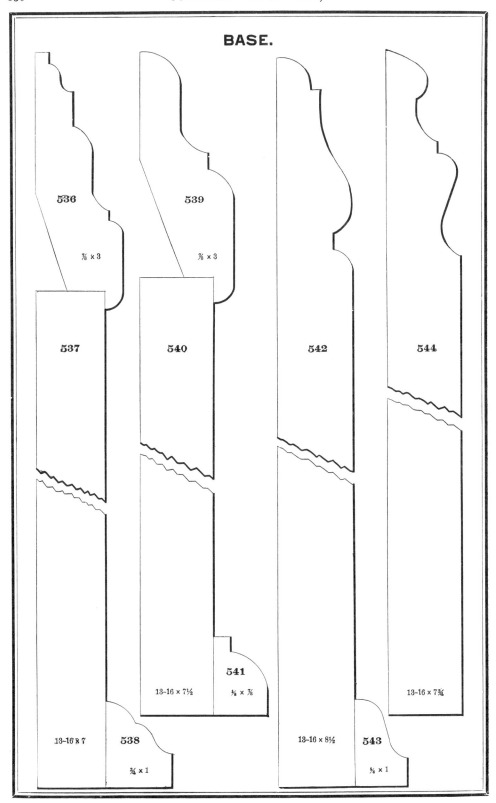

536

⅞ × 3

539

⅞ × 3

537

540

542

544

541

13–16 × 7½

⅝ × ⅞

13–16 × 7¾

13–16 × 7

538

¾ × 1

13–16 × 8½

543

⅝ × 1

PRICE OF MOULDINGS,

PER HUNDRED FEET (*Lineal Measure*).

Adopted by the Wholesale Sash, Door, and Blind Manufacturers' Association of the Northwest.

This list supersedes all former issues in conflict with it.

No.	Price.	No.	Price.	No.	Price.	No.	Price.	No.	Price.	No.	Price.
1	$2.50	63	$1.70	125	$2.20	187	$8.75	249	$3.00	311	$1.40
2	5.00	64	2.50	126	2.00	188	5.40	250	1.75	312	2.10
3	4.50	65	4.40	127	1.80	189	4.75	251	2.00	313	2.75
4	2.00	66	16.50	128	1.60	190	3.75	252	2.25	314	4.50
5	5.50	67	11.25	129	1.25	191	1.40	253	2.50	315	5.25
6	9.00	68	6.25	130	1.10	192	1.75	254	2.75	316	3.60
7	3.00	69	4.40	131	1.10	193	2.00	255	3.00	317	3.75
8	3.50	70	1.00	132	1.25	194	3.40	256	5.65	318	3.05
9	12.60	71	1.00	133	1.60	195	5.00	257	7.45	319	4.15
10	14.40	72	4.40	134	1.80	196	8.15	258	2.50	320	2.75
11	4.00	73	1.00	135	2.00	197	5.40	259	2.25	321	2.50
12	2.50	74	1.00	136	1.00	198	4.15	260	2.25	322	2.50
13	8.25	75	1.00	137	1.00	199	3.75	261	2.00	323	2.50
14	3.50	76	1.65	138	1.50	200	2.25	262	1.75	324	1.40
15	4.50	77	2.00	139	1.90	201	2.00	263	1.40	325	1.80
16	5.00	78	2.50	140	3.40	202	1.75	264	2.25	326	2.10
17	3.00	79	4.50	141	3.75	203	1.50	265	2.65	327	2.00
18	4.00	80	3.40	142	5.40	204	1.65	266	2.50	328	2.10
19	4.00	81	1.75	143	5.00	205	3.20	267	2.75	329	2.35
20	9.00	82	1.40	144	3.40	206	2.00	268	3.15	330	2.56
21	10.50	83	1.15	145	1.75	207	2.25	269	5.65	331	2.20
22	12.60	84	1.00	146	1.00	208	3.75	270	8.10	332	2.00
23	5.00	85	1.00	147	3.40	209	5.40	271	4.90	333	2.35
24	3.00	86	1.00	148	1.75	210	1.75	272	2.50	334	2.35
25	9.00	87	1.00	149	1.50	211	3.60	273	2.15	335	2.35
26	3.50	88	1.00	150	1.25	212	2.15	274	1.90	336	2.75
27	6.75	89	1.15	151	1.00	213	2.25	275	1.50	337	2.90
28	2.50	90	1.75	152	1.00	214	5.20	276	1.40	338	1.50
29	7.50	91	2.25	153	1.00	215	3.40	277	1.80	339	2.00
30	4.00	92	.90	154	1.15	216	1.90	278	2.20	340	4.15
31	2.00	93	1.00	155	1.40	217	2.50	279	2.75	341	2.25
32	2.00	94	1.20	156	2.65	218	4.15	280	3.30	342	2.25
33	7.50	95	1.40	157	3.60	219	4.90	281	5.25	343	2.40
34	3.00	96	1.60	158	6.00	220	4.70	282	6.20	344	4.50
35	6.00	97	1.75	159	6.60	221	5.65	283	3.60	345	2.25
36	6.75	98	1.80	160	3.85	222	7.65	284	3.45	346	
37	2.50	99	1.55	161	2.80	223	4.00	285	2.90	347	
38	3.50	100	1.35	162	1.50	224	2.75	286	2.50	348	
39	4.50	101	1.10	163	1.15	225	2.75	287	2.20	349	
40	7.20	102	1.00	164	1.00	226	4.15	288	1.65	350	
41	1.15	103	2.00	165	1.00	227	2.50	289	1.40	351	
42	1.15	104	1.80	166	1.00	228	3.00	290	2.00	352	2.25
43	1.15	105	1.60	167	1.15	229	3.25	291	2.20	353	2.15
44	1.40	106	1.40	168	1.50	230	6.00	292	3.00	354	4.00
45	2.00	107	1.10	169	1.65	231	2.50	293	7.20	355	7.25
46	2.10	108	1.00	170	2.80	232	2.50	294	8.10	356	13.30
47	1.65	109	1.10	171	4.00	233	3.00	295	3.30	357	19.60
48	2.65	110	1.25	172	7.80	234	3.50	296	2.75	358	1.50
49	6.30	111	1.60	173	4.30	235	5.25	297	2.35	359	3.00
50	2.50	112	1.80	174	3.20	236	2.50	298	1.55	360	2.50
51	3.15	113	2.00	175	1.75	237	2.50	299	2.50	361	2.00
52	3.60	114	1.00	176	1.50	238	2.50	300	2.20	362	1.65
53	1.00	115	1.10	177	1.25	239	3.00	301	2.50	363	1.00
54	5.00	116	1.35	178	1.00	240	2.90	302	4.15	364	3.00
55	1.00	117	1.55	179	1.00	241	5.25	303	1.80	365	2.50
56	4.10	118	1.80	180	1.15	242	2.75	304	2.00	366	2.65
57	1.00	119	2.00	181	1.40	243	5.10	305	3.20	367	3.40
58	4.90	120	1.80	182	1.40	244	3.25	306	4.35	368	3.15
59	1.00	121	1.55	183	1.50	245	3.25	307	2.50	369	4.00
60	1.00	122	1.35	184	1.65	246	3.00	308	2.20	370	4.50
61	1.00	123	1.10	185	1.90	247	2.75	309	2.75	371	3.75
62	1.00	124	1.00	186	2.15	248	2.50	310	2.20	372	2.15

N. B.—An extra price will be charged for all Mouldings not included in the above list.

PRICE OF MOULDINGS,

PER HUNDRED FEET (*Lineal Measure*).

Adopted by the Wholesale Sash, Door and Blind Manufacturers' Association of the Northwest.

This list supersedes all former issues in conflict with it.

No.	Price.	No.	Price.	No.	Price.	No.	Price.	No.	Price.	No.	Price.
373	$1.00	402	$1.20	431	$4.50	460	$5 00	489	$3.75	518	$2.85
374	4.40	403	6.25	432	5.40	461	5.00	490	7.50	519	1.25
375	3.30	404	6.25	433	6 30	462	5.00	491		520	4.75
376	1.75	405	1.80	434	8.10	463	5.00	492		521	2 65
377	1.75	406	5 50	435	9.00	464	5.50	493		522	1.00
378	1.75	407	7.50	436		465	5.00	494		523	4.75
379	1.75	408	3.50	437		466	4.50	495		524	2.85
380	1.75	409	3 50	438		467	6.25	496		525	1.00
381	1.75	410	6.40	439		468	5.50	497	5.50	526	3.60
382	1.75	411	2.75	440		469	4.50	498	5.50	527	7.00
383	2 00	412	8.55	441	6.75	470	5.50	499	5.50	528	1.00
384	2.00	413	1.50	442	3.60	471	5.50	500	5.50	529	3.60
385	1.00	414	1.75	443	6.75	472	5.50	501	5.50	530	7 00
386	1.15	415	2.75	444	2.50	473	5.50	502	5.50	531	1.00
387	1.00	416	7.65	445	5.00	474	5.50	503	4.50	532	3.30
388	1.00	417	2.00	446	2.50	475	5.50	504	4.50	533	7.50
389	1.40	418	2.00	447	5.50	476	5.50	505	4.50	534	1.25
390	1.50	419	3.00	448	4.15	477	5.50	506	4.50	535	7 50
391	1.65	420	3.75	449	5.50	478	3.50	507	4.50	536	3.30
392	1 90	421	2.40	450	4.50	479	4.50	508	4.50	537	7.00
393	1.65	422	3.20	451	5.50	480	5.50	509	5.00	538	1.00
394	1.15	423	.90	452	2.75	481	6.50	510	5.00	539	3.30
395	1.75	424	3.40	453	5.50	482	7.50	511	5.00	540	7.50
396	2.65	425	5.25	454	2.25	483	3.30	512	5.00	541	1 00
397	3.20	426	1.50	455	5 50	484	7.00	513	5.00	542	8.50
398	3.40	427	4.00	456	2.25	485	7.25	514	5 00	543	1.00
399	3.40	428	2 65	457	5.50	486	1.00	515	4.00	544	7.75
400	1.00	429	10.00	458	2.50	487	7.50	516	1.25		
401	1.00	430	4.80	459	5.50	488	1.00	517	4 75		

EQUATION OF PAYMENTS.

A Good Rule for Common Purposes.—Multiply each debt by the number of days between its own date of maturity and that of the debt earliest due, and divide the sum of the products by the sum of the debts; the quotient will express the common time in days subsequent to the leading date.

Example:—

1886, April 10, $250.26, time 6 months, Due Oct. 10, ⎤
  "   June 25, 320.56,   " 6   "   " Dec. 25, ⎥
  "   July 10,   50.62,   " 3   "   " Oct. 10, ⎥
  "   Aug. 1, 210.84,   " 4   "   " Dec. 1, ⎬ Find Average Due.
  "   Aug. 18,   73.40,   " 5   "   " Jan. 18, ⎥
  "   Oct. 15, 100.00,   " Cash,   " Oct. 15, ⎦

Practical method of stating and working:

1886, Due Oct. 10, $301
  "   "   Dec. 25, 321 $\times$ 76 $=$ 24396
  "   "   Dec. 1, 211 $\times$ 52 $=$ 10972
  "   "   Jan. 18,   73 $\times$ 100 $=$ 7300
  "   "   Oct. 15, 100 $\times$ 5 $=$ 500

    $1,006   ) 43168 (43 days from Oct. 10.

Ans., Nov. 22, 1886.